R5PD 3 1,695/-
APP 12 | 7
AF658779

Society and State *in* Medieval India

Society and State *in* Medieval India

Dr. A.K. Saxena

ABD PUBLISHERS
Jaipur ■ New Delhi

ABD PUBLISHERS

Regd. Off. "Bony Residency", Gate No. 2
Opp. Tilak Public School, Vishweswariya Nagar,
Gopalpura Road, Jaipur - 302018, India
Ph: 0141 - 2761280, Telefax: 2761381
Email: abdpublishersjpr@gmail.com

Delhi Office: 102, 1st Floor, Satyam House,
4327/3, Ansari Road, Darya Ganj,
New Delhi - 110002, India
Ph: 011-45652440

visit us: www.oxfordbookcompany.com

Distributed By
KEYA INTERNATIONAL PRESS LLP
E-mail: keyainternationalpressllp@gmail.com

Published in India, 2023

© All Rights Reserved

ISBN: 9788183766975

All Rights Reserved. Neither this publication nor any part thereof may be reproduced, stored in a retrieval system, or transmitted, in any form or by any means, electronic, mechanical, photocopying, recording, scanning or otherwise, without the prior written permission of the copyright owner.

Typeset by Shivangi Computer, Jaipur

Printed and bound in India by Thomson Press Ltd.,
New Delhi

Contents

Preface

In Hindu society, there were four principal castes (Brahamanas, Kshatriyas, Vaisyas and Sudras) in order of rank and status, and indefinite number of so-called mixed castes of varying status and the despised castes who were placed at the bottom of society. The old position of the Brahamanas and Kshatriyas was materially affected by the Muslim conquest of India. The Brahamanas lost their royal patronage. They got no job in administration. They were no longer prosperous. They lost the opportunity of earning a lot of money by officiating as priests in sacrifices.

Even while Indo-Buddhist civilization expanded and flourished overseas, however, Buddhist institutions were steadily declining in eastern India. Since Buddhists there had left life-cycle rites in the hands of Brahman priests, Buddhist monastic establishments, so central for the religion's institutional survival, became disconnected from the laity and fatally dependent on court patronage for their support.

By the time of the Muslim conquest, then, the official cult of a cosmic overlord, monumental state temples, and royally patronized Brahman priests had all emerged as central components of the Senas' religious and political ideology. It was not the case, however, that by that time early Indo-Aryan civilization and its later Hindu offshoot had penetrated all quarters of the Bengal delta evenly.

The Qutb was the first monumental stamp of Islamic architecture in India and was the start of a long relationship between indigenous craftsmen and their Mamluk masters. The grandiosity of its concept encouraged several rulers to continue adding to the structure and adding further stages.

This book places this subject in its most modern context as the foundation of this subject.

— Dr. A.K. Saxena

Chapter 1

The Mughal Period

The Mughal Emperors of India were descendants of a highly cultured dynasty. Their great ancestor, Tumur, had embellished his capital city of Samarq and with exquisite palaces, mosques, mausoleums, and *madrasahs*. Babur, the founder of the Mughal Empire, too was a scholar-warrior of a remarkably refined taste. In his "Memoirs" he relates that a considerable amount of construction in India was undertaken under his order, although he ruled only for five years. Two mosques attributed to him still existone at Panipat in East Punjab and the other at Sambhal, a town east of Delhi. They are, however, built in the traditional style.

The first construction in pure Mughal style, a combination of Persian and Indian style, was erected at Delhi in 972/1564 by Emperor Humaydn's Queen in memory of her beloved consort. During Humayun's forced sojourn in Iran, she faithfully stood by him for twelve years. She must have acquired a taste for Persian architecture there. When she decided to build Humayun's tomb, she entrusted the task to an Iranian architect, Mirak Mirza Chiyath. The result was that for the first time a Persian conception was interpreted in Indian architecture. The introduction of bulbous domes, so common in Iran and Central Asia, and of arched alcoves, a complex of rooms, corridors and a vast garden surrounding the tomb was a significant landmark in Indian architecture. Added to these purely Persian innovations were certain Indian characteristics such as the fanciful kiosks with their elegant cupolas and excellent stone masonry combined with artistic marble-work. From these it is obvious that there emerged a new style under the Mongols, the origin of which can be easily traced in Humayun's tomb. This style was almost perfected by Akbar the Great, who constructed numerous buildings during his long reign. He built four great fortresses: at Agra in 972/1564, at Ajmer in 978/1570, at Allahabad in 991/1583, and at Lahore at almost the same time. According to *Ain-i Akbari,* "there were built upwards of 500 edifices of red stone in the fine styles of Bengal and Gujarat" in the Agra fort alone.

The most complete of these buildings is the palace called the Jahangir Mahal in Agra. The palace-fortress of Lahore is unique in this respect that its outer walls are decorated with glazed tiles with sport *motifs* such as elephant combats, games of polo, and hunting episodes. Figure compositions and floral devices also are found in the panels.

The most monumental achievement of Akbar is Fatehpur Sikri, his new capital city, twenty-six miles west of Agra. It is a complex of palaces, official residences, and religious buildings, so designed and executed as to form one of the most spectacular structural productions in the whole of India. These are all built in red stone. Famous among them is the Diwan-i Khas (private audience hall), the Jami' Masjid with its Buland Darwazah (high gate) and palaces of Queen Jodha Ba'i, Maryam Sultanah, Rajah Birbal and Haws Mahaal. The Diwan-i Khas is a rectangular hall with unique arrangements. It has a large and circular pillar in the centre, its massive capital supporting a circular platform. From this platform stone-bridges radiate along each diagonal of the hall to connect it with hanging galleries. The Emperor used to sit on the central platform and listen to discussions among scholars of different religions.

The most impressive single structure at Fatehpur Sikri is the Buland Darwazah which was built in 979/1571 to commemorate the conquest of the Deccan. It is 134 ft. high with a further flight of steps, 42 ft. high. Across its front, the gate measures 130 ft. It serves as entrance to the Jami' Masjid containing the tomb of Shaikh Salim Chishti.

Emperor Akbar's son, Jahangir, was not much interested in buildings. The only important construction undertaken during his reign was Akbar's tomb at Sikandarah in 1022/1613. Unlike previous mausoleums, Akbar's tomb has no dome. It seems that a new group of architects were trying to evolve a style different from the one followed by the earlier Mughals. Two more tombs were built in the same style in which the central dome was replaced by a rectangular pavilion. These were the tombs of I'timad al-Daulah built at Agra in 1036/1626 and the tomb of Jahangir built at Lahore. Both were constructed under orders of Queen Nur Jahan. Of these three, the tomb of I'timad al-Daulah is the most delicate and ornate piece of architecture. It is made of marble with its surface tastefully decorated with precious stones of different colours. This inlaid work is in *pictora dura* style.

The reign of the Emperor Shahjahan (1036-1069/1627-1658) is the golden age of Mughal architecture. While Akbar's monuments surpassed those of his predecessors in red-stone architecture, his illustrious grandson preferred the use of marble on a scale unparalleled in history. His was the age of marble and its architectural style was determined by marble forms with the result that the character of the arches had to be altered into a foliated one; white marble arcades of engrailed arches became a distinguishing feature of Shahjahan's buildings. The bulbous dome also got constricted at the neck and ornamental elements became curvilinear.

Shahjahan was almost possessed with a passion for buildings. He started with the Agra Fort wherein he built the marble hall of Diwan-i 'Am as soon as he ascended the throne in 1037/1627. Ten years later, the Diwan-i has, a hall also made of marble, was added to it. The double columns of this hall are amongst the most graceful constructions of his reign. From time to time several other palaces, pavilions, and mosques, e.g., the has Mahal, the Shish Mahal, the Muhamman Burj, the Moti Masjid, and the Naginah Masjid, were added to the complex inside the citadel.

In 1048/1638, Shahjahan decided to transfer his capital to Delhi where he laid the foundations of Shahjahanabad, a palace-fortress on the right bank of the river Jamuna. The vast, oblong complex is a city within a city. It is a well-planned enclosure and a product of the architectural genius of Shahjahan himself.

This citadel, made of red stone and marble, consists of four groups of buildings arranged symmetrically. The large central quadrangle contains the Diwan-i 'Am, the two square courtyards in the form of ornamental gardens on either side, and the range of marble palaces along the riverside. These palaces include the Rang Mahal and the Diwan-i Khas, two most lavishly ornate buildings considered to be the crowning jewels of Shahjahan's seraglio.

Since the citadel did not include any mosque, Shahjahan built the famous Jami' Masjid of Delhi on a site near his palace. It is erected on a lofty plinth and is one of the two largest and most famous mosques in the sub-continent, the other being the Badshahi Masjid of Lahore. Rectangular in shape, the Jami‘ Masjid has three entrances; the main and the most imposing entrance faces the east and much resembles Akbar's Buland Darwazah at Fatehpur Sikri. It is made in red stone and marble. The three domes are made of marble with vertical strips of black stone inset at regular intervals.

Several noteworthy buildings were erected by Shahjahan and his governor at Thattah, the then capital of the province of Sind. Among these are the Jami‘ Masjid, begun in 1057/1647, and a group of tombs built on the Makli Hill by Mirza ‘Isa Khan who governed Sind from 1037/1627 to 1054/1644. The Jami‘ Masjid is built of bricks decorated with glazed tiles of blue, white, and yellow colours. These tiles were cut in very small sizes, only half an inch wide; thus nearly one hundred such tiles have been used within one square foot producing a mosaic effect. The designs are chiefly geometrical, but the spandrils of the arches often show conventional floral compositions.

Since stone and wood were scarce in Sind, most of the construction was done in bricks and glazed tiles. The architectural style of Sind closely resembles that of contemporary Persia-brick-walls arcaded with Tudor-type arches, kiosks with cupolas, a "Lodhi"-style dome, and the outer surface embellished with glazed tile-work.

The greatest masterpiece of Shahjahan is the Taj Mahal (1042-1050/1632-1650), built by the Emperor in memory of his beloved Queen at Agra on the bank of the river Jamuna. This exquisite poetry in marble touches the highest pinnacle of Muslim architecture and is unsurpassed in history.

Its rhythmic proportion, its atmospheric setting, its feminine delicacy, its animated ornamentation, and its pleasing symmetry make the Taj Mahal one of the great wonders of the world.

While Shahjahan built in marble and red stone, brick and glazed tile were patronized by the nobility. The finest example of this type of buildings is the famous mosque of Wazir Khan in Lahore. Built on conventional lines, every portion of its structure, both inside and outside, is enriched with a variegated scheme of colours either by means of floral patterns painted in tempera or panels of more conventional designs executed in lustrous glaze.

The Mughals were very fond of landscape architecture. Nothing pleased them more than ornamental gardens, traces of which are found almost in *every* city where the Mughals had lived. The most famous among these are the Shalimar Gardens and the Nishat Bagh of Srinagar and the Shalimar Gardens of Lahore, all three of them built by Shahjahan. These gardens, like most of the Mughal buildings, are almost always symmetrical and geometrical. But their rectangular terraces, kiosks, balconies, pools, fountains, and cascades present a most pleasant effect and testify to the refined taste of their originators.

The Emperor Aurangzeb (1068-1119/1657-1707) was the last of the great Mughals. Although too much occupied in political affairs of the State to indulge in constructional work, he has left a famous monument in the Badshahi Masjid of Lahore, the present capital of West Pakistan. Built in red stone and marble, the Badshahi Masjid is one of the two biggest mosques in the Indo-Pakistan sub-continent and is an imposing example of strength, solidity, and expanse.

With the death of Aurangzeb in 1119/1707, the glorious chapter of Muslim architecture in this sub-continent came to an end. The decline of the Mughal Empire was so swift and the political conditions prevailing in Lahore, Delhi, and other important centres of Muslim culture so insecure and unsettled that traces of late twelfth/eighteenth-century Muslim structures are very rare.

BABUR

Zahir-ud-din Mohammad Babur (February 23 [O.S. February 14] 1483 — January 5 [O.S. December 26 1530] 1531) was a Turkic conqueror from Central Asia who, following a series of setbacks, finally succeeded in laying the basis for the Mughal dynasty of India. He was a direct descendant of Timur through his father, and a descendant also of Genghis Khan through his mother.

Babur identified his lineage as Timurid and Chaghatay-Turkic, while his origin, milieu, training, and culture were steeped in Persian culture and so he was largely responsible for the fostering of this culture by his descendants, and for the expansion of Persian cultural influence in the Indian subcontinent, with brilliant literary, artistic, and historiographical results.

Military Career

In 1494, at only twelve years of age, Babur obtained his first power position, succeeding his father as ruler of Farghana, in present-day

Uzbekistan. His uncles were relentless in their attempts to dislodge him from this position as well as many of his other territorial possessions to come. Thus, Babur spent a large portion of his life shelterless and in exile, aided only by friends and peasants. In 1497, Babur attacked the Uzbek city of Samarkand and after seven months succeeded in capturing the city. Meanwhile, a rebellion amongst nobles back home approximately 350 kilometers (200 miles) away robbed him of Farghana. As he was marching to recover it, Babur's troops deserted in Samarkand, leaving him with neither Samarkand nor Fergana.

By 1501, he was ready again to regain control of Samarkand, but was shortly thereafter defeated by his most formidable enemy, Mohammad Shaybani, khan of the Uzbeks. Samarkand, his lifelong obsession, was lost again. Escaping with a small band of followers from Fergana, for three years Babur concentrated on building up a strong army, recruiting widely amongst the Tajiks of Badakhshan in particular. In 1504, he was able to cross the snowy Hindu Kush mountains and capture Kabul from the Arghunids, who were forced to retreat to Kandahar. With this move, he gained a wealthy new kingdom and re-established his fortunes and assumed the title of *Badshah*. In the following year, Babur united with Husayn Bayqarah of Herat, a fellow Timurid and distant relative, against the usurper Mohammad Shaybani. However, the death of Husayn Bayqarah in 1506 delayed that venture. Babur instead occupied his allies' city of Herat, spending just two months there before being forced to leave due to diminishing resources.

Nevertheless, he marvelled at the intellectual abundance in Herat, which he stated was "filled with learned and matched men.", and became acquainted with the work of the Uzbek poet Mir Ali Shir Navai, who encouraged the use of Chagatai as a literary language. Navai's profiency with the language, which he is credited with founding, may have influenced Babur in his decision to use it for his memoirs, *Baburnama*.

A brewing rebellion finally induced him to return to Kabul from Herat. He prevailed on that occasion, but two years later a revolt among some of his leading generals drove him out of Kabul. Escaping with very few companions, Babur soon returned to the city, capturing Kabul again and regaining the allegiance of the rebels. Mohammad Shaybani was defeated and killed by Ismail I, Safavid ruler of Persia, in 1510, and Babur used this opportunity to attempt to reconquer his ancestral Timurid territories.

Over the following few years, Babur and Shah Ismail I would form a partnership in an attempt to take over parts of Central Asia. In return for Ismail's assistance, Babur permitted the Safavids to act as a suzerain over him and his followers. Conversely, Shah Ismail reunited Babur with his sister Khanzada, who had been imprisoned by and forced to marry the recently-deceased Shaybani. Ismail also provided Babur with a large wealth of luxury goods and military assistance, for which Babur reciprocated by adopting the dress and outward customs of the Shia Muslims.

The Shah's Persia had become the bastion of Shia Islam, and he claimed descent from Imam Musa al-kazim, the seventh Shia Imam. Coins were to be struck in Ismail's name, and the Khutba at the Mosque was also to be read in his name. In effect, Babur was supposed to be holding Samarkand as a vassal territory for the Persian Shah, though in Kabul, coins and the Khutba would remain in Babur's name.

With this assistance, Babur marched on Bukhara, where his army were apparently treated as liberators, Babur having greater legitimacy as a Timurid, unlike the Uzbegs. Towns and villages are said to have emptied in order to greet him, and aid and feed his army. At this point Babur dismissed his Persian aide, believing them no longer needed. In October 1511 Babur made a triumphant re-entry into Samarkand, ending a ten year absence.

Bazaars were draped in gold, and again villages and towns emptied to greet the liberator. Dressed as a Shia, Babur stood out starkly amongst the masses of Sunnis who had thronged to greet him. The original belief was that this show of Shivism was a ploy to garner Persian help which would soon be dropped. While it was indeed a ploy, Babur did not think it wise to drop the charade.

His cousin, Haidar, wrote that Babur was still too fearful of the Uzbegs to dismiss the Persian aid. Though Babur did not persecute the Sunni community, to please the Persian Shah, he did not drop the show of collaboration with the Shia either, resulting in popular disapproval and the re-conquering of the city by the Uzbegs eight months later.

Last Days

After Babar fell seriously ill, Humayun was told of a plot by the senior nobles of Babur's court to bypass the leader's sons and appoint Mahdi Khwaja, Babur's sister's husband, as his successor. He rushed to Agra and arrived there to see his father was well enough again, although Mahdi Khwaja had lost all hope of becoming ruler after arrogantly exceeding his authority during Babur's illness. Upon his arrival in Agra it was Humayun himself who fell ill, and was close to dying.

Babar is said to have circled the sick-bed, crying to God to take his life and not his son's. The traditions that follow this tell that Babur soon fell ill with a fever and Humayun began to get better again. This is not accurate, as there are months separating the recovery of Humayun and the death of Babur, and Babur's final illness was rather sudden. His last words apparently being to his son, Humayun, "Do nothing against your brothers, even though they may deserve it."

He died at the age of 47 on January 5 [O.S. 26 December 1530] 1531, and was succeeded by his eldest son, Humayun. Though he wished to be buried in his favourite garden in Kabul, a city he had always loved, he was first buried in a Mausoleum in the capital city of Agra. Roughly nine years later his wishes were fulfilled by Sher Shah Suri and Babur was buried in a beautiful garden Bagh-e Babur in Kabul, now in Afghanistan. The inscription on his tomb reads (in Persian):

If there is a paradise on earth, it is this, it is this, it is this!

Babar's legacy was a mixed one. He is considered a national hero in Uzbekistan and Kyrgyzstan, and is held in high esteem in Afghanistan where he is buried. However, the Sikh Guru, Nanak, wrote a series of complaints against Babur in the Guru Granth Sahib, claiming Babur "terrified Hindustan" and was a "messenger of death." He also claimed that women with braided hair "were shaved with scissors, and their throats were choked with dust" and that "the order was given to the soldiers, who dishonored them, and carried them away."

HUMAYUN

Humayun (March 17, 1508– March 4, 1556) was the second Mughal Emperor who ruled modern Afghanistan, Pakistan, and parts of northern India from 1530–1540 and again from 1555–1556. Like his father, Babur, he lost his kingdom early, but with Persian aid, he eventually regained an even larger one. On the eve of his death in 1556, the Mughal empire spanned almost one million square kilometers. He succeeded his father in India in 1530, while his half-brother Kamran Mirza, who was to become a rather bitter rival, obtained the sovereignty of Kabul and Lahore, the more northern parts of their father's empire.

He originally ascended the throne at the age of 22 and was somewhat inexperienced when he came to power. Humayun lost his Indian territories to the Pashtun (Afghan) noble, Sher Shah Suri, and, with Persian aid, regained them fifteen years later. Humayun's return from Persia, accompanied by a large retinue of Persian noblemen, signaled an important change in Mughal court culture, as the Central Asian origins of the dynasty were largely overshadowed by the influences of Persian art, architecture, language and literature. Subsequently, in a very short time, Humayun was able to expand the Empire further, leaving a substantial legacy for his son, Akbar.

Background

Babur's decision to divide the territories of his empire between two of his sons was unusual in India, but it had been a common Central Asian practice since the time of Genghis Khan. Unlike most European Monarchies which practised primogeniture, the Timurids, following Genghis Khan's example, did not leave an entire kingdom to the eldest son.

Although under that system only a Chingissid could claim sovereignty and khanal authority, any male Chinggisid within a given sub-branch (such as the Timurids) had an equal right to the throne.. While Genghis Khan's Empire had been peacefully divided between his sons upon his death, almost every Chinggisid succession since had resulted in fratricide. Timur himself had divided his territories between Pir Mohammad, Miran Shah, Khalil Sultan and Shah Rukh, which resulted in inter-family warfare. Upon Babur's death, Humayun's territories were the least secure. Babur had ruled only four years, and not all *umarah* (nobles) viewed Humayun as the rightful ruler. Indeed earlier, when Babur had become ill, some of the nobles had tried to install Humayun's uncle, Mahdi Khwaja, as ruler. Although this attempt failed, it was a sign of problems to come.

Early Reign

Upon his succession to the throne, Humayun had two major rivals interested in acquiring his lands — Sultan Bahadur of Gujarat to the south west and Sher Shah Suri (Sher Khan) currently settled along the river Ganges in Bihar to the east. Humayun's first campaign was to confront a Sher Khan Suri. Halfway through the counter offensive Humayun had to abandon it and concentrate on Gujarat, where a threat from Ahmed Shah had to be squelched. In this he succeeded and annexed Gujarat and Malwa. Champaner and the great fort of Mandu followed next.

During the first five years of Humayun's reign, these two rulers were quietly extending their rule, although Sultan Bahadur faced pressure in the east from sporadic conflicts with the Portuguese. While the Mughals had acquired firearms via the Ottoman Empire, Bahadur's Gujurat had acquired them through a series of contracts drawn up with the Portuguese, allowing the Portuguese to establish a strategic foothold in north western India.

Humayun was made aware that the Sultan of Gujarat was planning an assault on the Mughal territories with Portuguese aid. Showing an unusual resolve, Humayun gathered an army and marched on Bahadur. His assault was spectacular and within a month he had captured the forts of Mandu and Champaner. However, instead of pressing his attack and going after the enemy, Humayun ceased the campaign and began to enjoy life in his new forts. Bahadur, meanwhile, escaped and took up refuge with the Portuguese.

Shortly after Humayun had marched on Gujarat, Sher Shah saw an opportunity to wrest control of Agra from the Mughals. He began to gather his army together hoping for a rapid and decisive siege of the Mughal capital. Upon hearing this alarming news, Humayun quickly marched his troops back to Agra allowing Bahadur to easily regain control of the territories Humayun had recently taken. A few months later, however, Bahadur was dead, killed when a botched plan to kidnap the Portuguese viceroy ended in a fire-fight which the Sultan lost.

Whilst Humayun succeeded in protecting Agra from Sher Shah, the second city of the Empire, Gaur the capital of the *vilayat* of Bengal, was sacked. Humayun's troops had been delayed while trying to take Chunar, a fort occupied by Sher Shah's son, in order to protect his troops from an attack from the rear. The stores of grain at Gauri, the largest in the empire, were emptied and Humayun arrived to see corpses littering the roads. The vast wealth of Bengal was depleted and brought East giving Sher Shah a substantial war chest.

Sher Shah withdrew to the east, but Humayun did not follow: instead he "shut himself up for a considerable time in his Harem, and indulged himself in every kind of luxury." Hindal, Humayun's nineteen year old brother, had agreed to aid him in this battle and protect the rear from attack but abandoned his position and withdrew to Agra where he decreed himself acting emperor. When Humayun sent the grand *Mufti*, Sheikh Buhlul, to reason with him, the Sheikh was killed. Further provoking the rebellion, Hindal ordered that the *Khutba* or sermon in the main mosque at Agra be read in his name, a sign of assumption of sovereignty. When Hindal withdrew from protecting the rear of Humayun's troops, Sher Shah's troop quickly reclaimed these positions, leaving Humayun surrounded.

Humayun's other brother, Kamran, marched from his territories in the Punjab, ostensibly to aid Humayun. However, his return home had treacherous motives as he intended to stake a claim for Humayun's apparently collapsing empire. He brokered a deal with Hindal which provided that his brother would cease all acts of disloyalty in return for a share in the new empire which Kamran would create once Humayun was deposed.

Sher Shah met Humayun in battle on the banks of the Ganges, near Benares, in Chausa. This was to become an entrenched battle in which both sides spent a lot of time digging themselves into positions. The major part of the Mughal army, the artillery, was now immobile, and Humayun decided to engage in some diplomacy using Mohammad Aziz as ambassador. Humayun agreed to allow Sher Shah to rule over Bengal and Bihar, but only as provinces granted to him by his Emperor, Humayun, falling short of outright sovereignty. The two rulers also struck a bargain in order to save face: Humayun's troops would charge those of Sher Shah whose forces then retreat in feigned fear. Thus honour would, supposedly, be satisfied.

Once the Army of Humayun had made its charge and Sher Shah's troops made their agreed-upon retreat, the Mughal troops relaxed their defensive preparations and returned to their entrenchments without posting a proper guard. Observing the Mughals' vulnerability, Sher Shah reneged on his earlier agreement. That very night, his army approached the Mughal camp and finding the Mughal troops unprepared with a majority asleep, they advanced and killed most of them. The Emperor survived by swimming the Ganges using an air filled "water skin," and quietly returned to Agra.

Death and Legacy

On March 4, 1556, Humayun, his arms full of books, was descending the staircase from his library when the muezzin announced the Adhan (the call to prayer), reportedly after smoking a pipefull of opium. It was his habit, wherever he heard the summons, to bow his knee in holy reverence. Kneeling, he caught his foot in his robe, tumbled down several steps and hit his temple on a rugged stone edge. He died three days later, and was succeeded by the 13 year old Akbar.

Humayun loved astrology and astronomy and built observatories that lasted centuries. His life was chronicled in a slightly hagiographical work called the *Humayun-nama* written by his sister Gulbadan Begum at the request of his son, Akbar.

His most lasting impact was the importing of Persian ideas into the Indian empire, something which was expanded on by later leaders. His support for the arts, following exposure to Safavid art, saw him recruit painters to his court who developed the celebrated Mughal style of painting.

Humayun's greatest architectural creation was the Din-Panah (Refuge of Religion) citadel, also known as *Purana Qila* at Delhi which was destroyed by Sher Shah Suri. He is best remembered today for his great Tomb, built by his widow after his death between 1562 and 1571. The ultimate model for Humayun's tomb is the Gur-e Amir in Samarkand, and it is best-known as a precursor to the Taj Mahal in style. However, in its striking composition of dome and *iwan*, and its imaginative use of local materials, it is one of the finest Mughal monuments in India in its own right.

AKBAR THE GREAT

Jalaluddin Mohammad Akbar (October 15, 1542 – October 27, 1605) was the third Mughal Emperor of India. He was of Timurid descent; the son of Humayun, and the grandson of Babur who founded the dynasty. At the end of his reign in 1605 the Mughal empire covered most of Northern India. Akbar, widely considered the greatest of the Mughal emperors, was thirteen years old when he ascended the throne in Delhi, following the death of his father Humayun.

During his reign, he eliminated military threats from the Pashtun descendants of Sher Shah Suri, and at the Second Battle of Panipat he defeated the Hindu king Hemu. It took him nearly two more decades to consolidate his power and bring parts of northern and central India into his realm. The emperor solidified his rule by pursuing diplomacy with the powerful Rajput caste, and by admitting Rajput princesses in his harem. Akbar's reign significantly influenced art and culture in the region.

Akbar took a great interest in painting, and had the walls of his palaces adorned with murals. Besides encouraging the development of the Mughal school, he also patronised the European style of painting. He was fond of literature, and had several Sanskrit works translated into Persian, apart from getting many Persian works illustrated by painters from his court.

He also commissioned many major buildings, and invented the first prefabricated homes. Akbar began a series of religious debates where Muslim scholars would debate religious matters with Sikhs, Hindus, Carvaka atheists and Portuguese Roman Catholic Jesuits. He founded a religious cult, the *Din-i-Ilahi* (Divine Faith), but it amounted only to a form of personality cult for Akbar, and quickly dissolved after his death.

Early Years

Akbar was born on October 15, 1542 (the fourth day of Rajab, 949 AH), at the Rajput Fortress of Umerkot in Sindh, where Humayun and his recently wedded wife, Hamida Banu Begum were taking refuge. Humayun gave the child the name he had heard in his dream at Lahore, Jalalu-d-din Mohammad Akbar Ghazi Humayun had been driven into exile in Persia by the Pashtun leader Sher Shah Suri. Akbar did not go to Persia with his parents but grew up in the village of Mukundpur in Rewa (in present day Madhya Pradesh).

Akbar and prince Ram Singh I, who later became the Maharaja of Rewa, grew up together and stayed close friends through life. Later, Akbar moved to the eastern parts of the Safavid Empire (now a part of Afghanistan) where he was raised by his uncle Askari. He spent his youth learning to hunt, run, and fight, but he never learned to read or write. Nonetheless, Akbar matured into a well-informed ruler, with refined tastes in the arts, architecture, music and a love for literature.

Following the chaos over the succession of Sher Shah Suri's son Islam Shah, Humayun reconquered Delhi in 1555, leading an army partly provided by his Persian ally Tahmasp I. A few months later, Humayun died.

Akbar's guardian, Bairam Khan concealed the death in order to prepare for Akbar's succession. Akbar succeeded Humayun on February 14, 1556, while in the midst of a war against Sikandar Shah to reclaim the Mughal throne. In Kalanaur, Punjab, the 13 year old Akbar donned a golden robe and Dark Tiara was enthroned by Bairam Khan on a newly constructed platform, which still stands. He was proclaimed *Shahanshah* (Persian for "King of Kings"). Bairam Khan ruled on his behalf until he came of age.

The Name Akbar

Akbar was originally named Badruddin Akbar, because he was born on the night of a *badr* (full moon). After the capture of Kabul by Humayun his date of birth and name were changed to throw off evil sorcerers. Contrary to some popular traditions, the name Akbar-meaning "Great"-was a not an honorific given to Akbar; rather he was named for his maternal grandfather, Shaikh Ali *Akbar* Jami.

Military Achievements

Early conquests: Akbar decided early in his reign that he should eliminate the threat of Sher Shah's dynasty, and decided to lead an army against the strongest of the three, Sikandar Shah Suri, in the Punjab. He left Delhi under the regency of Tardi Baig Khan. Sikandar Shah Suri presented no major concern for Akbar, and often withdrew from territory as Akbar approached.

The Hindu king Hemu, however, commanding the Afghan forces, defeated the Mughal army and captured Delhi on 6 October 1556. Tardi Beg Khan promptly fled the city. News of the capitulation of Delhi spread quickly to Akbar, and he was advised to withdraw to Kabul, which was relatively secure. But urged by Bairam Khan, Akbar marched on Delhi to reclaim it. Tardi Beg and his retreating troops joined the march, and also urged Akbar to retreat to Kabul, but he refused again. Later, Bairam Khan had the former regent executed for cowardice, though Abul Fazl and Jahangir both record that they believed that Bairam Khan was merely using the retreat from Delhi as an excuse to eliminate a rival. Akbar's army, led by Bairam Khan, met the larger forces of Hemu on 5 November 1556 at the Second Battle of Panipat, 50 miles (80 km) north of Delhi. The battle was going in Hemu's favour when an arrow pierced Hemu's eye, rendering him unconscious. The leader less army soon capitulated and Hemu was captured and executed.

The victory also left Akbar with over 1,500 war elephants which he used to re-engage Sikandar Shah at the siege of Mankot. Sikandar, along with several local chieftains who were assisting him, surrendered and so was spared death. With this, the whole of Punjab was annexed to the Mughal empire. Before returning to Agra, Akbar sent a detachment of his army to Jammu, which defeated the ruler Raja Kapur Chand and captured the kingdom. Between 1558 and 1560, Akbar further expanded the empire by capturing and annexing the kingdoms of Gwalior, northern Rajputana and Jaunpur.

After a dispute at court, Akbar dismissed Bairam Khan in the spring of 1560 and ordered him to leave on Hajj to Mecca. Bairam left for Mecca, but on his way was goaded by his opponents to rebel. He was defeated by the Mughal army in the Punjab and forced to submit. Akbar, however forgave him and gave him the option of either continuing in his court or resuming his pilgrimage, of which Bairam chose the latter.

JAHANGIR

Nur-ud-din Salim Jahangir (full title: *Al-Sultan al-Azam wal Khaqan al-Mukarram, Khushru-i-Giti Panah, Abul-Fath Nur-ud-din Mohammad Jahangir Padshah Ghazi [Jannat-Makaani]*) (September 20, 1569 – November 8, 1627) (OS August 31, 1569 – NS November 8, 1627) was the ruler of the Mughal Empire from 1605 until his death. The name Jahangir is from Persian Acoin, meaning "Conqueror of the World". Nur-ud-din or Nur al-Din is an Arabic name which means " Light of the Faith." Born as Prince Mohammad Salim, he was the third and eldest surviving son of Mughal Emperor Akbar.

Akbar's twin sons, Hasan and Hussain, died in infancy. His mother was the Rajput Princess of Amber, Jodhabai (born Rajkumari Hira Kunwari, eldest daughter of Raja Bihar Mal or Bharmal, Raja of Amber, India). Jahangir was a child of many prayers.

It is said to be by the blessing of Shaikh Salim Chishti (one of the revered sages of his times) that Akbar's first surviving child, the future Jahangir, was born. He was born at the dargah of the Shaikh Salim Chishti, within the fortress at Fatehpur Sikri near Agra. The child was named Salim after the darvesh and was affectionately addressed by Akbar as Sheikhu Baba. Akbar developed an emotional attachment with the village Sikri (abode of Chishti). Therefore, he developed the town of Sikri and shifted his imperial court and residence from Agra to Sikri, later renamed as Fatehpur Sikri. Shaikh Salim Chishti's daughter was appointed Jahangir's foster mother as a mark of respect to the Shaikh. Jahangir's foster brother Nawab Kutb-ud-din Khan was private secretary to the emperor Jahangir and afterwards governor of Bengal. Nawab Kutb-ud-din Khan's son Nawab Mohtashim. Khan was granted by Jahangir 4,000 bigas of land in Badaun District (United Provinces) where he built a small fort named Sheikhupur, Badaun after Jahangir, who was caned Sheikhu-baba in his childhood.

Jahangir and Religion

While Sunni Islam was the state religion, there was no widespread pressure to convert; indeed, Jahangir specifically warned his nobles that they "should not force Islam on anyone." In the first century of Islamic expansion this attitude was taken partially because of concerns that an absence of non-Muslims would deprive the state of a valuable source of revenue. However, as the jizya was not imposed by Jahangir, there might have been more behind this policy of toleration than mere economic reasoning.

Jahangir was certainly willing to engage with other religions, and Edward Terry, an English chaplain in India at the time, saw a ruler under which "all Religions are tolerated and their Priests [held] in good esteeme." Brahmins on the banks of the Ganges received gifts from the emperor, while following a meeting with Jadrup, a Hindu ascetic, Jahangir felt compelled to comment that "association with him is a great privilege."

He enjoyed debating theological subtleties with Brahmins, especially about the possible existence of avatars. Both Sunnis and Shias were welcome at court, and members of both sects gained high office. When drunk, Jahangir swore to Sir Thomas Roe, England's first ambassador to the Mughal court, that he would protect all the peoples of the book. Many contemporary chroniclers were not even sure quite how to describe his personal belief structure.

Roe labelled him an atheist, and although most others shied away from that term, they did not feel as though they could call him an orthodox Sunni. He relied greatly on astrologers, though that was not seen as unusual for a ruler at the time, even to the extent that he required that they work out the most auspicious time for the imperial camp to enter a city.

Roe believed Jahangir's religion to be of his own making, "for he envyes Mahomett, and wisely sees no reason why he should not bee as great a prophet as he, and therefore proffeseth him selfe soe ... he hath found many disciples that flatter or follow him." At this time, one of those disciples happened to be the current English ambassador, though his initiation into Jahangir's inner circle of disciples was devoid of religious significance for Roe, as he did not understand the full extent of what he was doing: Jahangir hung "a picture of him selfe sett in gold hanging at a wire gold chaine, with one pendent soule pearle" round Roe's neck. Roe thought it "an specially favour, for that all the great men that were the Kings image (which none may doe but to whom it is given) receive no other then a meddall of gold as bigg as six pence."

Had Roe intentionally converted, it would have caused quite a scandal in London. But since there was no intent, there was no resultant problem. Such disciples were an elite group of imperial servants, with one of them being promoted to Chief Justice. However, it is not clear that any of those who became disciples renounced their previous religion, so it is probable to see this as a way in which the emperor strengthened the bond between himself and his nobles. Despite Roe's somewhat casual use of the term 'atheist', he could not quite put his finger on Jahangir's real beliefs.

Roe lamented that the emperor was either "the most impossible man in the world to be converted, or the most easy; for he loves to heare, and hath so little religion yet, that he can well abide to have any derided." Broad toleration for other religions made little sense to Europeans forged in the heat of religious conflict, while the lifestyle and pretensions Jahangir afforded himself meant that it was difficult to see him as a devout Muslim. Sri Ram Sharma argues though that contemporaries and some historians have been too disparaging about Jahangir's beliefs, simply because he did not persecute non-believers and enforce his views on others.

This should not imply that the multi-confessional state appealed to all, or that all Muslims were happy with the situation in India. In a book written on statecraft for Jahangir, the author advised him to direct "all his energies to understanding the counsel of the sages and to comprehending the intimations of the 'ulama."

At the start of his regime many staunch Sunnis were hopeful, because he seemed less tolerant to other faiths than his father had been. At the time of his accession and the elimination of Abul Fazl, his father's chief minister and architect of his eclectic religious stance, a strong orthodox nucleus of noblemen had gained power in administration." Jahangir did not always benevolently regard some Hindu customs and rituals. On visiting a Hindu temple, he found a statue of a man with a pig's head, which was supposed to represent God, so he "ordered them to break that hideous form and throw it in the tank." If the Tuzuk is reliable on this subject (and there is no reason to suspect that it is not), then this was an isolated case.

J. F. Richards argues that "Jahangir seems to have been persistently hostile to popularly venerated religious figures." This is perhaps misleading. Hindu ascetics like Jadrup were treated with respect, and it was only those who upset the order of the state that were seen as a threat to the state, with their popularity making them even more dangerous. A Muslim, who had gained some followers by claiming that he had surpassed the understanding of the companions of Mohammad, was imprisoned in Gwalior Fort. If he had been allowed to spread his message there was potential for serious disturbance, so he had to be stopped.

Most notorious was the execution of the Sikh Guru Arjun. It is unclear that Jahangir even understood what a Sikh was, referring to Guru Arjun as a Hindu, who had "captured many of the simple-hearted of the Hindus, and even of the ignorant and foolish followers of Islam, by his ways and manners ... for three or four generations (of spiritual successors) they had kept this shop warm." The trigger for Guru Arjun's execution was his support for Jahangir's rebel son Khusrau, yet it is clear from Jahangir's own memoirs that he disliked Guru Arjun before then: "many times it occurred to me to put a stop to this vain affair or bring him into the assembly of the people of Islam."

Guru Arjun was handed over to the Mughal governor of Lahore, and was tortured to death for refusing to convert to Islam. Jahangir ordered his execution, but it is unlikely that he also ordered Guru Arjun to be tortured and converted, for two reasons; one, because we have no other examples from Jahangir's generally tolerant reign to support the idea that he forced people to convert to Islam, and two, because Jahangir makes no note of Guru Arjun's torture, yet cheerfully describes the torture of two other rebels, as well as Guru Arjun's execution. Jahangir maintained his hostility towards the Sikhs, imprisoning Guru Hargobind, the successor of Guru Arjun, for several years.

A rana was described as an infidel, but only because he was fighting against the Mughals, and infidel was used as an everyday phrase to describe all non-Muslims anyway. Admittedly Muslims were discouraged from performing most Hindu rites, with Jahangir lamenting that many Muslims prayed at a temple dedicated to Durga, and worshipped at a black stone. With Jahangir himself occasionally taking part in Hindu ceremonies, the aforementioned example was probably one way of showing support for the idea that Muslim and Hindus should not mix their rituals. His attitude to religion in his domain was relaxed yet diligent. He saw himself as doing Allah's bidding, yet he was inquisitive enough to explore new ideas about religion, intelligent enough to understand that Hindus were in the majority and grand enough in his pretensions not to need to obey every line of the Qur'an.

Such a religious situation allowed the more recently arrived form of Christianity to have opportunity to grow. Jahangir did not seem to have anything against Christianity. He wrote fondly of Akbar's reign, when "Sunnis and Shias met in one mosque, and Franks and Jews in one church, and observed their own forms of worship." Roe noted that "of Christ he never utters any word un-reverently."

His prayer room in Agra contained pictures of "our Lady and Christ." In the imperial palace in Lahore, over one of the doors, according to William Finch, a merchant, was "the Picture of our Sauiour," with an image of the Virgin Mary facing it. Elsewhere, the emperor had pictures of angels and demons, with the demons having a "most ugly shape, with long hornes, staring eyes ... with such horrible difformity and deformity, that I wonder the poore women are not frightened therewith."

It is possible that Jahangir might have seen these images in their Islamic persona, as the Qur'an features such creatures, yet depiction of living things was harem (forbidden), so the images could well have been created by a Christian artist. However, as Mughal art was still heavily Persian-influenced, images of living beings were allowed, and widespread, so perhaps the other worldly images had nothing to do with Christianity at all; they nonetheless caught Finch's eye. Muqarrab Khan sent to Jahangir "a European curtain (tapestry) the like of which in beauty no other work of the Frank painters has ever been seen." One of his audience halls was "adorned with European screens." Christian themes attracted Jahangir, and even merited a mention in the Tuzuk. One of his slaves gave him a piece of ivory into which had been carved four scenes. In the last scene "there is a tree, below which the figure of the revered (hazrat) Jesus is shown. One person has placed his head at Jesus' feet, and an old man is conversing with Jesus and four others are standing by."

Though Jahangir believed it to be the work of the slave who presented it to him, Sayyid Ahmad and Henry Beveridge suggest that it was of European origin, and possibly showed the Transfiguration.

Wherever it came from, and whatever it represented, it was clear that a European style had come to influence Mughal art, otherwise the slave would not have claimed it as his own design, nor would he have been believed by Jahangir. There was even some baseless suggestion that Jahangir had converted to Christianity. Thrown by the religious tolerance of Akbar and Jahangir's rule, the Jesuits had long thought that they were always on the verge of conversion.

Finch recounted how there "was much stirre with the King about Chrytianitie, he affirming before his Nobles, that it was the soundest faith, and that of Mahomet lies and fables." This is an extremely implausible story, yet the fact that Finch told it at all shows the extent to which Christianity was evident in the Mughal court.

Jahangir apparently allowed a Jesuit to teach some Indian boys Portuguese and elements of Christian doctrine, and the Jesuits were also allowed to open churches in Ahmadabad and Hooghly. Christians were allowed to openly celebrate Christmas, Easter and other such festivals, and the Jesuits were even given an allowance and gifts in order to carry on with their work, with a few Indians converting to Christianity. Given the toleration of Hinduism, such imperial leeway was not shocking. Christianity occupied a special place in Islamic canon, as did Isa (Jesus), who was considered to be amongst the greatest prophets. What did surprise some observers was the forcible conversion of three sons of Jahangir's brother, Prince Daniyal, to Christianity, followed by a parade to celebrate their conversions. This was seen by the Jesuits as a gigantic step forward, but the English and the locals knew better. Hawkins dryly commented that Jahangir made his nephews Christian "not for any zeale he had to Christianitie, as the [Jesuit] Fathers, and all Christians thought; but upon the prophecie of certain learned Gentiles [Hindus], who told him that the sonnes of his should be disinherited, and the children of his brother should raigne. And therefore he did it, to make these children hatefull to all Moores."

This highlighted the likely limits of Christianity in India. Its inhabitants already had mono-and poly-theistic religions from which to choose, and the European Christians had done little to demonstrate the attractiveness of conversion. A few did convert, though Terry believed that this was only for Jesuit money, as they did not appear to know anything about their new religion, and Roe agreed on this matter. Even Jahangir's nephews were allowed to return to the Islamic fold, because "the King of Portugall sent them no presents nor wives."

Christianity was tolerated because it posed no real threat. It certainly had an effect on the arts, but it is difficult to discern any other lasting impact on Mughal India.

Death

The health of Jahangir was completely shattered by too much drinking of alcohol. He was trying to restore it by visiting Kashmir and Kabul. He went from Kabul to Kashmir but returned to Lahore on account of a severe cold.

Jahangir died on the way from Kashmir in 1627 and was buried in Shahdara Bagh, a suburb of Lahore, Punjab, Pakistan. He was succeeded by his third son, Prince Khurram who took the title of Shah Jahan. Jahangir's elegant mausoleum is located in the Shahdara locale of Lahore and is a popular tourist attraction in Lahore. On his death in 1627 he uttered 'Kashmir only Kashmir'.

SHAH JAHAN

Shahab-ud-din Mohammad Shah Jahan I (also spelled Shah Jehan, Shahjehan, January 5, 1592 – January 22, 1666) was the ruler of the Mughal Empire in the Indian subcontinent from 1628 until 1658. The name Shah Jahan comes from Persian meaning "King of the World." He was the fifth Mughal ruler after Babur, Humayun, Akbar, and Jahangir. While young, he was a favourite of Akbar. Even while very young, he could be pointed out to be the successor to the Mughal throne after the death of Jahangir.

He succeeded to the throne upon his father's death in 1627. He is considered to be one of the greatest Mughals and his reign has been called the Golden Age of Mughals. Like Akbar, he was eager to expand his empire. The chief events of his reign were the destruction of the kingdom of Ahmadnagar (1636), the loss of Kandahar to the Persians (1653), and a second war against the Deccan princes (1655). In 1658 he fell ill, and was confined by his son Aurangzeb in the citadel of Agra until his death in 1666. On the eve of his death in 1666, the Mughal Empire spanned almost 750,000,000 acres (3,000,000 km^2), about 9/10 the size of modern India. The period of his reign was the golden age of Mughal architecture.

Shah Jahan erected many splendid monuments, the most famous of which is the Taj Mahal at Agra built as a tomb for his wife Mumtaz Mahal (birth name Arjumand Banu Begum). The Pearl Mosque at

Agra, the palace and great mosque at Delhi also commemorate him. The celebrated Peacock Throne, said to be worth millions of dollars by modern estimates, also dates from his reign. He was the founder of Shahjahanabad, now known as 'Old Delhi'. The important buildings of Shah Jahan were the Diwan-i-Am and Diwan-i-Khas in the fort of Delhi, the Jama Masjid, the Moti Masjid and the Taj. It is pointed out that the Palace of Delhi is the most magnificent in the East.

Biography

Birth And Early Years: Shah Jahan was born as Prince Khurram Shihab-ud-din Mohammad, in 1592 in Lahore as the third and favourite son of the emperor Jahangir, his mother being a Rathore Rajput Princess, known as Princess Jagat Gosain who was Jahangir's second wife. The name Khurram-Persian for 'joyful'- was given by his grandfather Akbar. His early years saw him receive a cultured, broad education and he distinguished himself in the martial arts and as a military commander while leading his father's armies in numerous campaigns-Mewar (1615 CE, 1024 AH), the Deccan (1617 and 1621 CE, 1026 and 1030 AH), Kangra (1618 CE, 1027AH). He was responsible for most of the territorial gains during his father's reign. He also demonstrated a precocious talent for building, impressing his father at the age of 16 when he built his quarters within Babur's Kabul fort and redesigned buildings within Agra fort.

Marriage: In 1607 CE (1025 AH), at the age of fifteen, Khurram was to marry Arjumand Banu Begum, the grand daughter of a Persian noble, who was 14 years old at the time. She would become the unquestioned love of his life. They would, however, have to wait five years before they were married in 1612 CE (1021 AH). After their wedding celebrations, Khurram "finding her in appearance and character elect among all the women of the time," gave her the title Mumtaz Mahal (Jewel of the Palace). She had 18 children. Despite her frequent pregnancies, Mumtaz Mahal travelled with Shah Jahan's entourage throughout his earlier military campaigns and the subsequent rebellion against his father. Mumtaz Mahal was utterly devoted— she was his constant companion and trusted confidante and their relationship was intense.

She is portrayed by Shah Jahan's chroniclers as the perfect wife with no aspirations to political power. This is in direct opposition to how Nur Jahan had been perceived.

AURANGZEB

Muhi-ud-din Mohammad Aurangzeb Bahadur Alamgir I, more commonly known as Aurangzeb (November 4, 1618– March 3, 1707), also known by his chosen imperial title Alamgir I (Conqueror of the Universe), was the 6th Mughal Emperor whose reign lasted from 1658 until his death in 1707. Aurangzeb's reign as the Mughal monarch was marked by many wars of expansion. Aurangzeb, having ruled most of the Indian subcontinent for nearly half a century, was the second longest reigning Mughal emperor after Akbar.

In this period he successfully brought a larger area, notably in southern India, under Mughal rule than ever before. A devout Muslim, Aurangzeb tried to encourage all his people to follow the doctrines of Islam. He destroyed many works of art because he feared that they might be worshipped as idols. After his death, the Mughal Empire gradually shrunk. Aurangzeb's successors, the "Later Mughals", lacked his strong hand and the great fortunes amassed by his predecessors.

Rise to Throne

Early life: Aurangzeb was the third son of the fifth Mughal emperor Shah Jahan and Mumtaz Mahal (Arjumand Banu Begum). After a rebellion by his father, part of Aurangzeb's childhood was spent as a virtual hostage at his grandfather Jahangir's court. Mohammad Saleh Kamboh Salafi had been one of his childhood teachers. After Jahangir's death in 1627, Aurangzeb returned to live with his parents. Shah Jahan followed the Mughal practice of assigning authority to his sons, and in 1634 put Aurangzeb in charge of the Deccan campaign. Following his success in 1636, Aurangzeb became Subahdar (governor) of the Deccan. At this time, he began building a new city near the former capital of Khirki which he named Aurangabad after himself. In 1637, he married Rabia Durrani. During this period the Deccan was relatively peaceful. In the Mughal court, however, Shah Jahan began to show greater and greater favouritism to his eldest son Dara Shikoh.

In 1644, Aurangzeb's sister Jahanara Begum was accidentally burned in Agra. This event precipitated a family crisis which had political consequences. Aurangzeb suffered his father's displeasure when he returned to Agra three weeks after the event, instead of immediately. Shah Jahan dismissed him as the governor of the Deccan. Aurangzeb later claimed (1654) that he had resigned in protest of his father favouring Dara.

In 1645, he was barred from the court for seven months. But later, Shah Jahan appointed him governor of Gujarat; he performed well and was rewarded. In 1647, Shah Jahan made him governor of Balkh and Badakhshan (in modern Afghanistan and Tajikistan), replacing Aurangzeb's ineffective brother Murad Baksh. These areas at the time were under attack from various forces and Aurangzeb's military skill proved successful.

He was appointed governor of Multan and Sindh, and began a protracted military struggle against the Safavid army in an effort to capture the city of Kandahar. He failed, and fell again into his father's disfavour.

In 1652, Aurangzeb was re-appointed governor of the Deccan. In an effort to extend the empire, Aurangzeb attacked the border kingdoms of Golconda (1657), and Bijapur (1658). Both times, Shah Jahan called off the attacks near the moment of Aurangzeb's triumph. In each case Dara Shikoh interceded and arranged a peaceful end to the attacks.

Aurangzeb's Reign

Enforcement of Islamic law: Francois Bernier (1625–1688), a French physician and traveler, became for 12 years the personal physician of Aurangzeb. He described his experiences in *Travels in the Mughal Empire*.

Soon after his ascension, Aurangzeb purportedly abandoned the "liberal" religious viewpoints of his predecessors. Though Akbar, Jahangir and Shah Jahan's approach to faith was more syncretic than the empire's founder, Aurangzeb's position is not so obvious. While his conservative interpretation of Islam and belief in the Sharia (Islamic law) is well documented, how this effected the empire remains unclear. Despite claims of sweeping edicts and policies, contradictory accounts exist. Specifically, his compilation of the Fatawa-e-Alamgiri, a digest of Muslim law, was either intended for personal use, never enforced, or only poorly done. While some assert the lack of broad adoption was due to an inherent flaw, others insist they were only intended for his observance. While it's possible the war of succession and a continued incursions combined with Shah Jahan's spending made cultural expenditures impossible, Aurangzeb's orthodoxy is also used to explain his infamous "burial" of music. The scene describing the "death of music" (and all other forms of performance) is paradoxically dramatic.

Niccolao Manucci's Storia do Mogor and Khafi Khan's Muntakhab al-Lubab are the only documents which describe the aforementioned event. In Storia do Mogor, Manucci describes the ramifications of Aurangzeb's 1668 decree. Here, Aurangzeb's instructions for the muhtasib seem particularly damning:

In Hindustan both Moguls and Hindus are very fond of listening to songs and instrumental music. He therefore ordered the same official to stop music. If in any house or elsewhere he heard the sound of singing and instruments, he should forthwith hasten there and arrest as many as he could, breaking the instruments. Thus was caused a great destruction of musical instruments.

Finding themselves in this difficulty, their large earnings likely to cease, without there being any other mode of seeking a livelihood, the musicians took counsel together and tried to appease the king in the following way: About one thousand of them assembled on a Friday when Aurangzeb was going to the mosque.

They came out with over twenty highly-ornamental biers, as is the custom of the country, crying aloud with great grief and many signs of feeling, as if they were escorting to the grave some distinguished defunct. From afar Aurangzeb saw this multitude and heard their great weeping and lamentation, and, wondering, sent to know the cause of so much sorrow. The musicians redoubled their outcry and their tears, fancying the king would take compassion upon them. Lamenting, they replied with sobs that the king's orders had killed Music, therefore they were bearing her to the grave. Report was made to the king, who quite calmly remarked that they should pray for the soul of Music, and see that she was thoroughly well buried. In spite of this, the nobles did not cease to listen to songs in secret. This strictness was enforced in the principal cities.

This implies he not only placed a prohibition on music, but actively sought and crushed any resistance. Without music, and implicitly dance, many Hindu-inspired practices would have been impossible. Lavish celebrations of the Emperor's birthday, commonplace since the time of Akbar, would certainly be forbidden under such conditions. Oddly, artistic work not only steadied during Aurangzeb's reign, it increased. Amidst these and other contradictions, the validity and bias of Manucci and Khafi Khan's work is being questioned.

Another particularly heinous claim against Aurangzeb, was his policy of temple destruction. Though figures vary wildly from 80 to 60,000, it clearly took place to some extent. However, Aurangzeb's

Firmans on behalf of the Balaji or Vishnu Temple and his land grant for famous Hindu religious sites in Kasi, Varanasi insist these events weren't universal. Noted Historian Richard Eaton believes the overall understanding of temples to be flawed. As early as the sixth century, temples became vital political landmarks as well as religious ones. In fact, not only was temple desecration widely practiced and accepted, it was a necessary part of political struggle.

Alexander Hamilton, a British historian, toured India towards the end of Aurangzeb's fifty year reign and observed that every one was free to serve and worship God in his own way. Francois Bernier, travelled and chronicled Mughal India during the war of succession, notes that both Shah Jahan and Aurangzeb's distaste for Christians.

This led to the demolition of Christian settlements near the British/ European Factories and enslavement of Christian converts by Shah Jahan. Furthermore, Aurangzeb stopped all aid to Christian Missionaries (Frankish Padres) initiated by Akbar and Jahangir. Even Aurangzeb's dislike of non-Muslims has become the subject of scrutiny. Historian Shri Sharma states that while Emperor Akbar had fourteen Hindu Mansabdars (high officials) in his court, Aurangzeb actually had 148 Hindu high officials in his court." But this fact is somewhat less known, and all the more hidden and purposefully concealed in books ranging from general magazines to national curricula"

Aurangzeb's Views on the Jizya

From Aurangzeb's Fatwa: [Jizyah] refers to what is taken from the Dhimmis, according to [what is stated in] al-Nihayah. It is obligatory upon the free, adult members of [those] who are generally fought, who are fully in possession of their mental faculties, and gainfully employed, even if [their] profession is not noble, as is [stated in] al-Sarajiyyah. There are two types of [Jizyah]. [The first is] the Jizyah that is imposed by treaty or consent, such that it is established in accordance with mutual agreement, according to [what is stated in] al-Kafi. [The amount] does not go above or below [the stipulated] amount, as is stated in al-Nahr al-Faiq. [The second type] is the Jizyah that the leader imposes when he conquers the unbelievers (kuffar), and [whose amount] he imposes upon the populace in accordance with the amount of property [they own], as in al-Kafi. This is an amount that is pre-established, regardless of whether they agree or disagree, consent to it or not.

The wealthy [are obligated to pay] each year forty-eight dirhams [of a specified weight], payable per month at the rate of 4 dirhams. The next, middle group (wast al-hal) [must pay] Twenty-four dirhams, payable per month at the rate of 2 dirhams. The employed poor are obligated to pay twelve dirhams, in each month paying only one dirham, as stipulated in Fath al-Qadir, al-Hidayah, and al-Kafi. [The scholars] address the meaning of "gainfully employed", and the correct meaning is that it refers to one who has the capacity to work, even if his profession is not noble.

The scholars also address the meaning of wealthy, poor, and the middle group. Al-Shaykh al-Imam Abu Jafar, may Allah the most high have mercy on him, considered the custom of each region decisive as to whom the people considered in their land to be poor, of the middle group, or rich. This is as such, and it is the most correct view, as stated in al-Muhit.

Al-Karakhi says that the poor person is one who owns two hundred dirhams or less, while the middle group owns more than two hundred and up to ten thousand dirhams, and the wealthy [are those] who own more than ten thousand dirhams...The support for this, according to al-Karakhi is provided by the fatawa of Qadi Khan (d. 592/1196). It is necessary that in the case of the employed person, he must have good health for most of the year, as is stated in al-Hidayah. It is mentioned in al-Idah that if a dhimmi is ill for the entire year such that he cannot work and he is well off, he is not obligated to pay the Jizyah, and likewise if he is sick for half of the year or more. If he quits his work while having the capacity [to work] he [is still liable] as one gainfully employed, as is [stated in] al-Nihayah. No Jizyah is imposed upon their women, children, ill persons or the blind, or likewise on the paraplegic, the very old, or on the unemployed poor, as is stated in al-Hidayah.

BADSHAHI MOSQUE

The Badshahi Mosque or the 'King's Mosque' in Lahore, commissioned by the Mughal Emperor Aurangzeb in 1671 and completed in 1673, is the second largest mosque in Pakistan and South Asia and the fifth largest mosque in the world. Epitomising the beauty, passion and grandeur of the Mughal era, it is Lahore's most famous landmark and a major tourist attraction.

Capable of accommodating 5,000 worshippers in its main prayer hall and a further 95,000 in its courtyard and porticoes, it remained the largest mosque in the world from 1673 to 1986 (a period of 313 years), when overtaken in size by the completion of the Faisal Mosque in Islamabad. Today, it remains the second largest mosque in Pakistan and South Asia and the sixth largest mosque in the world after the Masjid al-Haram (Grand Mosque) of Mecca, the Al-Masjid al-Nabawi (Prophet's Mosque) in Medina, the Hassan II Mosque in Casablanca, the Istiqlal Mosque in Jakarta and the Faisal Mosque in Islamabad.

To appreciate its large size, the four minarets of the Badshahi Mosque are 13.9 ft (4.2 m) taller than those of the Taj Mahal and the main platform of the Taj Mahal can fit inside the 278,784 sq ft (25,899.9 m^2) courtyard of the Badshahi Mosque, which is the largest mosque courtyard in the world.

In 1993, the Government of Pakistan recommended the inclusion of the Badshahi Mosque as a World Heritage Site in UNESCO's World Heritage List, where it has been included in Pakistan's Tentative List for possible nomination to the World Heritage List by UNESCO.

HISTORY

Construction

Construction of the Badshahi Mosque was ordered in May 1671 by the sixth Mughal Emperor, Aurangzeb, who assumed the title *Alamgir* (meaning "Conqueror of the World"). Construction took about two years and was completed in April 1673. The Badshahi Mosque was built opposite the Lahore Fort, emphasizing its stature in the Mughal Empire. It was constructed on a raised platform to avoid inundation from the nearby Ravi River during flooding. The Mosque's foundation and structure was constructed using bricks and compacted clay. The structure was then cladded with red sandstone tiles brought from a stone quarry near Jaipur in Rajasthan.

The construction work was carried out under the supervision of Aurangzeb's foster brother, Muzaffar Hussain (also known as Fidai Khan Koka), who was appointed Governor of Lahore by Aurangzeb in May 1671 to specifically oversee the construction of the Mosque and held that post until 1675. He was also Master of Ordnance to Aurangzeb. In conjunction with the building of the Badshahi Mosque, a new gate was built at the Lahore Fort opening into the Hazuri Bagh and facing the main entrance of the Badshahi Mosque, which was named Alamgiri Gate after Aurangzeb. Inscribed in a marble tablet on the entrance of the Badshahi Mosque are the following words in Persian:

"The Mosque of Abul Muzaffar Muhy-ud-Din Muhammad Aurangzeb Alamgir, Victorious King, constructed and completed under the superintendence of the Humblest Servant of the Royal Household, Fidai Khan Koka, in 1084 A.H."

Mosque under Mughal Rule (1673-1752)

When it was completed in 1673, the Badshahi Mosque was not only the largest mosque in the Mughal Empire, but also the largest mosque in the world- a record it would hold for 313 years until 1986. It was also one of the largest buildings in the Mughal Empire and the world. On a clear day, it could be seen from a distance of 15 km. The Badshahi Mosque elevated Lahore to greater political, economic and cultural importance for the Mughal Empire.

Mosque under Sikh Rule (1799-1849)

On 7 July 1799, the Sikh militia of the Sukerchakia chief, Ranjit Singh, took control of Lahore. After the capture of the city, the Badshahi Mosque was severely damaged when Ranjit Singh used its vast courtyard as a stable for his army's horses and its 80 *hujras* (small study rooms surrounding the courtyard) as quarters for his soldiers and as magazines for military stores. Ranjit Singh used the Hazuri Bagh, the enclosed garden next to the Mosque as his official royal court of audience. In 1841, during the Sikh civil war, Ranjit Singh's son, Sher Singh, used the Mosque's large minarets for placement of *zamburahs* or light guns, which were placed atop the minarets to bombard the supporters of the Sikh Maharani Chand Kaur taking refuge in the besieged Lahore Fort, inflicting great damage to the Fort itself. In one of these bombardments, the Fort's Diwan-e-Aam (Hall of Public Audience) was destroyed (it was subsequently rebuilt by the British but never regained its original architectural splendour). During this time, Henri De la Rouche, a French cavalry officer employed in the army of Sher Singh, used a tunnel connecting the Badshahi Mosque to the Lahore Fort to temporarily store gunpowder.

Mosque under British Rule (1858-1947)

When the British took control of India, they continued the Sikh practice of using the Mosque and the adjoining Fort as a military garrison. The 80 cells (*hujras*) built into the walls surrounding the Mosque's vast courtyard on three sides were originally study rooms, which were used by the Sikhs under Ranjit Singh to house troops and military stores. The British demolished them so as to prevent them from being used for anti-British activities and rebuilt them to form open arcades or *dalans*, which continue to this day.

Mosque's Return to Muslims and Restoration

Sensing increasing Muslim resentment against the use of the Mosque as a military garrison, which was continuing since Sikh Rule, the British set up the Badshahi Mosque Authority in 1852 to oversee the restoration and return of the Mosque to Muslims as a place of religious worship. From 1852 onwards, piecemeal repairs were carried out under the supervision of the Badshahi Mosque Authority. Extensive repairs commenced from 1939 onwards. The blueprint for the repairs was prepared by the architect Nawab Zen Yar Jang Bahadur.

Mosque under Pakistan (1947-present)

Restoration work at the Mosque continued after Lahore became part of the new Muslim State of Pakistan on 14 August 1947. By 1960, the Badshahi Mosque stood restored to its original condition at a total cost of 4.8 million rupees (1939-1960). The Government of Pakistan established a small museum inside the Main Gateway Entrance of the Mosque. It contains relics of the Prophet Muhammad, his cousin Ali, and his daughter, Fatimah.

On the occasion of the 2nd Islamic Summit held at Lahore on February 22, 1974, thirty-nine heads of Muslim states offered their Friday prayers in the Badshahi Mosque, which were led by Mawlana Abdul Qadir Azad, the then *Khatib* of the Mosque.

In 1993, the Government of Pakistan recommended the inclusion of the Badshahi Mosque as a World Heritage Site in UNESCO's World Heritage List, where it has been included in Pakistan's Tentative List for possible nomination to the World Heritage List by UNESCO.

In 2000, the marble inlay in the Main Prayer Hall was repaired. In 2008, replacement work on the red sandstone tiles on the Mosque's large courtyard commenced and was completed in 2010, using red sandstone especially imported from the original source near Jaipur, Rajasthan, India.

Architecture & Design

The architecture and design of the Badshahi Mosque closely resembles that of the slightly smaller Jama Mosque in Delhi, India, which was built in 1648 by Aurangzeb's father and predecessor, Emperor Shahjahan. Its design was inspired by Islamic, Persian, Central Asian and Indian influences. Like the character of its founder, the Mosque is bold, vast and majestic in its expression.

The steps leading to the Main Prayer Hall and its floor are in *Sang-e-Alvi* (variegated marble). The Main Prayer Hall is divided into seven sections by means of multi-foil arches supported on heavy piers, three of which bear the double domes finished externally in white marble. The remaining four sections are roofed with flat domes.

The interior of Main Prayer Hall is richly embellished with stucco tracery (Manbatkari), fresco work, and inlaid marble.

The exterior is decorated with stone carving as well as marble inlay on red sandstone, specially of lotiform motifs in bold relief. The embellishment has Indo-Greek, Central Asian and Indian architectural influence both in technique and motifs.

The skyline is furnished by beautiful ornamental merlons inlaid with marble lining adding grace to the perimeter of the mosque. In its various architectural features like the vast square courtyard, the side aisles (*dalans*), the four corner minarets (*minars*), the projecting central transept of the prayer chamber and the grand entrance gate, is summed up the history of development of mosque architecture of the Muslim world over the thousand years prior to its construction in 1673.

The north enclosure wall of the Mosque was laid close to the Ravi River bank, so a majestic gateway could not be provided on that side and, to keep the symmetry the gate had to be omitted on the south wall as well. Thus, a four Aiwan plan like the earlier Jama Mosque in Delhi, could not be replicated at the Badshahi Mosque.

The walls were built with small kiln-burnt bricks laid in *kankar*, lime mortar (a kind of hydraulic lime) but have a veneer of red sandstone. The steps leading to the prayer chamber and its plinth are in variegated marble.

The main prayer chamber is very deep and is divided into seven compartments by rich engraved arches carried on very heavy piers. Out of the 7 compartments, three double domes finished in marble have superb curvature, whilst the rest have curvilinear domes with a central rib in their interior and flat roof above. In the eastern front aisle, the ceiling of the compartment is flat (*qalamdani*) with a curved border (*ghalatan*) at the cornice level.

The original floor of the courtyard was laid with small kiln-burnt bricks laid in the *Mussalah* pattern. The present red sandstone flooring was laid during the last major refurbishhment (1939-60). Similarly, the original floor of the main prayer chamber was in cut and dressed bricks with marble and *Sang-i-Abri* lining forming *Mussalah* and was also replaced by marble *Mussalah* during the last major repairs.

There are only two inscriptions in the Mosque:

- one on the main gateway entrance
- the other of Kalimah in the prayer chamber under the main high vault.

Dimensions

- Courtyard: 528 ft 8 in (161.14 m) x 528 ft 4 in (161.04 m) (area: 278,784 sq ft (25,899.9 m^2)) (the world's largest mosque courtyard) (compared to 186 × 186 ft (57 × 57 m) for the main platform of the Taj Mahal), divided into two levels: the upper and the lower. In the latter, funeral prayers can also be offered.
- Prayer Chamber: 275 ft 8 in (84.02 m) x 83 ft 7 in (25.48 m) x 50 ft 6 in (15.39 m) high, with its main vault 37 ft 3 in (11.35 m) x 59 ft 4 in (18.08 m) high but with the merlons 74 ft (22.555200 m). (area: 22,825 sq ft (2,120.5 m^2))
- 4 Corner Minarets: 176 ft 4 in (53.75 m) high and 67 ft (20 m) in circumference, are in four stages and have a contained staircase with 204 steps (compared with 162.5 ft (49.5 m) for the minarats of the Taj Mahal).
- Central Dome: Diameter 65 ft (20 m) at bottom (at bulging 70 ft 6 in (21.49 m)); height 49 ft (15 m); pinnacle 24 ft (7.3 m) and neck 15 ft (4.6 m) high.
- 2 Side Domes: Diameter 51 ft 6 in (15.70 m) (at bulging 54 ft (16.46 m)); height 32 ft (9.8 m); pinnacle 19 ft (5.8 m); neck 9 ft 6 in (2.90 m) high.
- Gateway: 66 ft 7 in (20.29 m) x 62 ft 10 in (19.15 m) x 65 ft (20 m) high including domelets; vault 21 ft 6 in (6.55 m) x 32 ft 6 in (9.91 m) high. Its three-sided approach steps are 22 in number.
- Side Aisles (Dalans): 80 in number. Height above floor 23 ft 9 in (7.24 m); plinth 2 ft 7 in (0.79 m).
- Central Tank: 50 ft (15 m) x 50 ft (15 m) x 3 ft (0.91 m) deep (area: 2,500 sq ft (230 m^2))

Architectural Influence

The Badshahi Mosque has architecturally influenced the design of the following mosques:

- Sheikh Zayed Mosque, Abu Dhabi, U.A.E.
- Sir Syed Masjid, Aligarh, India
- Taj-ul-Masajid, Bhopal, India.

REFERENCES

Armand Maass: *Social Problems as Social Movements.* Philadelphia: Lippincott, 1975.

Asher, Catherine: *Architecture of Mughal India*, Cambridge, New York, 1992.

Edwin, M.: *Social Pathology A Systematic Approach to the Theory of Sociopathic Behaviour,* New York: McGraw-Hill, 1951.

Elizabeth B.: *Paradise as a Garden In Persia and Mughal India.* New York, George Braziller, 1979.

Moin, A.: *Evolution of Muslim Political Thought in India,* New Delhi: S. Chand, 1975.

Chapter 2

Middle Kingdoms of India

Middle kingdoms of India (or Classical India) refers to the political entities in India from the 3rd century BC after the decline of the Maurya Empire, and the corresponding rise of the Satavahana dynasty, beginning with Simuka, from 230 BC. This is known as the classical period of India, during which India is estimated to have had the largest economy of the world controlling between one third and one fourth of the world's wealth. The "Middle" period lasts for some 1,500 years, and ends in the 13th century, with the rise of the Delhi Sultanate and the end of the Chalukya Cholas (Rajendra Chola III died 1279).

THE NORTHWEST

The Mauryan Empire, during the 2nd century BC, became a collage of regional powers with overlapping boundaries. The whole of north-west attracted a series of invaders between 200 BC and 300 AD. The Puranas speak of many of these tribes as foreigners and impure barbarians (Mlechhas). First the Satavahanas and later the Gupta Empire, both successor states to the Mauryan Empire, attempt to contain the expansions of the successive before eventually crumbling internally due pressure exerted by these wars.

The invading tribes were influenced by Buddhism which continued to flourish under the patronage of both the invaders and the Satavahanas and Guptas and provides a cultural bridge between the two cultures. Over time, the invaders became "Indianized" as they influence society and philosophy across the Gangetic plains and are conversely influenced by it. This period is marked by both intellectual and artistic achievements inspired by cultural diffusion and syncretism as the new kingdoms straddle the Silk route.

THE INDO-SCYTHIAN SAKAS

The Indo-Scythians are a branch of Sakas (Scythians), who migrated from southern Siberia into Bactria, Sogdiana, Arachosia, Gandhara, Kashmir, Punjab, and into parts of Western and Central India, Gujarat, Maharashtra and Rajasthan, from the middle of the 2nd century BCE to the 4th century CE. The first Saka king in India was Maues or Moga who established Saka power in Gandhara and gradually extended supremacy over north-western India. Indo-Scythian rule in India ended with the last Western Satrap Rudrasimha III in 395 CE.

The invasion of India by Scythian tribes from Central Asia, often referred to as the Indo-Scythian invasion, played a significant part in the history of India as well as nearby countries. In fact, the Indo-Scythian war is just one chapter in the events triggered by the nomadic flight of Central Asians from conflict with Chinese tribes which had lasting effects on Bactria, Kabul, Parthia and India as well as far off Rome in the west. The Scythian groups that invaded India and set up various kingdoms, included besides the Sakas other allied tribes, such as the Medii, Xanthii,Massagetae, Getae, Parama Kambojas, Avars, Bahlikas, Rishikas and Paradas.

The Indo-Greeks

The Indo-Greek Kingdom (or sometimes Graeco-Indian Kingdom) covered various parts of the north-west and northern Indian subcontinent during the last two centuries BCE, and was ruled by more than 30 Hellenistic kings, often in conflict with each other. The kingdom was founded when the Greco-Bactrianking Demetrius invaded India early in the 2nd century BC; in this context the boundary of "India" is the Hindu Kush. The Greeks in India were eventually divided from the Greco-Bactrian Kingdom centered in Bactria (now the border between Afghanistan and Uzbekistan). The expression "Indo-Greek Kingdom" loosely describes a number of various dynastic polities. There were numerous cities, such as Taxila Pakistan's Punjab, or Pushkalavati and Sagala. These cities would house a number of dynasties in their times, and based on Ptolemy's *Geographia* and the nomenclature of later kings, a certain Theophila in the south was also probably a satrapal or royal seat at some point.

During the two centuries of their rule, the Indo-Greek kings combined the Greek and Indian languages and symbols, as seen on their coins, and blended ancient Greek, Hindu and Buddhist religious practices, as seen in the archaeological remains of their cities and in the indications of their support of Buddhism, pointing to a rich fusion of Indian and Hellenistic influences. The diffusion of Indo-Greek culture had consequences which are still felt today, particularly through the influence of Greco-Buddhist art. The Indo-Greeks ultimately disappeared as a political entity around 10 AD following the invasions of the Indo-Scythians, although pockets of Greek populations probably remained for several centuries longer under the subsequent rule of the Indo-Parthians and Kushans.

The Yavanas

The Yavanas or Yonas were described as living beyond Gandhara. There was another country mentioned in the epic as Parama Yona, in the far west of Yavana. This could be the Ionia of Greece, somehow related to Indian Ionians or Yavanas. The name Yavana could be the Sanskritized form of the name Ionia. Some believes that the name Ionia originated from the Sanskrit word*Ayonija* meaning *one who born not from a (human) womb* or *people with extra ordinary origins*. Yavanas, Sakas, Pahlavas and Hunas were sometimes described as Mlechhas. Sometimes along with them, the Madras, Kambojas, Kekeyas, Sindhus and Gandharas were included. This name was used to indicate their cultural differences with the Vedic culture, prevailed in the Kuru–Panchala Kingdoms.

The Indo-Parthians

With the rise of the Parthians, the Indus Valley was once again brought under the influence of Persia as they conquered the Indo-Scythians. The Indo-Parthian Kingdom was founded by Gondophares around 20 BCE when he declared his Independence from the Parthians. The kingdom last only briefly until its conquest by the Kushans in the late 1st century CE, and was a loose framework where many smaller dynasts maintained their independence.

The Pahlavas

The Pahlavas are a people mentioned in ancient Indian texts like the Manu Smriti, various Puranas, the Ramayana, the Mahabharata, and the Brhatsamhita. In some texts the Pahlavas are synonymous with the Pallavas, a dynasty of Southern India: While the Vayu Purana distinguishes between *Pahlava* and *Pahnava*, the Vamana Purana and Matsya Purana refer to both as *Pallava*. The Brahmanda Purana and Markendeya Purana refer to both as *Pahlava* or *Pallava*. *Bhishama Parava* of the Mahabharata does not distinguish between the Pahlavas and Pallavas. The Pahlavas are said to be same as the Parasikas. According to P. Carnegy, the Pahlava are probably those people who spoke Paluvi or Pehlvi, that is the Parthian language. Buhler similarly suggests Pahlava is an Indic form of *Parthava* meaning 'Parthian'. In a 4th century BCE, Vartika of Katyayana mentions the *Sakah-Parthavah* demonstrating an awareness of these Saka-Parthians, probably by way of commerce.

The Western Satraps

The Western Satraps, or Western Kshatrapas (35–405) were Saka rulers of the western and central part of India (Saurashtra and Malwa: modern Gujarat, Southern Sindh, Maharashtra, Rajasthan and Madhya Pradesh states). Their state, or at least part of it, was called "Ariaca" according to the Periplus of the Erythraean Sea. They were successors to the Indo-Scythians, and were contemporaneous with the Kushans who ruled the northern part of the Indian subcontinent and were possibly their overlords, and the Satavahana (Andhra) who ruled in Central India. They are called "Western" in contrast to the "Northern" Indo-Scythian satraps who ruled in the area of Mathura, such as Rajuvula, and his successors under the Kushans, the "Great Satrap" Kharapallana and the "Satrap" Vanaspara. Although they called themselves "Satraps" on their coins, leading to their modern designation of "Western Satraps", Ptolemy in his 2nd century *Geographia* still called them "Indo-Scythians". Altogether, there were 27 independent Western Satrap rulers during a period of about 350 years. The word *Kshatrapa* stands for *satrap*, and its equivalent inPersian *Ksatrapavan*, which means viceroy or governor of a province.

The Kushans

The Kushan Empire (c. 1st–3rd centuries) originally formed in Bactria on either side of the middle course of the Oxus River or Amu Darya in what is now northern Afghanistan, Tajikistan and Uzbekistan; during the 1st century CE, they expanded their territory to include the Punjab and much of the Gangesbasin, conquering a number of kingdoms across the northern part of the Indian subcontinent in the process. The

Kushans conquered the central section of the main Silk Routes and, therefore, had control of the overland trade between India, Persia, China and the Roman Empire.

The Indo-Sassanid Kushanshahs

The rise of a new Persian dynasty, the Sassanids saw them re-exert their influence into the Indus region and conquer lands from the Kushans setting up the Kushanshahs around 240 AD. They were to maintain their influence in the region until they were overthrown by the rising Caliphate. Afterwards they were displaced in 410 CE by the invasions of the Indo-Hephthalites.

The Hephthalite Hunas

The Hephthalite were another Central Asian nomadic tribe to invade. They are also linked to the Yuezhi who founded the Kushan Empire. From their capital in Bamiyan, Afghanistan they extended their rule across the Indus and Northern India thereby pressuring the collapse of the Gupta Empire. They were eventually defeated by the Sassanid Empire in alliance with other Turkic tribes.

The Rais

The Rai Dynasty of Sindh were patrons of Buddhism even though they also established a huge temple of Shiva in present-day Sukkur, derived from original Shankar, close to their capital in Alor. This is consistent with the historical accounts from the times of Emperor Ashoka and Harsha because Indian monarchs never sponsored a state religion and usually patronized more than one faith. The influence of the Rai state exdended from Kashmir and Kannaujin the east, Makran and Debal (Karachi) port in the west, Surat port in south, Kandahar, Sistan, Suleyman, Ferdan and Kikanan hills in the north.

The Gandharan Kambojas

The Gandhara Satrapy became an independent kingdom based from Afghanistan and vied with the Tang dynasty, Tibet, the Islamic Caliphate and Turkic tribes for domination in the region.

The Shahis

The Shahialso called Shahiya dynasties ruled portions of the Kabul Valley (in eastern Afghanistan) and the old province of Gandhara (northern Pakistan from the decline of the Kushan Empire in 3rd century to the early 9th century. The kingdom was known as Kabul-shahan or Ratbel-shahan from (565–670 CE) when the capitals were located inKapisa and Kabul, and later Udabhandapura (also known as *Hund*) for its new capital. In ancient time, the title Shahi appears to be a quite popular royal title in Afghanistan and the north-western areas of the Indian sub-continent. It was used by Achaemenids, Sakas, Kushanas, Hunas, Bactrians, by the rulers of Kapisa/Kabul and Gilgit. In Persian form, the title appears as *Kshathiya, Kshathiya Kshathiyanam*, Shao of the Kushanas and the *Ssaha* of Mihirakula (Huna chief). The Kushanas are stated to have adopted the title *Shah-in-shahi("Shaonano shao")* in imitation of Achaemenid practice. The Shahis of Kabul/Gandhara are generally split up into two eras—the Buddhist-Shahis and the Hindu-Shahis, with the change-over thought to have occurred sometime around 870 AD.

The Gangetic Plains and Deccan

Following the demise of the Mauryan Empires the Satavahanas rose as the successor state to check and contend with the influx of the Central Asian tribes from the Northwest. The Satavahanas straddling the Deccan plateau also provided a link for transmission of Buddhism and contact between the Northern Gangetic plains and the Southern regions even as the Upanishads were gaining ground. Eventually weakened both by contention with the northwestern invaders and internal strife they broke up and gave rise to several nations around Deccan and central India regions even as the Gupta Empire arose in the Indo-Gangetic Plain and ushered in a "Golden Age" and rebirth of empire as decentralized local administrative model and the spread of Indian culture until collapse under the Huna invasions. After the fall of Gupta Empire the Gangetic region broke up into several states temporarily reunited under Harsha then giving rise to the Rajput dynasties. In the Deccan, the Chalukyas arose forming a formidable nation marking the migration of the centres of cultural and military power long held in the Indo-Gangetic Plain to the new nations forming in the southern regions of India.

The Satavahanas

The Sâtavâhana Empire started out as feudatories to the Mauryan Empire but declared independence with its decline. They were the first Indic rulers to issue coins struck with their rulers embossed and are known for their patronage of Buddhism resulting in Buddhist monuments from Ellora to Amaravati. They formed a cultural bridge and played a vital role in trade and the transfer of ideas and culture to and from the Gangetic plains to the southern tip of India.

They had to compete with the Sungas and then the Kanvas of Magadha to establish their rule. Later they had to contend in protecting their domain from the incursions of Sakas, Yavanas and Pahlavas. In particular their struggles with the Western Kshatrapas weakened them and the empire split into smaller states.

The Mahameghavahana Dynasty

The Mahameghavahana dynasty (c. 250s BC to 400s AD) was an ancient ruling dynasty of Kalinga after the decline of the Mauryan Empire. The third ruler of the dynasty, Kharavela, conquered much of India in a series of campaigns at the beginning of the common era. Kaingan military might was reinstated by Khârabsa: under Khârabsa's generalship, the Kalinga state had a formidable maritime reach with trade routes linking it to the then-Simhala (Sri Lanka), Burma (Myanmar), Siam (Thailand), Vietnam, Kamboja (Cambodia), Borneo, Bali, Samudra (Sumatra) and Jabadwipa (Java). Khârabsa led many successful campaigns against states of Magadha, Anga, Satavahanas and the South Indian regions of Pandyan Empire (modern Andhra Pradesh) and expanded Kalinga as far as the Ganges and the Kaveri.

The Kharavelan state had a formidable maritime empire with trading routes linking it to Sri Lanka, Burma, Thailand, Vietnam, Cambodia, Borneo, Bali, Sumatra and Java. Colonists from Kalinga settled in Sri Lanka, Burma, as well as the Maldives and Maritime Southeast Asia. Even today Indians are referred to as Keling in Malaysia because of this.

Although religiously tolerant, Khârabç7a patronised Jainism and was responsible for the propagation of Jainism in the Indian Subcontinent but his importance is neglected in many accounts of Indian history. The main source of information about Khârabesa is his famous seventeen line rock-cut Hâtigumphâ inscription in a cave in the Udayagiri hills near Bhubaneswar, Orissa. According to the Hathigumpha inscription, he attacked Rajagriha in Magadha, thus inducing the Indo-Greek king Demetrius to retreat to Mathura.

The Guptas

The Classical Age refers to the period when much of the Indian

Subcontinent was reunited under the Gupta Empire (ca. 320 AD–550 AD). This period is called the Golden Age of India and was marked by extensive achievements in science, technology, engineering, art, dialectic, literature, logic, mathematics, astronomy, religion and philosophy that crystallized the elements of what is generally known as Hindu culture. The decimal numeral system, including the concept of zero, was invented in India during this period. The peace and prosperity created under leadership of Guptas enabled the pursuit of scientific and artistic endeavours in India.

The high points of this cultural creativity are magnificent architectures, sculptures and paintings. The Gupta period produced scholars such as Kalidasa, Aryabhata, Varahamihira, Vishnu Sharma, and Vatsyayana who made great advancements in many academic fields. Science and political administration reached new heights during the Gupta era. Strong trade ties also made the region an important cultural centre and set the region up as a base that would influence nearby kingdoms and regions in Burma, Sri Lanka, Malay Archipelago and Indochina.

The Gupta period marked a watershed of Indian culture: the Guptas performed Vedic sacrifices to legitimize their rule, but they also patronized Buddhism, which continued to provide an alternative to Brahmanical orthodoxy.

The military exploits of the first three rulers - Chandragupta I (ca. 319–335), Samudragupta (ca. 335–376), and Chandragupta II (ca. 376–415) —brought much of India under their leadership. They successfully resisted the North-Western Kingdoms until the arrival of the Hunas who established themselves in Afghanistan by the first half of the 5th century, with their capital at Bamiyan. Nevertheless, much of the Deccan and southern India were largely unaffected by this state of flux in the north.

The Vakatakas

The Vakataka Empire was the contemporaries of the Gupta Empire and the successor state of the Satavahanas they formed the southern boundaries of the north and ruled over today's modern day states of Madhya Pradesh and Maharashtra during the 3rd and 5th centuries. The rock-cut Buddhist viharas and chaityas of Ajanta Caves (a UNESCO World Heritage Site), built under the patronage of the Vakataka rulers. They were eventually overrun by the Chalukyas.

The Harsha Vardhana

After the collapse of the Gupta Empire, the gangetic plains fractured into numerous small nations. Harsha of Kannauj was able to briefly bind them together under his rulership. Only a defeat at the hands of the Chalukyas (Pulakesi II) prevented him from expanding his reign south of the Narmada River. This unity did not last long beyond his reign and his empire fractured soon after his death in 647 AD.

The Gurjars

From 550 to 1018 AD, the Gurjars played a great part in history of Northern India nearly for 500 years. Present day Rajasthan was under the rule of Gurjars for centuries with capital at Bhilmal (Bhinmal or Srimal), situated nearly 50 miles to the north west of Mount Abu. The Gurjars of Bhilmal conquered Kannuaj on the Ganges at the beginning of 9th century and transferred their capital to Kannuaj and founded an empire which at its peak was bounded on the east by Bihar, on the west by the *lost river*, the Hakra, and the Arabian Sea, on the North By the Himalaya andSutlaj, and on the South by the Jumna and Narmada. The region round Broach, which was offshoot of this kingdom, was also ruled by the Gurjaras of Nandipuri (or Nadol).

The Vishnukundinas

The Vishnukundina Empire was an Indian dynasty that ruled over the Deccan, Orissa and parts of South India during the 5th and 6th centuries carving land out from the Vakataka Empire. The Vishnukundin reign came to an end with the conquest of the eastern Deccan by the Chalukya, Pulakesi II. Pulakesi appointed his brother Kubja Vishnuvardhana as Viceroy to rule over the conquered lands. Eventually Vishnuvardhana declared his independence and started the Eastern Chalukya dynasty.

The Maitrakas

The Maitraka Empire ruled Gujarat in western India from the c. 475 to 767. The founder of the dynasty, *Senapati* (general) Bhatarka, was a military governor of Saurashtra peninsula under Gupta Empire, who had established himself as the independent ruler of Gujarat approximately in the last quarter of 5th century. The first two Maitraka rulers Bhatarka and Dharasena I used only the title of *Senapati* (general). The third ruler Dronasimha declared himself as the *Maharaja*. King Guhasena stopped using the term *Paramabhattaraka*

Padanudhyata along his name like his predecessors, which denotes the cessation of displaying of the nominal allegiance to the Gupta overlords. He was succeeded by his son Dharasena II, who used the title of *Mahadhiraja*. His son, the next ruler Siladitya I, Dharmaditya was described by Hiuen Tsang as a "monarch of great administrative ability and of rare kindness and compassion". Siladitya I was succeeded by his younger brother Kharagraha I. Virdi copperplate grant (616 CE) of Kharagraha I proves that his territories included Ujjain.

The Gurjara Pratiharas

The Gurjara Pratihara Empire formed an Indian dynasty that ruled much of Northern India from the 6th to the 11th centuries. At its peak of prosperity and power (c. 836–910), it rivaled the Gupta Empire in the extent of its territory.

Pointing out the importance of the Gurjara Pratihara empire in the history of India Dr. R.C. Majumdar has observed, "the *Gurjara Pratihara Empire* which continued in full glory for nearly a century, was the last great empire in Northern India before the Muslim conquest. This honour is accorded to the empire of Harsha by many historians of repute but without any real justification, for the Pratihara empire was probably larger, certainly not less in extent rivalled the Gupta Empire and brought political unity and its attendant blessings upon a large part of Northern India. But its chief credit lies in its succecessful resistance to the foreign invasions from the west, from the days of Junaid. This was frankly recognised by the Arab writers themselves.

Historians of India, since the days of Eliphinstone, has wondered at slow progress of Muslim invaders in India compared to their rapid advance in other parts of the world. Arguments of doubtful validity have often been put forward to explain this unique phenomenon. Now there can be little doubt that it was the power of the Gurjara Pratihara army that effectively barred the progress of the Muslims beyond the confines of Sindh, their first conquest for nearly three hundred years. In the light of later events this might be regarded as the "chief contribution of the Gurjara Pratiharas to the history of India".

The Rajputs

The Rajput were a Hindu clan who rose to power across a region stretching from the gangaetic plains to the Afghan mountains, and refer to the various dynasties of the many kingdoms in the region in the wake of the collapse of the Sassanid Empire and Gupta Empire and marks the transition of Buddhist ruling dynasties to Hindu ruling dynasties.

The Chauhans

The Chauhan dynasty flourished from the 8th to 12th centuries AD. It was one of the four main Rajput dynasties of that era, the others being Pratiharas, Paramaras and Chalukyas. Chauhan dynasties established themselves in several places in North India and in the state of Gujarat in Western India.

They were also prominent at Sirohi in the southwest of Rajputana, and at Bundi and Kota in the east.

Inscriptions also associate them with Sambhar, the salt lake area in the Amber (later Jaipur) district (the Sakhambari branch remained near lake Sambhar and married into the ruling Gurjara–Pratihara, who then ruled an empire in Northern India).

Chauhans adopted a political policy that saw them indulge largely in campaigns against the Chalukyas and the invading Muslim hordes. In the 11th century they founded the city of Ajayameru (Ajmer) in the southern part of their kingdom, and in the 12th century captured Dhilika (the ancient name of Delhi) from the Tomaras and annexed some of their territory along the Yamuna River.

The Chauhan Kingdom became the leading state in Northern India under King Prithviraj III (1165–1192), also known as Prithvi Raj Chauhan or Rai Pithora. Prithviraj III has become famous in folk tales and historical literature as the Chauhan king of Delhi who resisted and repelled the invasion by Mohammed of Ghor at the first Battle of Tarain in 1191. Armies from other Rajput kingdoms, including Mewar, assisted him. The Chauhan kingdom collapsed after Prithviraj and his armies fled the battle ground against Mohammed of Ghor in 1192 at the Second Battle of Tarain.

The Kachwaha

The Kachwaha originated as tributaries of the preceding powers of the region. Some scholars point out that it was only following the downfall, in the 8th-10th century, of Kannauj (the regional seat-of-power, following the break-up of Harsha's empire), that the Kacchapaghata state emerged as a principal power in the Chambal valley of present-day Madhya Pradesh.

The Paramaras

The Paramara dynasty was an early medieval Indian dynasty who ruled over Malwa region in central India. This dynasty was founded by Upendra in c.800. The most significant ruler of this dynasty was Bhoja I who was a philosopher king and polymath. The seat of the Paramara kingdom was *Dhara Nagari* (the present day Dhar city in Madhya Pradesh state).

The Solankis

The Solanki were Hindu The name *Solanki* comes from *Chalukya* the ancient Indian dynasty. During 543-566, Pulakesi I, established the kingdom at*Vatapi* (present-day Badami, Bagalkot District in North Karnataka of Karnataka).

In Gujarat, Anhilwara (modern Siddhpur Patan) served as their capital. Gujarat was a major centre of Indian Ocean trade, and Anhilwara was one of the largest cities in India, with population estimated at 100,000 in the year 1000. The Solankis were patrons of the great seaside temple of Shiva at Somnath Patan in Kathiawar; Bhima Dev helped rebuild the temple after it was sacked by Mahmud of Ghazni in 1026. His son, Karandev, conquered the Bhil king Ashapall or Ashaval, and after his victory established a city named Karnavati on the banks of the Sabarmati River, at the site of modern Ahmedabad.

The Tanwars (Tomara)

The Tanwar dynasty flourished from 8th to 12th century AD. It ruled from Delhi and Anangpal Tuar in 10th century AD was justly titled 'Paramount Soveirgn of India'. This dynasty claimed to be genelogical descendants of Chandra Vanshi Pandavas and ruled small principalities and villages till Anangpal Tuar - I in 8th century expanded and established Tomar rule at Indraprastha (Delhi), the place of abode of his ancestors. They ruled from modern day Kannauj and Delhi and were later defeated by Gahadavala's at Kannauj and later by Chauhan's of Ajmer. The last Tomar King married his daughter to Chauhan ruling family and his maternal Grandson Prithviraj Chauhan was proclaimed his heir apparent. A total of 19 Tomar rulers ruled Thanesar (modern-day Haryana-Delhi). Jaipal Tuar was ruling at the time of Gaznavid invasion in 10th century.

The Palas

Pala Empire was a Buddhist dynasty that ruled from the north-eastern region of the Indian subcontinent. The name *Pala* means *protector* and was used as an ending to the names of all Pala monarchs. The Palas were followers of the Mahayana and Tantric schools of Buddhism. Gopala was the first ruler from the dynasty. He came to power in 750 in Gaur by ademocratic election. This event is recognized as one of the first democratic elections in South Asia since the time of the Mahâ Janapadas. He reigned from 750-770 and consolidated his position by extending his control over all of Bengal. The Buddhist dynastylasted for four centuries (750-1120 AD) and ushered in a period of stability and prosperity in Bengal. They created many temples and works of art as well as supported the Universities of Nalanda and Vikramashila. Somapura Mahavihara built by Dharmapala is the greatest Buddhist Vihara in the Indian Subcontinent.

The empire reached its peak under Dharmapala and Devapala. Dharmapala extended the empire into the northern parts of the Indian Subcontinent. This triggered once again the power struggle for the control of the subcontinent. Devapala, successor of Dharmapala, expanded the empire to cover much of South Asia and beyond. His empire stretched from Assam and Utkala in the east, Kamboja(modern day Afghanistan) in the northwest and Deccan in the south. According to Pala copperplate inscription Devapala exterminated the Utkalas, conquered the Pragjyotisha (Assam), shattered the pride of the Huna, and humbled the lords of Pratiharas, Gurjara and the Dravidas.

The death of Devapala ended the period of ascendancy of the Pala Empire and several independent dynasties and kingdoms emerged during this time. However, Mahipala I rejuvenated the reign of the Palas. He recovered control over all of Bengal and expanded the empire. He survived the invasions of Rajendra Chola and the Chalukyas. After Mahipala I the Pala dynasty again saw its decline until Ramapala, the last great ruler of the dynasty, managed to retrieve the position of the dynasty to some extent. He crushed the Varendra rebellion and extended his empire farther to Kamarupa, Orissa and Northern India. The Pala Empire can be considered as the golden era of Bengal. Never had the Bengali people reached such height of power and glory to that extent. Palas were responsible for the introduction of Mahayana Buddhism in Tibet, Bhutan and Myanmar. The Palas had extensive trade as well as influence in southeast Asia. This can be seen in the sculptures and architectural style of the Sailendra Empire (presentday Malaya, Java, Sumatra).

The Candras

The Candra Dynasty who ruled over eastern Bengal and were contemporaries of the Palas.

The Eastern Gangas

The Eastern Ganga dynasty rulers reigned over Kalinga which consisted of the parts of the modern day Indian states of Orissa, West Bengal, Jharkhand, Chattisgarh, Madhya Pradesh and Andhra Pradesh from the 11th century to the early 15th century. Their capital was known by the name Kalinganagar, which is the modern Srimukhalingam in Srikakulam District of Andhra Pradesh bordering Orissa. Today they are most remembered as the builders of the Konark Sun Temple a World Heritage site at Konark, Orissa. It was built by King Narasimhadeva I (1238–1264). During their reign (1078-1434) a new style of temple architecture came into being, commonly called as Indo-Aryan architecture. This dynasty was founded by King Anantavarma Chodaganga Deva (1078–1147). He was a religious person and a patron of art and literature. He is credited for having built the famous Jagannath Temple of Puri in Orissa. King Anantavarman Chodagangadeva was succeeded by a long line of illustrious rulers such as Narasimhadeva I (1238–1264). The rulers of Eastern Ganga dynasty not only defended their kingdom from the constant attacks of the Muslim rulers from both northern and southern India but were perhaps one of the few empires to have successfully invaded and defeated their Muslim adversaries. The Eastern Ganga King Narasimha Deva I invaded the Muslim kingdom of Bengal and handed a heavy defeat to the Sultan. This ensured that Sultanate never encroached upon the domains of the Ganga Emperors for nearly a century. His military exploits still survive today as folklore in Orissa. This kingdom prospered through trade and commerce and the wealth was mostly used in the construction of temples. The rule of the dynasty came to end under the reign of King Bhanudeva IV (1414–34), in the early 15th century.

The Senas

The Palas were followed by the Sena dynasty who brought Bengal under one ruler during the 12th century. Vijay Sen the second ruler of this dynasty defeated the last Pala emperor Madanapalaand established his reign. Ballal Sena introduced caste system in Bengal and made Nabadwip the capital. The fourth king of this dynasty Lakshman Sen expanded the empire beyond Bengal to Bihar, Assam, northern Orissa and probably to Varanasi. Lakshman was later defeated by the Muslims and fled to eastern Bengal were he ruled few more years. The Sena dynasty brought a revival of Hinduism and cultivated Sanskrit literature in India.

The Varmans

The Varman Dynasty (not to be confused with the Varman dynasty of Kamarupa) ruled over eastern Bengal and were contemporaries of the Senas.

THE NORTHEAST

The Varman Dynasty of Kamarupa

The Varman dynasty was the first historical dynasty of the Kamarupa kingdom, established by Pushyavarman in the 4th century. The kingdom under the Varman rulers, especially under Kumar Bhaskara Varman, extended up to the Karatoya river in the west and Sadiya in the east and included the Sylhet division of presentday Bangladesh. This dynasty ruled from their capital in the vicinity of presentday Guwahati till the middle of the 7th century.

The Mlechchha dynasty of Kamarupa

The Mlechchha dynasty succeeded the Varman dynasty in Kamarupa and ruled to the end of the 10th century. They ruled from their capital in the vicinity of the presentday Tezpur.

The Pala dynasty of Kamarupa

The Pala dynasty of Kamarupa succeeded the Mlechchha dynasty in Kamarupa and ruled till the end of the 12th century.

The Twipras

The Twipra kingdom and dynasty ruled in the Tripura region.

The Deccan plateau and South

In the first half of the millennium the South saw various smalled kingdoms rise and fall mostly independent to the turmoil in the Gangetic plains and the spread of the Buddhism and Jainism to the southern tip of India. During the second half of the millennium after the fall of the Gupta Empire we see a gradual shift of the balance of power both military and cultural from the northern states to the rise of large southern states.

In fact, from the mid-seventh to the mid-13th centuries, regionalism was the dominant theme of political or dynastic history of South Asia. Three features commonly characterize the sociopolitical realities of this period.

- First, the spread of Brahmanical religions was a two-way process of Sanskritization of local cults and localization of Brahmanical social order.
- Second was the ascendancy of the Brahman priestly and landowning groups that later dominated regional institutions and political developments.
- Third, because of the seesawing of numerous dynasties that had a remarkable ability to survive perennial military attacks, regional kingdoms faced frequent defeats but seldom total annihilation.

Peninsular India was involved in an 8th-century tripartite power struggle among the Chalukyas (556–757), the Pallavas (300–888) of Kanchipuram, and the Pandyas. The Chalukya rulers were overthrown by their subordinates, the Rashtrakutas (753-973). Although both the Pallava and Pandya kingdoms were enemies, the real struggle for political domination was between the Pallavaand Chalukya realms.

The emergence of the Rashtrakutas heralded a new era in the history of South India. The idiom of a Pan-Indian empire had moved to south. South Indian kingdoms had hitherto ruled areas only up to and south of the Narmada River. It was the Rashtrakutas who first forged north to the Gangetic plains and successfully contested their might against the Palas of Bengal and the Rajput Prathiharas of Gujarat.

Despite interregional conflicts, local autonomy was preserved to a far greater degree in the south where it had prevailed for centuries. The absence of a highly centralized government was associated with a corresponding local autonomy in the administration of villages and districts. Extensive and well-documented overland and maritime trade flourished with the Arabs on the west coast and with Southeast Asia. Trade facilitated cultural diffusion in Southeast Asia, where local elites selectively but willingly adopted Indian art, architecture, literature, and social customs.

The interdynastic rivalry and seasonal raids into each other's territory notwithstanding, the rulers in the Deccan and South India patronized all three religions - Buddhism, Hinduism, and Jainism. The religions vied with each other for royal favour, expressed in land grants but more importantly in the creation of monumental temples, which remain architectural wonders. The cave temples of Elephanta Island (near Mumbai or Bombay, as it was known formerly), Ajanta, and Ellora (in Maharashtra), and structural temples of Pattadakal, Aihole, Badami in Karnataka and Mahaballipuram and Kanchipuram in Tamil Nadu are enduring legacies of otherwise warring regional rulers. By the mid-7th century, Buddhism and Jainism began to decline as sectarian Hindu devotional cults of Shiva and Vishnu vigorously competed for popular support.

Although Sanskrit was the language of learning and theology in South India, as it was in the north, the growth of the bhakti (devotional) movements enhanced the crystallization of vernacular literature in all four major Dravidian languages: Tamil, Telugu, Malayalam, and Kannada; they often borrowed themes and vocabulary from Sanskrit but preserved much local cultural lore. Examples of Tamil literature include two major poems, Cilappatikaram (The Jewelled Anklet) and Manimekalai (The Jewelled Belt); the body of devotional literature of Shaivism and Vaishnavism—Hindu devotional movements; and the reworking of the Ramayana by Kamban in the 12th century. A nationwide cultural synthesis had taken place with a minimum of common characteristics in the various regions of South Asia, but the process of cultural infusion and assimilation would continue to shape and influence India's history through the centuries.

The Sangam Era Kingdoms

Farther south were three ancient Tamil states - Chera (on the west), Chola (on the east), and Pandya (in the south) —. They were involved in internecine warfare seeking regional supremacy. They are mentioned in Greek and Ashokan sources as important Indian kingdoms beyond the Mauryan Empire. A corpus of ancient Tamil literature, known as Sangam (academy) works, provides much useful information about life in these kingdoms in the era 300 BC to 200 AD. There is clear evidence of encroachment by Aryan traditions from the north into a predominantly indigenous Dravidian culture in transition.

Dravidian social order was based on different ecoregions rather than on the Aryan varna paradigm, although the Brahmans had a high status at a very early stage. Segments of society were characterized by matriarchy and matrilineal succession—which survived well into the 19th century—crosscousin marriage, and strong regional identity. Tribal chieftains emerged as "kings" just as people moved from pastoralism toward agriculture sustained by irrigation based on rivers by small-scale water tanks (as man-made ponds are called in India) and wells, as well as maritime trade with Rome and Southeast Asia.

Discoveries of Roman gold coins in various sites attest to extensive South Indian links with the outside world. As with Patliputra in the northeast and Taxilain the northwest (in modern Pakistan), the city of Madurai, the capital of the Pandyan Kingdom (in modern Tamil Nadu), was the centre of intellectual and literary activity. Poets and bards assembled there under royal patronage at successive concourses to composed anthologies of poems and expositions on Tamil grammar. By the end of the 1st century BC, South Asia was crisscrossed by overland trade routes, which facilitated the movements of Buddhist and Jain missionaries and other travelers and opened the area to a synthesis of many cultures.

The Cheras

From early pre-historic times, Tamil Nadu was the home of the four Tamil states of the Chera, Chola, Pandya and Pallavas. The oldest extant literature, dated between 300 BC and 600 AD mentions the exploits of the kings and the princes, and of the poets who extolled them. Cherans, who spoke Tamil language ruled from the capital of Karur in the west and traded extensively with West Asian kingdoms.

An unknown dynasty called Kalabhras invaded and displaced the three Tamil kingdoms between the 4th and the 7th centuries. This is referred to as the Dark Age in Tamil history. They were eventually expelled by the Pallavas and the Pandyas.

The Kalabhras

Little of their origins or the time during which they ruled is known beyond that they ruled over the entirety of the southern tip of India during the 3rd to the 6th century, overcoming the Sangam era kingdoms. The appear to be patrons of Jainism and Buddhism as the only source of information on them is the scattered mentions in the many Buddhist and Jain literature of the time. They were contemporaries of the Kadambas and the Western Ganga Dynasty. They were overcome by the rise of the Pallavas and the resurgence of the Pandyan Kingdom.

The Kadambas

The Kadamba Dynasty (345–525 CE) was an ancient royal family of Karnataka that ruled from Banavasi in present day Uttara Kannada district. The dynasty later continued to rule as a feudatory of larger Kannada empires, the Chalukya and the Rashtrakuta empires for over five hundred years during which time they branched into Goa and Hanagal. At the peak of their power under King Kakushtavarma, they ruled large parts of Karnataka. During the pre-Kadamba era the ruling families that controlled Karnataka, the Mauryas, Satavahanas and Chutus were not natives of the region and the nucleus of power resided outside present day Karnataka. The Kadambas were the first indigenous dynasty to use Kannada, the language of the soil at an administrative level. In the history of Karnataka, this era serves as a broad based historical starting point in the study of the development of region as an enduring geo-political entity and Kannada as an important regional language.

The dynasty was founded by Mayurasharma in 345 which at times showed the potential of developing into imperial proportions, an indication to which is provided by the titles and epithets assumed by its rulers. One of his successors, Kakusthavarma was a powerful ruler and even the kings of imperial Gupta Dynasty of northern India cultivated marital relationships with his family, giving a fair indication of the sovereign nature of their kingdom. Tiring of the endless battles and bloodshed, one of the later descendants, King Shivakoti adopted Jainism. The Kadambas were contemporaries of the Western Ganga Dynastyof Talakad and together they formed the earliest native kingdoms to rule the land with absolute autonomy.

The Western Gangas

The Western Ganga Dynasty (350–1000 CE) was an important ruling dynasty of ancient Karnataka in India. They are known as Western Gangas to distinguish them from the Eastern Gangas, who in later centuries ruled over modern Orissa. The general belief is the Western Gangas began their rule during a time when multiple native clans asserted their freedom due to the weakening of the Pallava dynasty of South India, a geo-political event sometimes attributed to the southern conquests of Samudragupta. The Western Ganga sovereignty lasted from about 350 to 550 CE, initially ruling from Kolar and later moving their capital to Talakad on the banks of the Kaveri in modern Mysore district.

After the rise of the imperial Chalukya dynasty of Badami, the Gangas accepted Chalukya overlordship and fought for the cause of their overlords against the Pallavas of Kanchipuram. The Chalukyas were replaced by the Rashtrakutas of Manyakheta in 753 CE as the dominant power in the Deccan. After a century of struggle for autonomy, the Western Gangas finally accepted Rashtrakuta overlordship and successfully fought alongside them against their foes, the Chola dynasty of Tanjavur. In the late 10th century, north of Tungabhadra river, the Rashtrakutas were replaced by the emerging Western Chalukya Empire and the Chola Dynasty saw renewed power south of the Kaveri. The defeat of the Western Gangas by Cholas around 1000 resulted in the end of Ganga influence over the region.

Though territorially a small kingdom, the Western Ganga contribution to polity, culture and literature of the modern south Karnataka region is considered important. The Western Ganga kings showed benevolent tolerance to all faiths but are most famous for their patronage towards Jainism resulting in the construction of monuments in places such as Shravanabelagola and Kambadahalli. The kings of this dynasty encouraged the fine arts due to which literature in Kannada and Sanskrit flourished. Chavundaraya's writing, *Chavundaraya Purana* of 978 CE, is an important work in Kannada prose. Many classics were written on subjects ranging from religious topics to elephant management.

The Badami Chalukyas

The Chalukya Empire, natives of the Aihole and Badami region in Karnataka, were at first a feudatory of the Kadambas. They encouraged the use of Kannada in addition to the Sanskrit language in their administration. In the middle of the 6th century the Chalukyas came into their own when Pulakesi I made the hill fortress in Badami his centre of power. During the rule of Pulakesi II a south Indian empire sent expeditions to the north past the Tapti River and Narmada River for the first time and successfully defied Harshavardhana, the King of Northern India (*Uttarapatheswara*). The Aihole inscription of Pulakesi II, written in classical Sanskrit language and old Kannada script dated 634, proclaims his victories against the Kingdoms of Kadambas, Western Gangas, Alupas of South Canara, Mauryas of Puri, Kingdom of Kosala, Malwa, Lata and Gurjaras of southern Rajasthan. The inscription describes how King Harsha of Kannauj lost his *Harsha* (joyful disposition) on seeing a large number of his war elephants die in battle against Pulakesi II.

These victories earned him the title *Dakshinapatha Prithviswamy* (lord of the south). Pulakesi II continued his conquests in the east where he conquered all kingdoms in his way and reached the Bay of Bengal in present day Orissa. A Chalukya viceroyalty was set up in Gujarat and Vengi (coastal Andhra) and princes from the Badami family were dispatched to rule them. Having subdued the Pallavas of Kanchipuram, he accepted tributes from the Pandyas of Madurai, Chola dynasty and Cheras of the Kerala region. Pulakesi II thus became the master of India, south of the Narmada River. Pulakesi II is widely regarded as one of the great kings in Indian history.

Hiuen-Tsiang, a Chinese traveller visited the court of Pulakesi II at this time and Persian emperor Khosrau II exchanged ambassadors. However, the continuous wars with Pallavas took a turn for the worse in 642 when the Pallava king Narasimhavarman I avenged his father's defeat, conquered and plundered the capital of Pulakesi II who may have died in battle. A century later, Chalukya Vikramaditya II marched victoriously into Kanchipuram, the Pallava capital and occupied it on three occasions, the third time under the leadership of his son and crown prince Kirtivarman II. He thus avenged the earlier humiliation of the Chalukyas by the Pallavas and engraved a Kannada inscription on the victory pillar at the Kailasanatha Temple. He later overran the other traditional kingdoms of Tamil country, the Pandyas, Cholas and Keralas in addition to subduing a Kalabhra ruler.

The Kappe Arabhatta record from this period (700) in *tripadi* (three line) metre is considered the earliest available record in Kannada poetics. The most enduring legacy of the Chalukya dynasty is the architecture and art that they left behind. More than one hundred and fifty monuments attributed to the them, built between 450 and 700, have survived in the Malaprabha basin in Karnataka. The constructions are centred in a relatively small area within the Chalukyan heartland. The structural temples at Pattadakal, a UNESCO World Heritage Site, the cave temples of Badami, the temples at Mahakuta and early experiments in temple building at Aihole are their most celebrated monuments. Two of the famous paintings at Ajanta cave no. 1, "The Temptation of the Buddha" and "The Persian Embassy" are also credited to them. Further, they influenced the architecture in far off places like Gujarat and Vengi as evidenced in the Nava Brahma temples at Alampur.

The Pallavas

The 7th century Tamil Nadu saw the rise of the Pallavas under Mahendravarman I and his son *Mamalla* Narasimhavarman I. The

Pallavas were not a recognised political power before the 2nd century. It has been widely accepted by scholars that they were originally executive officers under the Satavahana Empire. After the fall of the Satavahanas, they began to get control over parts of Andhra and the Tamil country. Later they had marital ties with the Vishnukundina who ruled over the Deccan. It was around 550 AD under King Simhavishnu that the Pallavas emerged into prominence. They subjugated the Cholas and reigned as far south as the Kaveri River. Pallavas ruled a large portion of South India with Kanchipuram as their capital. Dravidian architecture reached its peak during the Pallava rule. Narasimhavarman II built the Shore Temple which is a UNESCO World Heritage Site. Many sources describe Bodhidharma, the founder of the Zen school of Buddhism in China, as a prince of the Pallava dynasty.

The Eastern Chalukyas

Eastern Chalukyas were a South Indian dynasty whose kingdom was located in the present day Andhra Pradesh. Their capital was Vengi and their dynasty lasted for around 500 years from the 7th century until c. 1130 CE when the Vengi kingdom merged with the Chola empire.

The Vengi kingdom was continued to be ruled by Eastern Chalukyan kings under the protection of the Chola empire until 1189 CE, when the kingdom succumbed to the Hoysalas and the Yadavas. They had their capital originally at Vengi now (Pedavegi, Chinavegi and Denduluru) near Eluru of the West Godavari district end later changed to Rajamahendravaram (Rajamundry).

Eastern Chalukyas were closely related to the Chalukyas of Vatapi (Badami). Throughout their history they were the cause of many wars between the more powerful Cholas and Western Chalukyas over the control of the strategic Vengi country.

The five centuries of the Eastern Chalukya rule of Vengi saw not only the consolidation of this region into a unified whole, but also saw the efflorescence of Telugu culture, literature, poetry and art during the later half of their rule. It can be said to be the golden period of Andhra history.

The Pandyas

Pallavas were replaced by the Pandyas in the 8th century. Their capital Madurai was in the deep south away from the coast. They had extensive trade links with the Southeast Asian maritime empires of Srivijaya and their successors. As well as contacts, even diplomatic, reaching as far as the Roman Empire. During the 13th century of the Christian era Marco Polo mentioned it as therichest empire in existence. Temples like Meenakshi Amman Temple at Madurai and Nellaiappar Temple at Tirunelveli are the best examples of Pandyan Temple architecture. The Pandyas excelled in both trade as well as literature and they controlled the pearl fisheries along the South Indian coast, between Sri Lanka and India, which produced some of the finest pearls in the known ancient world.

The Rashtrakutas

In the middle of 8th century the Chalukya rule was ended by their feudatory, the Rashtrakuta family rulers of Berar (in present day Amravati district of Maharashtra). Sensing an opportunity during a weak period in the Chalukya rule, Dantidurga trounced the great Chalukyan "Karnatabala" (power of Karnata). Having overthrown the Chalukyas, the Rashtrakutas made Manyakheta their capital (modern Malkhed in Gulbarga district). Although the origins of the early Rashtrakuta ruling families in central India and the Deccan in the 6th and 7th centuries is controversial, during the eighth through the 10th centuries they emphasised the importance of the Kannada language in conjunction with Sanskrit in their administration. Rashtrakuta inscriptions are in Kannada and Sanskrit only. They encouraged literature in both languages and thus literature flowered under their rule.

The Rashtrakutas quickly became the most powerful Deccan empire, making their initial successful forays into the doab region of Ganges River and Jamuna River during the rule of Dhruva Dharavarsha. The rule of his son Govinda III signaled a new era with Rashtrakuta victories against the Pala Dynasty of Bengal and Gurjara Pratihara of north western India resulting in the capture of Kannauj. The Rashtrakutas held Kannauj intermittently during a period of a tripartite struggle for the resources of the rich Gangetic plains. Because of Govinda III's victories, historians have compared him to Alexander the Great and Pandava Arjuna of the Hindu epic Mahabharata. The Sanjan inscription states the horses of Govinda III drank the icy water of the Himalayan stream and his war elephants tasted the sacred waters of the Ganges River. Amoghavarsha I, eulogised by contemporary

Arab traveller Sulaiman as one among the four great emperors of the world, succeeded Govinda III to the throne and ruled during an important cultural period that produced landmark writings in Kannada and Sanskrit. The benevolent development of Jain religion was a hallmark of his rule. Because of his religious temperament, his interest in the arts and literature and his peace loving nature, he has been compared to emperor Ashoka. The rule of Indra III in the 10th century enhanced the Rashtrakuta position as an imperial power as they conquered and held Kannauj again. Krishna III followed Indra III to the throne in 939. A patron of Kannada literature and a powerful warrior, his reign marked the submission of the Paramara of Ujjain in the north and Cholas in the south.

An Arabic writing *Silsilatuttavarikh* (851) called the Rashtrakutas one among the four principle empires of the world. *Kitab-ul-Masalik-ul-Mumalik* (912) called them the "greatest kings of India" and there were many other contemporaneous books written in their praise. The Rashtrakuta empire at its peak spread from Cape Comorin in the south to Kannauj in the north and from Banaras in the east to Broach (Bharuch) in the west. While the Rashtrakutas built many fine monuments in the Deccan, the most extensive and sumptuous of their work is the monolithic Kailasanatha temple at Ellora, the temple being a splendid achievement. In Karnataka their most famous temples are the Kashivishvanatha temple and the Jain Narayana temple at Pattadakal. All of the monuments are designated UNESCO World Heritage Sites.

The Western Chalukyas

In the late 10th century, the Western Chalukyas, also known as the Kalyani Chalukyas or 'Later' Chalukyas rose to power by overthrowing the Rashtrakutas under whom they had been serving as feudatories. Manyakheta was their capital early on before they moved it to Kalyani (modern Basavakalyan). Whether the kings of this empire belonged to the same family line as their namesakes, the Badami Chalukyas is still debated. Whatever the Western Chalukya origins, Kannada remained their language of administration and the Kannada and Sanskrit literature of their time was prolific. Tailapa II, a feudatory ruler from Tardavadi (modern Bijapur district), re-established the Chalukya rule by defeating the Rashtrakutas during the reign of Karka II. He timed his rebellion to coincide with the confusion caused by the invading Paramara of Central India to the Rashtrakutas capital in 973. This era produced prolonged warfare with the Chola dynasty of Tamilakam for control of the resources of the Godavari River–Krishna River doab region in Vengi. Somesvara I, a brave Chalukyan king, successfully curtailed the growth of the Chola Empire to the south of the Tungabhadra River region despite suffering some defeats while maintaining control over his feudatories in the Konkan, Gujarat, Malwa and Kalingaregions. For approximately 100 years, beginning in the early 11th century, the Cholas occupied large areas of South Karnataka region (Gangavadi).

In 1076, the ascent of the most famous king of this Chalukya family, Vikramaditya VI, changed the balance of power in favour of the Chalukyas. His fifty year reign was an important period in Karnataka's history and is referred to as the "Chalukya Vikrama era". His victories over the Cholas in the late 11th and early 12th centuries put an end to the Chola influence in the Vengi region permanently. Some of the well known contemporaneous feudatory families of the Deccan under Chalukya control were the Hoysalas, the Seuna Yadavas of Devagiri, the Kakatiya dynasty and the Southern Kalachuri. At their peak, the Western Chalukyas ruled a vast empire stretching from the Narmada River in the north to the Kaveri River in the south. Vikramaditya VI is considered one of the most influential kings of Indian history. Important architectural works were created by these Chalukyas, especially in the Tungabhadra river valley, that served as a conceptual link between the building idioms of the early Badami Chalukyas and the later Hoysalas. With the weakening of the Chalukyas in the decades following the death of Vikramaditya VI in 1126, the feudatories of the Chalukyas gained their independence.

The Kalachuris of Karnataka, whose ancestors were immigrants into the southern deccan from central India, had ruled as a feudatory from Mangalavada (modern Mangalavedhe in Maharashtra). Bijjala II, the most powerful ruler of this dynasty, was a commander (*mahamandaleswar*) during the reign of Chalukya Vikramaditya VI. Seizing an opportune moment in the waning power of the Chalukyas, Bijjala II declared independence in 1157 and annexed their capital Kalyani. His rule was cut short by his assassination in 1167 and the ensuing civil war caused by his sons fighting over the throne ended the dynasty as the last Chalukya scion regained control of Kalyani. This victory however, was short-lived as the Chalukyas were eventually driven out by the Seuna Yadavas.

The Yadavas

The Seuna, *Sevuna* or Yadava dynasty (850–1334) was an Indian dynasty, which at its peak ruled a kingdom stretching from the Tungabhadra to theNarmada rivers, including presentday Maharashtra, north Karnataka and parts of Madhya Pradesh, from its capital at Devagiri (presentday Daulatabad in Maharashtra). The Yadavas initially ruled as feudatories of the Western Chalukyas. Around the middle of the 12th century, they declared independence and established rule that reached its peak under Singhana II. The foundations of Marathi culture was laid by the Yadavas and the peculiarities of Maharashtra's social life developed during their rule.

The Kakatiyas

The Kakatiya dynasty was a South Indian dynasty that ruled parts of what is now Andhra Pradesh, India from 1083 to 1323. They were one of the great Telugu kingdoms that lasted for centuries.

The Kalachuris

Kalachuri Empire is this the name used by two kingdoms who had a succession of dynasties from the 10th-12th centuries, one ruling over areas in Central India (west Madhya Pradesh, Rajasthan) and were called Chedi or *Haihaya* (*Heyheya*) (northern branch) and the other southern Kalachuri who ruled over parts of Karnataka. They are disparately placed in time and space. Apart from the dynastic name and perhaps a belief in common ancestry, there is little in known sources to connect them. The earliest known Kalachuri family (550–620 AD) ruled over northern Maharashtra, Malwa and western Deccan. Their capital was Mahismati situated in the Narmada river valley. There were three prominent members; Krishnaraja, Shankaragana and Buddharaja. They distributed coins and epigraphs around this area.

Southern Kalachuris (1130–1184) at their peak ruled parts of the Deccan extending over regions of present day North Karnatakaand parts of Maharashtra. This dynasty rose to power in the Deccan between 1156 and 1181 AD. They traced their origins to *Krishna* who was the conqueror of *Kalinjar* and Dahala in Madhya Pradesh. It is said that *Bijjala* a viceroy of this dynasty established the authority over Karnataka. He wrested power from the Chalukya king Taila III. Bijjala was succeeded by his sons Someshwara and Sangama but after 1181 AD, the Chalukyas gradually retrieved the territory. Their rule was a short and turbulent and yet very important from the socio-religious movement point of view; a new sect called the Lingayat or Virashaiva sect was founded during these times. A unique and purely native form of Kannada literature-poetry called the *Vachanas* was also born during this time. The writers of *Vachanas* were called *Vachanakaras* (poets). Many other important works like Virupaksha Pandita's *Chennabasava-purana*, Dharani Pandita's *Bijjalarayacharite* and Chandrasagara Varni's *Bijjalarayapurana* were also written.

Northern Kalachuris ruled in central India with its base at the ancient city of Tripuri (Tewar); it originated in the 8th century, expanded significantly in the 11th century, and declined in the 12th–13th centuries.

The Hoysalas

The Hoysalas had become a powerful force even during their rule from Belur in the 11th century as a feudatory of the Chalukyas (in the south Karnataka region). In the early 12th century they successfully fought the Cholas in the south, convincingly defeating them in the battle of Talakad and moved their capital to nearby Halebidu. Historians refer to the founders of the dynasty as natives of Malnad Karnataka, based on the numerous inscriptions calling them *Maleparolganda* or "Lord of the Male (hills) chiefs" (*Malepas*). With the waning of the Western Chalukya power, the Hoysalas declared their independence in the late 12th century.

During this period of Hoysala control, distinctive Kannada literary metres such as *Ragale* (blank verse), *Sangatya* (meant to be sung to the accompaniment of a musical instrument), *Shatpadi* (seven line) etc. became widely accepted. The Hoysalas expanded the Vesara architecture stemming from the Chalukyas, culminating in the Hoysala architectural articulation and style as exemplified in the construction of the Chennakesava Temple at Belur and the Hoysaleswara temple at Halebidu. Both these temples were built in commemoration of the victories of the Hoysala Vishnuvardhanaagainst the Cholas in 1116. Veera Ballala II, the most effective of the Hoysala rulers, defeated the aggressive Pandya when they invaded the Chola kingdom and assumed the titles "Establisher of the Chola Kingdom" (*Cholarajyapratish-tacharya*), "Emperor of the south" (*Dakshina Chakravarthi*) and "Hoysala emperor" (*Hoysala Chakravarthi*). The Hoysalas extended their foothold in areas known today as Tamil Nadu around 1225, making the city of Kannanur Kuppam near Srirangam a provincial capital. This gave them control over South Indian politics that began a period of Hoysala hegemony in the southern Deccan.

In the early 13th century, with the Hoysala power remaining unchallenged, the first of the Muslim incursions into South India began. After over two decades of waging war against a foreign power, the Hoysala ruler at the time, Veera Ballala III, died in the battle of Madurai in 1343. This resulted in the merger of the sovereign territories of the Hoysala empire with the areas administered by Harihara I, founder of the Vijayanagara Empire, located in the Tungabhadra region in present day Karnataka. The new kingdom thrived for another two centuries with Vijayanagara as its capital.

The Cholas

By the 9th century, under Rajaraja Chola and his son Rajendra Chola, the Cholas rose as a notable power in south Asia. The Chola Empire stretched as far as Bengal. At its peak, the empire spanned almost 3,600,000 km^2 (1,389,968 sq mi). Rajaraja Chola conquered all of peninsular South India and parts of the Sri Lanka. Rajendra Chola's navies went even further, occupying coasts from Burma (now Myanmar) to Vietnam, the Andaman and Nicobar Islands, Lakshadweep, Sumatra, Java, Malaya in South East Asia and Pegu islands. He defeated Mahipala, the king of the Bengal, and to commemorate his victory he built a new capital and named it Gangaikonda Cholapuram.

The Cholas excelled in building magnificent temples. Brihadeshwara Temple in Thanjavur is a classical example of the magnificent architecture of the Chola kingdom. Brihadshwara temple is an UNESCO Heritage Site under "Great Living Chola Temples." Another example is the Chidambaram Temple in the heart of the temple town of Chidambaram.

REFERENCES

Atul Chandra: *History of Bengal: Mughal Period (1526-1765 A.D.)*. Calcutta, 1968.

Augustine, P.A.: *Social Equality in Indian Society*, New Delhi, Concept 1991.

Evans, T.F. : *On Three Copper Cakes found at Bryndu*, Oxford, Anglesey, 1873.

Gascoigne, Bamber : *The Great Moghuls*. London: Jonathan Cape, 1971.

Muhammed Zaki: *History of Muslim Rule : The Prophet and the Early Rulers*, Beacon Pub, Delhi, 2006.

Chapter 3

Mongol Invasions of India

The Mongol Empire launched several invasions into the Indian subcontinent from 1221 to 1327. Some of those later raids were made by the unruly Qaraunas of Mongol origin. The Mongols made Kashmir their vassal state. The Mongol Empire also occupied most of modern Pakistan and Punjab for decades. However, the campaigns against the Delhi Sultanate proved unsuccessful, in spite of constant Mongol incursions.

Background

After pursuing Jalal ad-Din into India from Samarkand and defeating him at the battle of Indus in 1221, Genghis Khan sent two tumens (20,000 soldiers) under commanders Dorbei the Fierce and Bala to continue the chase. The Mongol commander Bala chased Jalal ad-Din throughout the Punjab region and attacked outlying towns like Bhera and Multan and had even sacked the outskirts of Lahore. Jalal ad-Din regrouped, forming a small army from survivors of the battle and sought an alliance, or even an asylum, with the Turkic rulers of Delhi Sultanate, but was turned down.

Jalal ad-Din fought against the local rulers in the Punjab, and usually defeated them in the open but could not occupy their lands. At last he proposed an alliance with the khokhar chieftain of the Salt Range and married his daughter. The Khokhar Rai's son joined Jalal ad-Din's army along with his clansmen and received the title of Kalich (sword) Khan. Jalal ad-Din's soldiers were under his officers Uzbek Pai and Hassan Qarlugh. Khokhar tribe of Punjab was in alliance with Mongols during their invasion of India.

While fighting against the local governor of Sindh, Jalal ad-Din heard of an uprising in the Kirman province of southern Iran and he immediately set out for that place, passing through southern Baluchistan on the way. Jalal ad-Din was also joined by forces from Ghor and Peshawar, including members of the Khilji, Turkoman, andGhori tribes. With his new allies he marched on Ghazni and defeated a Mongol division under Turtai, which had been assigned the task of hunting him down. The victorious allies quarreled over the division of the captured booty; subsequently the Khilji, Turkoman, and Ghori tribesmen deserted Jalal ad-Din and returned to Peshawar. By this time Ögedei Khan, third son of Genghis Khan, had become Great Khan of the Mongol Empire. A Mongol general named Chormaqan sent by the Khan attacked and defeated him, thus ending the Khwârazm-Shâh dynasty.

Mongol conquest of Kashmir and conflicts with the Delhi Sultanate

Some time after 1235 another Mongol force invaded Kashmir, stationing a darughachi (administrative governor) there for several years, and Kashmir became a Mongolian dependency. Around the same time, a Kashmiri Buddhist master, Otochi, and his brother Namo arrived at the court of Ögedei. Another Mongol general named Pakchak attacked Peshawar and defeated the army of tribes who had deserted Jalal ad-Din but were still a threat to the Mongols. These men, mostly Khiljis, escaped to Multan and were recruited into the army of the Delhi Sultanate. In winter 1241 the Mongol force invaded the Indus valley and besieged Lahore. General Dayir was killed while storming the town. However, on December 30, 1241, the Mongols under Munggetu butchered the town before withdrawing from the Delhi Sultanate. At the same time the Great Khan Ögedei died (1241).

The Kashmiris revolted in 1254-1255, and Möngke Khan, who became Great Khan in 1251, appointed his generals, Sali and Takudar, to replace the court and appointed the Buddhist master, Otochi, as darugachi of Kashmir. However, the Kashmiri king killed Otochi at Srinagar. Sali invaded Kashmir, killing the king, and put down the rebellion, after which the country remained subject to the Mongol Empire for many years. The Delhi prince, Jalal al-Din Masud, traveled to the Mongol capital at Karakorum to seek the assistance of Möngke Khan in seizing the throne from his elder brother in 1248. When

Möngke was crowned as Great Khan, Jalal al-Din Masud attended the ceremony and asked for help from Möngke. Möngke ordered Sali to assist him to recover his ancestral realm. Sali made successive attacks on Multan and Lahore. Sham al-Din Muhammad Kart, the client malik (ruling prince) of Herat, accompanied the Mongols. Jalal al-Din was installed as client ruler of Lahore, Kujah and Sodra. In 1257 the governor of Sindh offered his entire province to Hulagu Khan, Mongke's brother, and sought Mongol protection from his overlord in Delhi. Hulagu led a strong force under Sali Bahadur into Sindh. In the winter of 1257 - beginning of 1258, Sali Noyan entered Sind in strength and dismantled the fortifications of Multan; his forces may also have invested the island fortress of Bakhkar on the Indus.

But Hulagu refused to sanction a grand invasion of the Delhi Sultanate and a few years later diplomatic correspondence between the two rulers confirmed the growing desire for peace. Hulagu had many other areas of conquests to take care of in Syria and southwestern Asia. Large-scale Mongol invasions of India ceased and the Delhi Sultans used the respite to recover the frontier towns like Multan, Uch, and Lahore, and to punish the local Ranas and Rais who had joined hands with either the Khwarazim or the Mongol invaders.

Large numbers of tribes that took shelter in the Delhi Sultanate as a result of the Mongol invasions changed the balance of power in North India. The Khilji tribe usurped power from the older Delhi Sultans and began to rapidly project their power into other parts of India. At about this time the Mongol raids into India were also renewed (1300).

The Chagatai Mongols vs. Delhi Sultanate

The Tushar sources claim invasions by hundreds of thousands of Mongols, numbers approximating (and probably based on) the size of the entire cavalry armies of the Mongol realms of Central Asia or the Middle East: about 150,000 men. A count of the Mongol commanders named in the sources as participating in the various invasions might give a better indication of the numbers involved, as these commanders probably led tumens, units nominally of 10,000 men. These invasions were led by either various descendants of Genghis Khan or by Mongol divisional commanders; the size of such armies was always between 10,000-30,000 cavalry although the Muslim chroniclers of Delhi exaggerated the number to 100,000-200,000 cavalry, which was their norm in describing enemy forces.

After civil war broke out in the Mongol Empire in the 1260s, the Chagatai Khanate controlled Central Asia and its leader since the 1280s was Duwa Khan who was second in command of KaiduKhan. Duwa was active in Afghanistan, and attempted to extend Mongol rule into India. Negudari governor Abdullah, who was a son of Chagatai Khan's great grandson, invaded Punjab with his force in 1292, but their advance guard under Ulghu was defeated and taken prisoner by the Khalji Sultan. He was intimidated by the main Mongol army and bought off their attacks for a price. The 4000 Mongol captives of the advance guard converted to Islam and came to live in Delhi as "new Muslims". The suburb they lived in was appropriately named Mughalpura. Chagatai tumens were beaten by the Delhi Sultanate several times in 1296-1297. The Mongols thereafter repeatedly invaded northern India. On at least two occasions, they came in strength.

The two armies met at Jalandhar in 1297. Zafar Khan defeated the Mongols in this first invasion. The Mongols attacked again under the command of Saldi and captured the fort at Siri. Zafar Khan, holding the honour of being one of the few undefeated military commanders in history, had no problem crushing this army. He recaptured the fort and brought 2,000 Mongol prisoners beforeAlauddin Khilji.

During Mongol incursions in 1298, a mixed Turk-Mongol army fought against the Rajput Kings. The Mongols quarreled with the Turk commander and killed his brother in an argument over the distribution of captured wealth. The wives and children of these Mongols were treated with ferocious cruelty and they escaped to the forts of the Rajputs.

Shortly afterward, Duwa Khan sought to end the ongoing conflict with the Yuan Khagan Temür Öljeytü, and around 1304 a general peace among the Mongol khanates was declared, bringing an end to the conflict between the Yuan Dynasty and western khanates that had lasted for the better part of a half century. Soon after, he proposed a joint Mongol attack on India, but the campaign did not materialize.

Late Mongol Invasions

In 1299, against advice, Delhi sultan Alauddin Khilji attacked the Mongols. The advance guard of the Khilji army was led by Zafar Khan himself. He defeated the Mongols and pursued of them as they withdrew. However, the Mongol general Qutlugh Khwaja tricked Zafar into a position where he was surrounded and killed by the Mongols. However, in face of Alauddin Khilji's continued offensives, they had to retreat to the heights from where they had come.

The Mongols took a long time to rally from this setback. Then they attacked at the worst time possible for Alauddin Khilji – when he was busy laying siege to Chittor. This time the Mongols traveled light. An army of 12,000 under Targhi's leadership moved to Delhi in a swift attack; many governors could not send their troops to Delhi in time.

Alauddin Khilji was forced to retreat to Siri for about two months. The Mongols attacked and pillaged not only the surrounding areas, but Delhi itself.

Alauddin Khilji continued to hold the fortress at Siri; Targhi withdrew the siege after a few months and left the area. Barani, a contemporary historian at that time, attributed this "marvel" to the prayers of the Sufi mystic Shaikh Nizamuddin Auliya.

Alauddin Khilji had the forts along the border strengthened and equipped with larger garrisons. New, more effective fortifications were built in the area. A whole new army with its own special governor was created whose portfolio was managing and guarding the border areas. Despite these measures, the Mongols under the leadership of Ali Beg and Tartaq suddenly appeared in Punjab and the neighbourhood of Amroha. The Mongols plundered Punjab and burnt everything along the way.

Alauddin Khilji sent a strong army led by two of his toughest generals: Ghazi Malik and the famous Malik Kafur to engage the invaders. They surprised the Mongols on their way back to Central Asia with their plunder. At the Battle of Amroha Kubak and other Mongol generals were captured and brought back to Siri, along with other prisoners. Alauddin Khilji had the generals trampled to death by elephants while the other prisoners were put to death and their heads hung from the walls of the fort.

The Mongols returned under the leadership of Kebek, who became a khan later in 1306. They crossed the Indus River near Multan and were moving towards the Himalayas, when Ghazi Malik, governor of Punjab, intercepted them. About 50,000 Mongols were made prisoners including one of their generals. Alauddin Khilji put them all to death and sold their wives and children as slaves.

The last Mongol invasion of this period took place in 1307-8 under Iqbalmand and Tai Bu. They had just about managed to cross the

Indus when Alauddin Khilji's armies overtook them and put them all to the sword. In that same year the Mongol Khan, Duwa, died and in the dispute over his succession this spate of Mongol raids into India ended.

Alauddin Khilji was an original thinker and brilliant as a strategist. He sent plundering armies under the veteran general Ghazi Malik to Kandhar, Ghazni and Kabul. These offensives effectively crippled the Mongol line of control leading to India.

After besieging and taking Siwana, Jalor, and Warangal, the Indian army, led by the Alauddin Khilji Indian slave commander Malik Kafur, invaded Malababar from Devagiri in 1311. They returned with immense amounts of gold and other booty. After the Mongol commander Abachi tried to kill Kafur, Alauddin had him executed. Believing that thousands of Mongols who were captives and later converted into Islam in Delhi were conspiring to kill him, the Sultan ordered all Mongols arrested, and about 20,000 were reported to have been executed. The court of Delhi also executed emissaries of Oljeitu, the Ilkhan of Mongol Persia. In 1320 the Qaraunas under Zulju (Dulucha) entered Kashmir by the Jehlam Valley without meeting any serious resistance. The Kashmiri king, Suhadeva, tried to persuade Zulju to withdraw by paying a large ransom. After he failed to organize resistance, Suhadeva fled to Kishtwar, leaving the people of Kashmir to the mercy of Zulju. The Mongols burned the dwellings, massacred the men and made women and children slaves. Only refugees under Ramacandra, commander in chief of the king, in the fort of Lar remained safe. The invaders continued to pillage for eight months until the commencement of winter. When Zulju was departing via Brinal, he lost most of his men and prisoners due to a severe snowfall in Divasar district.

The next major Mongol invasion took place after the Khiljis had been replaced by the Tughlaq dynasty in the Sultanate. In 1327 the Chagatai Mongols under Tarmashirin, who had sent envoys to Delhi to negotiate peace the previous year, sacked the frontier towns of Lamghan and Multan and besieged Delhi. The Tughlaq ruler paid a large ransom to spare his Sultanate from further ravages. Muhammad bin Tughluq asked the Ilkhan Abu Sa'id to form an alliance against Tarmashirin, who had invaded Khorasan, but an attack didn't materialize. Tarmashirin was a Buddhist who later converted to Islam. Religious tensions in the Chagatai Khanate were a divisive factor among the Mongols.

No more large-scale invasions or even raids took place in India; by this time the Mongol attempt to conquer India had finally ended in failure. However, small groups of Mongol adventurers hired out their swords to the many local powers in the northwest. Amir Qazaghan raided northern India with his Qara'unas. He also sent several thousand troops to aid the Delhi Sultan Muhammad bin Tughluq in suppressing the rebellion in his country in 1350.

Timur and Babur

The Delhi sultans had developed cordial relations with the Yuan Dynasty in Mongolia and China and the Ilkhanate in Persia and the Middle East. Around 1338, Sultan Muhammad bin Tughluq of the Delhi Sultanate appointed Moroccan traveller Ibn Battuta an ambassador to the Mongol court of Emperor Huizong of Yuan China. The gifts he was to take included 200 slaves.

The Chagatai Khanate had split up by this time and an ambitious Mongol Turk chieftain named Timur had brought Central Asia and the regions beyond under his control. He followed the twin policies of Imperialism and Islamization, shifting various Mongol tribes to different parts of his empire and giving primacy to the Turkic people in his own army. Timur also reinforced the Islamic faith over the Chagatai Khanate and gave primacy to the laws of the Quran over Genghis Khan's shaminist laws. He invaded India in 1398 to make war and plunder the wealth of the country.

Timur's empire broke up and his descendants failed to hold on to Central Asia, which split up into numerous principalities. The descendants of the Mongol Chagtais and the descendants of Timur empire lived side by side, occasionally fighting and occasionally inter-marrying.

One of the products of such a marriage was Babur, founder of the Mughal Empire. His mother belonged to the family of the Mongol Khans of Tashkent. Babur was a true descendant of Timur and shared his beliefs: he believed that rules and regulations of Genghis Khan were deficient as he remarked, "they had no divine authority."

Even though his own mother was a Mongol, Babur hated the Mongol race and wrote a stinging verse in his autobiography:

"Were the Mughals an angel race, it would be bad,

Even writ in gold, the Mughal name would be bad."

When Babur occupied Kabul and began invading the Indian

subcontinent, he was called a Mughal like all the earlier invaders from the Chagatai Khanate. Even the invasion of Timur had been considered a Mongol invasion since the Mongols had ruled over Central Asia for so long and had given their name to its people.

The military heritage of the Mongols, unlike their secular laws, had no conflict with the question of religion. Hence both Timur and Babur continued the military system of Genghis Khan. One part of this system was the name Ordu - used for the collective of tents that formed the military camp — it was now pronounced Urdu. In all their campaigns in India the Mughal camp was called the Urdu and this word became current in the languages of the various soldiers that formed the body of this camp.

In time these Indian and foreign languages mingled together in the Urdu and a new language of that name was born. This language of the military camp survived in some of the North Indian cities after the fall of the Mughal Empire. The Urdu that passed through all these centuries of political changes ultimately became the language of poetry, of music, and of other forms of cultural expression—today it is recognized as one of the languages of Pakistan and modern India.

REFERENCES

Baird, Robert: *Religion in Medieval India*, New Delhi, Manohar, 1981.

Basham, A.L.: *A Cultural History of India*, Oxford, Clarendon Press, 1975.

Goodwin, Godfrey: *A History of Ottoman Architecture,* Oxford, New York, 1992.

Habibullah, A. B. M.: *The Foundations of Muslim Rule in India.* Lahore, 1945.

Nagel, Stuart: *Public Policy: Coals, Means, Methods.* New York: St Martins, 1983.

Chapter 4

Tughlaq Dynasty

The Tughlaq Dynasty of north India started in 1321 in Delhi when Ghazi Tughlaq assumed the throne under the title of Ghiyath al-Din Tughluq. The Tughluqs were a Muslim family of Turkic origin. Their rule relied on their alliances with Turkic, Afghan, and other Muslim warriors from outside South Asia.

The empire grew under his son and successor Mohammed bin Tughlaq, but the latter became notorious for ill-advised policy experiments such as shifting the capital from Delhi to Daulatabad and introducing copper coins without effective regulation against forgery. Tughluqi has as a result become antonym for brilliant if stubborn eccentricity in the Hindustani language.

After Mohammed bin Tughlaq his cousin Feroz Shah Tughlaq assumed the throne. He was somewhat weak militarily mainly because of inept army. After Feroz died in 1388, the Tughlaq dynasty started to fade out and there were no able leaders; the dynasty was almost over within 10 years.

Rulers

- Ghiyas ud din Tughluq Shah I (1321-1325)
- Mohammed Shah II (1325-1351)
- Mahmud Ibn Mohammed (March 1351)
- Firuz Shah Tughluq (1351-1388)
- Ghiyas ud din Tughluq II (1388-1389)

- Abu Baker (1389-1390)
- Nasir ud din Mohammed Shah III (1390-1393)
- Sikander Shah I (March-April 1393)
- Mahmud Nasir ud din (Sultan Mahmud II) at Delhi (1393-1394)
- (1394-1398)

Nusrat Shah, grandson of Firuz Shah Tughluq, controlled the west from Firozabad

Nasiruddin Mahmud Shah, son of Mahmud Nasir ud din, controlled the east from Delhi.

GHIYASUDDIN TUGHLAQ

Ghiyasuddin Tughlaq laid down the foundation of a new dynasty known as the Tughlaq dynasty. He was a Turkish slave of Sultan Balban and by serving the Sultans of Delhi, he rose to a higher position. He was appointed as the governor of Dipalpur by Ala–ud–din Khilji. Ghiyasuddin revolted against Khusrav, killed him in the battle and became the Sultan in 1320A.D.

Ghiyasuddin faced internal and external problems when he ascended the throne. The administrative set-up established by Ala-ud-din was destroyed by his successors while no steps were taken to establish a new one. The nobles and the courtiers had become negligent towards their responsibilities and engaged themselves pleasures and entertainment. The Sultan had lost his prestige both among the nobles and the subjects. Ghiyasuddin faced these hurdles with courage and succeeded in solving them.

The first task of Ghiyasuddin was to strengthen his position on the throne and for that he tried to conciliate the nobles and the people. He pursued a policy of conciliation mixed up with sternness towards the nobles.

Ghiyasuddin attempted to improve the finances of the state and for that purpose, pursued the policy of encouraging agriculture and protecting cultivators. His twin objects were to increase the land under cultivation and improve the economic condition of the farmers. The practice of measurement and survey of land which was adopted during the reign of Ala-ud-din was abandoned. Instead, the old system of sharing of the produce was revived. He improved means of irrigation and plant-many gardens. Ghiyasuddin improved the means of communication. Roads were repaired and improved. Bridges and canals were also constructed. He improved the postal system. The judicial system was also improvised by Ghiyasuddin. The practice of rigorous punishment and that of torture for extracting truth was generally prohibited. Ghiyasuddin was a capable military commander and was affectionate towards his soldiers. He looked after their welfare and paid them well.

But he was a strict disciplinarian as well. Within two years after his accession, Ghiyasuddin succeeded in enhancing the strength of his army. Ghiyasuddin proved himself more aggressive imperialist than Ala-ud-din. He frankly pursued the policy of annexation. He annexes the territories of all those rulers who were defeated by him. He captured Telingana, raided Jajnagar and conquered Bengal.

Ghiyasuddin followed the principles of Islam honestly and respected religious men and saints. His policies towards the Hindus were not liberal yet it was not that of oppression. He was a powerful commander and under his leadership, the army of Delhi Sultanate once more became effectively powerful and helped in the extension of the empire.

Ghiyasuddin conquered Bengal and a large part of South India and thus became the master of a more extensive empire than that of Ala-ud-din Khilji. Ghiyasuddin was successful as an administrator as well. He followed a middle path in administration which combined firmness with fairness.

He established peace and order in the kingdom and thus saved it from the anarchy which prevailed after the death of Ala-ud-din. He rooted out dishonesty from the administration, looked after the happiness of peasants, increased the area under cultivation, improved means of communication, transport and postal system, constructed bridges and canals, developed gardens, increased the wages of his civil servants so that they might remain free from petty temptations, and restored the privileges and perquisites of his revenue officers. Ghiyasuddin Tughlaq had faith in his own capabilities and tried to find out capabilities among others and use them for the benefit of the state.

A DRAMATIC TALE OF GHIYASUDDIN TUGHLAQ BEING CROWNED

Under the influence of the enigmatic Malik Kafur, Ala-ud-din had disinherited his sons Khizr and Shadi Khan and then nominated his minor son Shihab-ud-din Umar as the heir and Malik Kafur as his regent. When Ala-ud-din died, Umar was hardly six years old and Malik Kafur of course seized advantage. He had Khizr Khan and Shadi

Khan blinded and set his men after Mubarak Khan, Ala-ud-din's third-born. Had the old sultan been alive, his heart would have warmed up to Mubarak Khan who managed to buy off Malik Kafur's agents and made them double-cross him.

After Mubarak Khan had Malik killed, he announced himself the regent of the hapless Shihab-ud-din Umar. Not two months were out before Mubarak dethroned the kid and had him blinded (of all beastly things!). Unfortunately Mubarak did not live up to the promise he showed early on. He went soft. In his quest to win friends and influence people he went too far and gave too much.

SPENDING TIME WITH MERRYMAKERS LEADS TO DOWN FALL

Zia-ud-din Barani tells us that during the rule of Mubarak Khan, the omnipotent and omnipresent dread of the state receded considerably. On top of this, the king was indiscreet and careless. His idea of warming up with the nobles was drinking and making merry with them, something which his illustrious predecessors like Ala-ud-din and Balban would have never even dreamt of. Word went round that the king was a pushover and naturally everyone who could take advantage of the situation did so. There were rebellions all round. Conspiracies, confusion and corruption became the order of the day. Then Mubarak Shah fell in love with Khusro Shah, an attendant of sorts, and things just got worse. Merrymakers and jesters soon began to occupy more of the king's time than courtiers. In the end the king was disposed of by his own lover, who then occupied the throne. Meanwhile in Punjab, Ghazi Malik, that seasoned old campaigner of Ala-ud-din, thought that enough was enough. He marched to Delhi, defeated Khusro Shah in battle and took over the throne, putting an end to this turbulent period.

GHAZI MALIK–A SENSIBLE CLEAR-HEADED EMPEROR

He stripped his court of all frippery and frivolity and made it more austere than it had ever been except perhaps at the time of Balban. He restored all land that had been taken away by Ala-ud-din Khalji but only after he had made secret inquiries into the claims and all unlawful grants had been filtered out. He tried to recover the treasure squandered by Khusro Shah and succeeded in some measure. Barani tells us that the king believed that people should 'be taxed so that they are not blinded with wealth and so become discontented and rebellious; nor, on the other hand, be so reduced to poverty and destitution as to be unable to pursue their daily bread.' Under Ghazi the judicial, police and postal arrangements improved out of all knowledge and became very efficient. Despite the fact that he was forever busy with war campaigns, he actually found time to think out social welfare schemes.

GHAZI'S DEFEAT

Yet Ghazi Malik's biggest defeat was to come not at the hands of some great conqueror, but at those of a mystic-the great and popular Sufi dervish Shaikh Nizamuddin Auliya. Throughout his reign Ghazi Malik remained at loggerheads with the Shaikh and although he repeatedly tried to curb the saint's power and hold over people, nothing came of it. In fact many believed at that time that it only helped bring about Ghazi's untimely demise.

There are lots of stories about Auliya and Ghazi's war of words. One of their earliest skirmishes occurred when Ghazi—better known as Ghiyasuddin Tughlaq-was building the capital city of Tuqhlaqabad, which is now about 5km east of Delhi. As it happened, the Auliya was building his baoli (step well) at the same time. The workers of the sultan offered to help the saint. When Ghazi came to know of this, he put a stop to it instantly and told the workers to stick to what they were being paid for. Miffed at this, the dervish predicted that the sultan's fort would be either populated by nomads or abandoned. Curiously this actually came to pass. Ghiyasuddin was killed by his own son Muhammad Tughlaq (which incidentally had also been predicted by Auliya, who was rather fond of Muhammad) after only five years of occupying the fort. Muhammad abandoned Tughlaqabad, preferring the old city of Delhi to it. For a long time thereafter Ghazi's city remained the hangout for nomads and it now stands in ruins.

ADMINISTRATION OF GHIYAS UD DIN TUGHLAQ

Administration of Ghiyasuddin Tughlaq was a success. Though he faced many problems initially but with his effective administrative measures he was successful in overcoming them. Ghiyasuddin faced both internal and external problems. The administrative set-up established by Ala-ud-din Khilji was destroyed by his successors while no steps were taken to establish new one. The nobles and the courtiers had become negligible towards their responsibilities and engaged themselves in fun and frolic. However, Ghiyasuddin faced difficulties and succeeded in overcoming them. The first task of Ghiyasuddin was to strengthen his position on the throne and for that he tried to conciliate the nobles and the people. He pursued a policy of conciliation with sternness towards the nobles. Ghiyasuddin was successful in getting loyalty of his subjects by the administrative measures.

Ghiyas–ud-din attempted to improve the finances of the state and for that purpose, pursued the policy of encouraging agriculture and nig cultivators. His twin objects were to increase the land cultivation and improve the economic condition of the farmers. State demand of revenue was fixed in between one fifth to one third of the produce.

The practice of measurement of land which was adopted during the reign of Ala-ud-din was abandoned. Instead, the old system of sharing of the produce was revived. The government officers were asked not to be cruel to the peasants but to look after their welfare. He also improved means of irrigation and plant-gardens. These measures of Ghiyasuddin succeeded. The area under cultivation increased and the condition of the farmers improved.

Ghiyasuddin improved the means of communication. Roads were repaired and improved. Bridges and canals were also constructed. He improved the postal system. Runners or horsemen were placed at a distance of two-thirds of a mile. The judicial system was also developed by Ghiyasuddin. Torture for extracting truth was prohibited. It continued only in cases of thieves or those who embezzled money of the state. Ghiyasuddin was a capable military commander and he loved his soldiers as a father loved his sons. He looked after their welfare and paid them well. But he was a strict disciplinarian as well.

He strictly enforced the practice of keeping of the soldiers and that of branding of the horses. Two years after his accession, Ghiyasuddin succeeded in increasing the strength of his army. Thus the administrative measures adopted by Ghiyasuddin were quite a success and helped him to consolidate his empire.

FALL OF KAKATIYA DYNASTY

In the Deccan Prataparudra, the Kakatiya ruler of Warangal refused to acknowledge the suzerainty of the new dynasty. Ghyas-ud-diin sent an expedition against Warangal under the Crown Prince Juna Khan. On his arrival at Warangal Juna Khan besieged the fort. Epidemics broke out in the camp. Besides a remour that the Sultan was dead in Delhi awas also spread.

Believing the story, Juna Khan raised the siege and returned to Delhi. Two years later, he led another expedition to Warangal and compelled Parataparudura to surrender. Then he was sent to Delhi. Barani tells us that Warangal was renamed as Sultanpur and Telingana was put under the control of Muslim officers. But epigraphic evidence refers to Prataparudra as the king reigning even in 1326.

DEATH OF GHIYASUDDIN TUGHLUQ

When Ghiyasuddin Tughluq returned from Bengal, his son Prince Juna Khan gave him reception. A special wooden pavilion was erected near Delhi to give reception to the King. The King entered into the pavilion. When he was having a view of the elephants brought from Bengal, some elephants came into contact with the wooden pavilion and the entire pavilion fell. Ghiyasuddin Tughluq was crushed along with his Prince Mahmud Khan. The King was found bent over the body of Mahmud Khan as if trying to protect him. It happened in 1325 A.D. Most of the historians believe that the death of the King was the result of a conspiracy in which Juna Khan took part and was not due to any accident.

MOHAMMED BIN TUGHLUQ

Mohammed bin Tughluq (also Prince Fakhr Malik, Jauna Khan and Ulugh Khan) (c.1300 – 1351) was the Turkic Sultan of Delhi from 1325 to 1351. He was the eldest son of Ghiyath al-Din Tughluq. Ghiyath al-din sent the young Mohammed to the Deccan to campaign against king Prataparudra of the Kakatiya dynasty whose capital was at Warangal. Mohammed succeeded to the Delhi throne upon his father's death in 1325.

Mohammed Tughluq was a scholar versed in logic, philosophy, mathematics, astronomy and physical sciences. He had knowledge of medicine and was skilful in dialectics. He was also a calligrapher. Ibn Batuta (Moroccan traveller) visited him during his reign.

Rule of Tughluq

Tughlaq was committed to maintaining the Sultanate's expansion into the newly conquered provinces of peninsular India. To strengthen the sultanate's hold on its southern parts, Tughlaq early in his reign moved the capital from Delhi to Devagiri, 700 miles (1500 km) south in the Deccan, renaming Devagiri as Daulatabad. Instead of moving just his government offices there, he forcibly moved the entire population of Delhi to the new capital. The plan proved disastrous due to Mongol

Attack on North.Inadequate water supply arrangements in Daulatabad; after only two years, the capital had to be shifted back again to Delhi. Multitudes died during the two moves, and it was said that Delhi was a ghost town for years after the move back. "When I entered Delhi, it was almost like a desert", wrote the famed North African travel writer, ibn Battuta. Tughlaq also introduced token currency for the first time in India, modelled after the Chinese example, using brass or copper coins, backed by silver and gold kept in the treasury. However, very few people exchanged their gold or silver coins for the new copper ones. Moreover, the tokens were easy to forge, which led to heavy losses. It is said that after the plan failed, there were heaps of copper coins lying around the royal offices for years.

Campaign against Mokhadaji Gohil in Gujarat

Mohammed bin Tughlaq was very ambitious and he was planning to attack surrounding countries, probably China. To fund his campaign he decided to accumulate wealth. He started to move his wealth from Devagiri to Delhi through the Gujarati port of Khambhat. During that time Mokhadaji Gohil ruled nearby Ghogha and Piram Bet (presently near Bhavnagar). In 1347, he got information about moving of treasure by the Delhi Sultanate through Khambhat. His navy seized the port and looted the Delhi Sultanate's cargoes. Tughlaq sent his army to defeat Mokhadaji Gohil, who skillfully waged a naval war from his base at Piram Bet. The sultanate's army's strategy was to cordon Piram Bet, but they were not well experienced in naval warfare and were easily defeated. Thereafter, Mohammed bin Tughlaq himself came to Gujarat to take charge. He established his base in Ghogha and resolved not to leave until Mokhadaji was killed. During the initial few months he didn't taste any success in his efforts to capture Piram Bet. He therefore schemed to entice Mokhadaji to come ashore in order to engage him in land battle. To this end he recruited a rich Vaishnav merchant of Khambhat, who was promised trade benefits if he could convince Mokhadaji to come on land to fight. The merchant went to Piram and emotionally told Mokhadaji that the local people felt very oppressed by the sultan's occupying army, and wished to wage battle for Mokhadaji if the latter would come to them. Mokhadaji heeded the plea, lost the battle, was taken prisoner near Khadarpar village, and was beheaded near Ghogha. But his force continued to fight. Mohammed bin Tughlaq is said to have been so upset to witness the horrible scene of a beheaded Mokhadaji in battle, that he didn't sleep for many nights.

Collapse of the Empire

Tughlaq died in 1351 on his way to Thatta. He had lived to see his empire fall apart. During the latter years of his reign new kingdoms broke away in the Deccan, such as the Bahmani kingdom founded by Hasan Gangu.

Experiments with Coinage

Muhammad bin Tughlaq is known for his active interest in experimenting with coinage. He memorialized himself and his activities through his coinage and produced more gold coins than had his predecessors. The coins boasted fine calligraphy. He issued a number of fractional denominations.

The large influx of gold from his plundering of south Indian campaign led him to increase coinage weights. He enlarged the gold dinar from 172 grains to 202 grains. He introduced a silver coin, the *adlis*, which was discontinued after seven years due to lack of popularity and acceptance among his subjects.

All his coins reflect a staunch religiosity, with such inscriptions as "The warrior in the cause of God", "The trustier in support of the four Khalifs-Abubakkar, Umar, Usman and Ali". The *kalimah* appeared in most of his coinage. Both at Delhi and at Daulatabad coins were minted in memory of his late father. There were also mints at Lakhnauti, Salgaun, Darul-I-Islam, Sultanpur (Warrangal), Tughlaqpur (Tirhut), and Mulk-I-Tilang. More than thirty varieties of billion coins are known so far, and the types show his numismatic interests.

Unique among his coinage was the "forced currency". Tughlaq had two scalable versions, issued in Delhi and Daulatabad. The currency obeyed two different standards, probably to satisfy the local standard which preexisted in the North and in the South respectively. Tughlaq's skill in forcing the two standards of currency is remarkable. He engraved "He who obeys the Sultan obeys the compassionate" to fascinate people in accepting the new coinage. Inscriptions were even engraved in the Nagari legend, but owing to the alloy used, the coinage underwent deterioration. As well, the copper and brass coins could easily be forged, turning every house into a mint. Tughlaq subsequently withdrew the forged currency by exchanging it with bulls and gold.

Religious Tolerance

Muhammad bin Tughlaq was relatively liberal and permitted Hindus and Jains to settle in Delhi. The policy was reversed by his nephew Firuz Shah Tughlaq.

The Consolidation of Muslim Rule

According to generally accepted accounts, Ghiyasuddin Tughlaq, who became sultan of Delhi in September, 1320, was the son of a Turkish slave of Balban and a Jat woman. With a distinguished record as a defender of the sultanate against the Mongols, he faced first the task of restoring the authority of the Delhi government, which had been weakened during the disorders that followed Alauddin's death. In the south, the tributary raja of Warangal had declared his independence; Ghiyasuddin met the challenge by annexing his kingdom. The governor of Bengal had also revolted, and while suppressing this rebellion Ghiyasuddin expanded his boundaries by the conquest of Tirhut (the ancient Mithila), which had remained outside Muslim rule. This was his last campaign, however, for he was killed in 1325 in the collapse of a victory pavilion erected to celebrate his triumphal return from Bengal.

The son who succeeded him was Muhammad Tughlaq, whose character was a puzzle both to contemporary and later historians. Highly gifted and accomplished, and possessing great purity of character, he endeavored throughout his reign to create a just and orderly society. Instead, he soon gained a reputation for barbarous cruelty, and his rule brought misery to his people and greatly weakened the power of the Delhi Sultanate.

Admittedly this was due partly to natural calamities, for his reign coincided with a long period of drought which in intensity and extent was one of the worst the subcontinent has ever known. From 1335 to 1342 there was widespread famine, and although the king tried to deal with the situation by opening poor-houses and distributing free grain, the problem was beyond his resources. But his misfortunes were not all due to natural and unavoidable causes.

A man of ideas, he continually conceived new schemes; and if they were not well received, he lost patience and resorted to ferocious cruelty to enforce them. The most famous incident of this kind occurred in 1327. He had decided, in view of repeated rebellions in the south, that it was necessary to shift the capital to a more central place. He selected Devagiri, which he named Daulatabad, as the new seat of government, and he forced the Muslim inhabitants of Delhi to migrate to the new capital. Many perished on the long march to Daulatabad, and eventually the sultan allowed them to return to Delhi. On the face of it, the operation seems to have been an act of folly, yet there is no doubt that the migration of a large Muslim population drawn from all sections of society helped to stabilize Muslim rule in the south. Like many of his schemes, it failed, not because his idea was wrong, but because his organization was not adequate to carry it out.

Another controversial measure was the sultan's issue of token currency. The prolonged famine, the expensive wars, and royal liberality had severely strained the exchequer. Muhammad Tughlaq's solution was to issue brass and copper tokens in place of silver coins. Again, the idea was probably sound enough, and one that has been adopted everywhere in the modern world. However the measure was too unfamiliar and too complex for fourteenth-century India. The result was severe dislocation of the economy. Counterfeiting became common and as Barani says, "every Hindu's house became a mint." The king had the good sense to acknowledge his failure, and the token currency was withdrawn from circulation after three or four years. Its introduction and failure neither enhanced public confidence in the sultan nor restored economic prosperity to the country.

There were widespread rebellions throughout Muhammad Tughlaq's reign, and the vast empire which Alauddin Khalji and Ghiyasuddin Tughlaq had governed with success began to fall apart. Early in his reign he had to deal with the revolt of Baha-ud-din Gurshashp, a cousin who was given shelter by the Hindu rajas of the south. Muhammad Tughlaq sent a powerful force against the defiant rajas, annexed Kampili, sacked Dvarasamudra, and forced its ruler to surrender Gurshashp and to reiterate his submission to the government of Delhi.

The cousin's fate was indicative of the sultan's treatment of rebels. He was flayed alive, his flesh was cooked with rice and was sent to his wife and children, while his skin, stuffed with straw, was exhibited in the principal cities of the kingdom. But even such ferocious punishments did not prevent rebellion; perhaps they drove men to rebel out of desperation and fear.

In 1335 Mabar, in the extreme south, became independent, followed three years later by Bengal. The Hindu rajas in the south organized a confederacy, and in 1336 Vijayanagar became the nucleus of a powerful Hindu state. A year later, when the Muslim chiefs in the Deccan set up the independent Bahmani kingdom, the entire area south of the Vindhyas was lost to Delhi. In the same year Gujarat and Kathiawar revolted, but the sultan was able to quell the rebellions in these two areas. Next it was Sind, and in 1351 he was marching towards Thatta to put down the revolt when he fell ill and died. As Badauni says, "The king was freed from his people and they from their king."

While the breakup of the Delhi Sultanate began in the reign of Muhammad Tughlaq, the disasters which overtook him during the last years of his reign need not be the only basis for assessing his character and abilities. Until extreme irritation at the failure of his plans had warped his judgment, driving him to revolting cruelties, he had tried, as a man of ideas, to steer his course according to certain intelligent plans and considerations.

His policy toward the Hindus, for example, was conciliatory, and he had tried to introduce social reforms, such as the abolition of sati. He appointed a Hindu as governor of Sind, and employed others in high positions. The Jain chroniclers remember with gratitude the respect with which he received their theologians. When northern India was afflicted by the seven-year famine, he built a new town on the Ganges near the worst affected area, giving it the Hindu name of Svargdvara, the "Gate of Heaven."

Muhammad Tughlaq's greatest achievement was in the south. Previous rulers, particularly Alauddin Khalji, had established suzerainty over the Hindu princes of the south, but in general had left them in possession of their territories as long as they paid tribute. Muhammad Tughlaq, however, set out to end Hindu rule in the south. Warangal and Madura had already been incorporated in the Tughlaq dominions, and now Kampili and a large part of the Hoysala dominions shared the same fate. Not all of these conquests were maintained, for even during Muhammad's lifetime a powerful Hindu reaction led to the foundation of Vijayanagar, but much remained. Above all, the creation of Daulatabad out of the old fortress city of Devagiri gave the Muslims a great stronghold.

Mention must be made also of the attempt by Muhammad Tughlaq to establish links with other Muslim countries. Among the many distinguished visitors who came to Delhi at this time perhaps the most famous was Ibn Battuta, the Moorish traveller who was appointed chief judge in the capital. He has left an interesting account of the capital as well as of places in Sind, Multan, and the Punjab which he visited on the way to Delhi. He was sent on a diplomatic mission to China, and although he did not return to India, his *Book of Travels* is a useful source for the history of Indo-Islamic society.

Muhammad Tughlaq's successor was his cousin, Firuz Tughlaq, who reigned from 1351 to 1388. While the commencement of the Tughlaq rule had seen a new emphasis on orthodoxy, Firuz's reign saw an even greater attempt to govern India in conformity with Islamic law. Until Aurangzeb, in fact, no other ruler made such a serious endeavor to champion orthodoxy as a guide for the state. The study of Islamic law was encouraged, and Firuz attempted to enforce the law not only among orthodox Muslims, but also among sects such as the Ismaili Shias and the non-Muslims. For the first time jizya was levied upon the Brahmans, who had hitherto remained exempt from the tax. On appeal, the king reduced the amount to be levied from 10 tankas to 50 jitals, but maintained the tax as a legal formality. In this support of orthodoxy Firuz was probably swayed by personal religious beliefs, even though he was not, in his private life, a strict follower of the Islamic code. Probably he was conscious also that one reason for Muhammad Tughlaq's failures was lack of support from the powerful religious leaders, and therefore he was anxious to win them to his side.

The measures by which Firuz helped to gain a reputation for orthodoxy were of a formal nature; the developments which shed luster on his reign were the steps taken in the furtherance of public welfare. In many ways he was the ablest of the Muslim rulers of Delhi previous to Akbar, and contemporary historians describe at length the steps he took to assist agriculture, promote employment, and secure the happiness and prosperity of the people. He initiated extensive irrigation schemes, digging five canals to distribute the water of the Sutlej and Jhelum over a large area. One of these continues to be used up to the present day. Also he set up an employment bureau where young men who were without work in the city of Delhi gave their qualifications, and occupations were found for them.

The greatest monuments of Firuz's rule, however, are the buildings and the towns founded by him. He is credited with the erection of 200 towns, 40 mosques, 30 colleges, 30 reservoirs, 50 dams, 100 hospitals, 100 public baths, and 150 bridges. He built a magnificent new capital near Delhi, and the two important towns of Jaunpur and Hissar were founded by him. He set up a regular Department of Public Works, which erected new buildings and took steps to restore the structures of former kings. He removed two gigantic monolithic pillars of the emperor Ashoka, one from a village in the Ambala District and the other from Meerut, and had them set up near Delhi. He also showed his interest in India's past by having translations made of a number of Sanskrit books which he found during his conquest of Kangra in 1361.

But Firuz did little to prevent the disintegration of the sultanate which had already set in during the last years of the reign of his predecessor. The process was speeded by his death, for a civil war broke out between his son and grandson. The Hindu chiefs threw off their allegiance and governors of provinces became independent. The weakness of the kingdom invited foreign invasion and in 1398 Timur, the Barlas Turkish chief who ruled at Samarqand, invaded India.

He had no intention of staying in India, but came, as had the invaders of four centuries before, to take back slaves and booty. After terrible destruction, including the sacking of Delhi, he returned home, but he had helped to destroy the Delhi Sultanate. Possibly it could not have survived long in any case, but certainly Timur's raid effectively prevented the Tughluqs from regaining their control.

The familiar story of dynastic decay thus repeated itself. In the decade following Firuz's death, six sultans briefly occupied the throne. The last of the Tughlaq line, Mahmud, fled from Delhi during Timur's invasion. Although he returned after his departure, managing to stay on the throne until 1413, he was not able to ensure the succession to a member of the house.

EXPERIMENTS AND REFORMS

The problems and approaches should be helpful in understanding the many experiments and reforms which Muhammad bin Tughlaq launched, and for which he is so well-known. Muhammad bin Tughlaq was keen to tone up the administration, and bring about uniformity in its functioning. Towards this end, according to Ibn Batturah, he issued large numbers of orders *(manshurs)*. However, only a few of these appear to have been taken up seriously, or to have made an impact. *These have been listed by Barani, and may be divided into two*:

1. Administrative and political measures,
2. Economic and agrarian reforms.

Of course, each influenced the other, so that no rigid demarcation can be made between them.

ADMINISTRATIVE AND POLITICAL MEASURES

One of the most controversial steps taken by Muhammad bin Tughlaq early in his reign was his so-called transfer of capital to Deogiri which was renamed Daultabad, and the alleged orders of the sultan ordering a mass transfer of the people from Delhi to the new capital. A careful analysis of the contemporary and later sources show that Barani grossly exaggerated when he alleges that the steps led to the ruination of Delhi which, till then, had equalled the leading cities of the Islamic world, Cairo and Baghdad, Some others have alleged that the step was taken by the sultan to punish the people of Delhi who had become hostile to him.

However, there is evidence that the step was not taken by Muhammad bin Tughlaq in a pique, but was the result of considerable thought, and had been carefully prepared for. The motive of the step taken by the sultan has been set out by Barani himself, *viz.*, that it was central to all parts of the empire. During the reign of Ghiyasuddin and the early years of Muhammad bin Tughlaq, the direct rule of Delhi had been extended to cover almost the entire south. Since the days of Alauddin, Deogiri had been the virtual base of operations in the Deccan. Muhammad bin Tughlq had spent a number of years in the south, both as a prince and as a ruler, campaigning, and was familiar with Deogiri which had a pleasant climate, being surrounded by hills.

He wanted to have a second capital in the south so that he could control it more easily. According to a 17th century author, Ferishta, some of the councilors of the sultan suggested Ujjain in Malwa which had been made his capital by Raja Vikramaditya for the same reason. But the sultan preferred Deogiri, both because he was more familiar with it, and because it was already one of the great cities of India. The decision to make Deogiri a second capital was apparently taken in 1327 when Muhammad bin Tughlaq passed Deogiri after his journey to the Karnataka to suppress the rebellion of his cousin, Cars hasp.

In preparation for the new step, he planted trees on both sides of the road and at a distance of every two miles set up halting stations. Provision was made for food and drink bring available for the travellers at the station. Land was allotted from the income of which the staff working there could draw their salaries. We are told that at each station, a sufi saint was stationed, and a *khnqah* (hospice for the saint) built. Soon afterwards the sultan's mother was sent to Deogiri or Daultabad. The sultan's mother was accompanied by many nobles, leading men of the city, and the entire royal household including slaves, servants, and treasures, Sometime afterwards, the sultan summoned all the sufis, *Ulema* and grandees of Delhi. This is placed in the year 1328-29. It is clear that no mass exodus of the population at Delhi was ordered.

However, it seems that a good deal of pressure was exerted upon the people to migrate, the royal orderlies even inspecting their houses for the purpose. Those travelling to Daultabad were divided into caravans for purposes of convenience. The journey was long, and undertaken during the hot months, so that many people died on the way. Full preparations had been made for welcoming those who reached Daultabad. The city had been divided into wards *(Mohallas),* with separate quarters for troops, the nobles, the civil servants, the judges and the learned men, the merchants and artisans. Mosques, markets, public baths, etc., were built in each *mohalla.*

The Sultan purchased the houses and dwelling of those at Delhi who had migrated and wanted the government to do so. Liberal grants were made to people, both at the time of their departure at Delhi and at their arrival at Daultabad where free boarding and lodging was provided to them. Nevertheless, most of the migrants were not happy. They had got used to Delhi where many of them had lived for more than a hundred years, and which they regarded as their home. That many of the Turks had started looking upon India with love and affection is obvious from the writings of the poet, Amir Khusrau. For them, Daultabad was an alien land, full of infidels.

Meanwhile, Delhi was not deserted. Coins struck at Delhi, two Sanskrit inscriptions in *baolis* (sunken wells with steps) built by some wealthy Hindus in the environs of Delhi at this time prove it. But, we are told, many of the houses had been shut up, and the bad characters in the city started looting them. Hence, Muhammad bin Tughlaq invited sufis, learned men and others living in neighbouring cities to move to Delhi. In 1334, when Ibn Battutah visited Delhi, it was fully settled. Nor was there any question of the capital being shifted from Delhi Rather, Daultabad became a second capital, as coins struck at Daultabad testify. However, the Sultan's ambitious project soon struck a reef. In 1334-35, there was a serious rebellion in Mabar (modern Coromandal in Tamilnadu). The sultan marched to the south to suppress the rebellion. While he was at Bidar, there was an out-break of bubonic plague in which many of his soldiers perished. Muhammad Tughlaq himself was taken ill, and retreated to Daultabad. Rumours spread of the sultan's death, and soon the entire south, including Mabar, Dwar-Samudra (Karnataka), and Warangal (Telingana) were lost to the Delhi sultanate. Thus the raison d'etre of keeping Doultabas as a second capital disappeared. It was around this time, *i.e.*, between 1335-37, that the Sultan permitted the people at Daultabad to return to Delhi,

Thus, the exodus to Daultabad proved to be a costly failure, and brought misery to many people. However, its effects were felt largely by the upper classes, not by the people of Delhi. It is not clear why Muhammad bin Tughlaq ordered the sufis, clergymen and the learned people to migrate to Daultabad. Perhaps he felt that he or the state could not function in an atmosphere where mystics and men of Islamic learning were not present. He might also have felt that by their example, the sufis and the men of learning would spread Islam, and the hold of the sultan there become more secure. Whatever may have been his motives, one long-term effect of Muhammad bin Tughlaq's exodus to Daultabad was that many of the sufis and men of learning decided to stay back at Daultabad, so that in course of time it became a centre of Islamic learning. But the beneficiaries of this were not the sultans of Delhi, but the Bahmani rulers who established their rule in the area soon afterwards.

The Khurasan and Karachil Expeditions

Although the Khurasan and Karachil expeditions, and the recruitment of a large army by Muhammad bin 'Tughlaq, are mentioned by Barani separately, we may take them together as they were interconnected.

The Khurasan expedition was closely connected to events in Central and West Asia, and with Muhammad bin Tughlaq's desire to make Sindh and the Punjab safe at all times from the danger of recurrent Mongol invasions. After the death of Chingez. Khan, one branch of his descendants, the Chaghtai branch, had dominated Turkistan and Transoxiana, while another branch, led by Halaku, had captured Iran, Iraq, etc., Ghur, Ghazni, Afghanistan, etc., which provided access to India was a bone of contention between the two. However, both the branches were in decay at this time, the conditions in Transoxiana being unsettled after the death of Tarmashirin whose invasion of India in 1326-27. We are told that Muhammad bin Tughlaq wanted to overthrow the descendants of Chingez. Khurasan was used vaguely to describe the area, and Barani adds Iraq and sometimes Trans-oxiana to it. To realise his objective, Muhammad bin Tughlaq invited and gave lavish grants to some of the leading men of those areas. He also raised a large army of 370,000 soldiers. They were paid by the grant of iqtas but, Barani says, no care was taken about enforcing the brand of the horses, or the description of the soldiers, or testing their swordsmanship. They were kept idle for a year, and then dispersed since it was not possible to pay them any longer.

The rapid raising of the army and its nature suggests that it was not meant to be a major enterprise, and perhaps only aimed at extending the sultan's control over Kabul, Ghazni, etc. Muhammad bin Tughlaq's interest in the area is shown by the fact that after the failure of Tarmashirin's invasion (1326-27), he frequently sent money to the government of Ghazni, and almost took the qazi of Ghazni into his pay, a fact which Barani deplores. However, conditions were not ripe even for this limited enterprise, and hence it was abandoned.

The Karachil expedition (1333) is placed soon after the Khurasan expedition. This expedition was apparently aimed at the Kulu-Kangra region of Himachal. However, Barani quite wrongly links it to the Khurasan expedition and says that its conquest would have enabled him to capture horses (from Turkistan), and provide an easier road to Transoxiana! Some later writers, such as Badayuni and Ferishta, call it the expedition to China and Himachal. Medieval ideas of geography were very vague, and these historians thought that Khitai or old China was just across the Himalayas. As it was, the expedition proved a failure. The commander of the Delhi armies advanced too far into the mountains so that his retreat was cut off by the defending forces, and almost the entire army of 10,000 was destroyed. However, this expedition was not a total failure because, after some time, the ruler of the area patched up a treaty with Muhammad bin Tughlaq, agreeing to pay him a certain sum of money for the use of the territory lying at the foot hills. He also accepted the sultan's overlordship.

ECONOMIC AND AGRARIAN REFORMS

Token Currency: One of Muhammad bin Tughlnq's ambition was to reform the coinage and, according to a modern historian, Dr. Ishwari Prasad, from his mints in different parts of the empire, various kinds of coins were issued which were unequalled in the artistic perfection of their design, execution and finish. An experiment which Muhammad bin Tughlaq launched after the exodus to Deogiri in 1329-30, was the token currency which has been little understood and much condemned.

He issued coins of copper and brass which were to exchange as equal with silver and gold. The idea of a token currency is known to everyone in the modern world, but it was a novelty in medieval times. However, it was not a totally new thing. Paper currency in China was known. The Mughal ruler, Kulai Khan, had introduced in the first year of his reign in 1260 a paper currency called the *chan* which had lasted throughout his reign till his death in 1294. It had been accepted by everyone including foreign traders. This fact was widely known, and it is referred to by Barani to explain the background of Muhammad bin Tughlaq's action. Later, in 1294, an Iranian king, Qai Katu, had tried to introduce the paper *chan* in his country, but it had led to serious disturbances, and had to be discontinued after eight days.

There has been a great deal of controversy regarding the motives of the sultan in introducing the token currency. According to Barani, it was part of his ambition to conquer all the inhabited quarters of the world for which a huge army was needed and a large treasury to pay them. Thus, it was for the purpose of supplementing the treasury. But Barani contradicts himself when he goes on to say that the sultan's treasury had been exhausted by his reck less grant of gifts and awards. However, shortage of gold and silver could not have been a major reason for the step because, when the experiment failed, the sultan called in the token coins, and paid gold and silver in exchange for them.

Trade and commerce began to be disrupted. Hence, in anger, Muhammad bin Tughlaq cancelled his orders, and redeemed the token coins by gold and silver coins. This could have been done only for the coins issued from the royal mints. The token coins issued by Muhammad bin Tughlaq were both in copper and brass. None of the earlier sultans had issued any coins in brass which was an alloy of copper with tin and zinc, etc. According to an eminent modern historian. Professor Muhammad Habib, Muhammad bin Tughlaq had issued coins of bronze which had distinct inscriptions in Persian and Arabic to mark the new coins. Confusion arose because ordinary people could not easily distinguish between these and the forged coins. The forged coins brought by people for redemption, but not accepted by the government, lay heaped in mounds outside the fort for a long time,

The experiment if successful, would have led to an expansion of India's trade and commerce because there was a world wide shortage of silver at the time. This is reflected in the reduction of the silver content of the tanka by Muhammad bin Tughlaq from 178 to 140 grains early in his reign. The failure of the token currency must certainly have affected the treasury adversely. But it was not too serious a blow, or upset public life. It was given up by 1333, three years after its introduction. Thus, no issues of the token coins are available after 732 *hijri* or 1332-33. The token coins are not mentioned by Ibn Battutah who came to Delhi in 1334. This shows that the entire episode had been speedily forgotten.

Agrarian Reforms

The failure of these three experiments—the exodus to Deogiri, the failure of the Khurasan expedition, and the withdrawal of the token currency as also the disastrous result of the Karchil campaign must have affected the public reputation of the Sultan, as also his treasury. However, the resources of the empire were still vast, and the loss to the treasury must have been quickly made up. But it seems to have encouraged the practice of letting out big tracts of land on revenue-farming terms *(muqata)*—a development to which we shall revert later on. Meanwhile, certain agrarian measures of Muhammad bin Tughlaq, epidemics, and a famine which lasted for six to seven years and affected large parts of the *doab* and Malwa, created serious public distress, and a widespread peasant uprising. We are told that Ghiyasuddin had replaced Alauddin's system of measurement for the fields by sharing of the produce. This was advantageous to the peasant because it made allowance for a total or partial failure of crops. According to Barani, the Sultan's policy was that increase in the incidence of taxation was to be gradual, and such that it did not affect the prosperity of the peasantry. Instructions were issued to the officials to see that cultivation increased from year to year, and that the revenue also increased proportionately. We do not know what he actually charged from the cultivators, but there seems no reason to believe that he reduced it to one-fifth, as argued by some modcm historians.

When Muhammad bin Tughlaq came to the throne, he attempted a substantial increase in the scale of the land-revenue demanded from the cultivators. Barani says that he increased it from "one to ten or one to twenty". This was only a figure of speech, and should not be taken literally to mean either increase from ten to twenty times, or one in ten or twenty, *i.e.*, ten to five per cent. Barani elsewhere uses the words "onc to hundrcd", or "one to thousand" to convey a sense of considerable increase. We are told that new cesses were levied, and the old cesses—grazing tax *(carai),* and house *(ghari)* tax were collected in a rigorous manner, the cattle being branded and the houses counted. Worse, when assessing the yield of a field, not the actual produce, but the standard yield was taken into account. Further, when commuting the state's share into cash, not the actual but the officially assumed prices were used.

These measures, we are told, led to the destruction of the peasantry and to an agrarian uprising which affected a large area near Delhi and the *doab*. *B*arani says that the Hindus, *i.e.*, the peasants set fire to the grain heaps, and drove away cattle from their homes. Thus, "Whole regions were devastated. Cultivation was totally aban-doned." The Sultan adopted the usual methods to suppress rebellion. Thus, shiqdars *and faujdars* (revenue collectors and military officials) were ordered to lay waste and plunder the country. In consequence, many of the *khuts and muqaddams* were killed, or took refuge in forests. The Sultan's troops surrounded the jungles and killed everyone whom they found within the jungle. Thus, the entire area from Kannauj to Dalmau was laid waste.

The range and extent of this agrarian rebellion need some explanation for we must remember that Alauddin Khalji had raised the land revenue in the doab to half, given no concessions to the *Khuts* and *muqaddams,* and insisted on measurement which put he cultivators in a position of disadvantage when the rains failed, wholly or partially. Yet the *khuts* and m*uqaddams,* or the peasants had not risen in rebellion. Fear of drastic punishment by Alauddin is no answer, for Muhammad bin Tughlaq was no less severe. Even if we imagine that Barani exaggerated, as he often does, the reality of a widespread peasant rebellion cannot be denied. Does it mean that Muhammad bin Tughlaq had, in effect, raised the land revenue to more than half, the share demanded by Alauddin? If that was so, Barani, who was critical of Muhammad bin Tughlaq, would have said so.

A possible explanation is that unlike Alauddin, Muhammad bin Tughlaq was not able to keep a tight control over the local revenue officials. Hence, in the name of realising the standard produce on the basis of officially accepted prices, many of them must have indulged in gross oppressions. Barani says, when peasants of distant regions heard of the ruin and destruction of the peasantry, and fearful that the same orders may be applied to them, they also rose in rebellion. However, this may have been an exaggeration for we do not hear that the rebellion spread to areas outside the *doab.*

Barani says that the contraction of cultivation in the doab, the ruin of its peasantry, the reduction in the number of graincarriers *(banjtaras),* and the failure of the grains to reach Delhi led to a famine. The rains, too, failed. Hence, the prices of grains rose very high. To cope with the famine, relief camps were opened at Delhi, foodgrains arriving from Awadh where there was no famine. Muhammad Tughlaq also advanced agricultural loans *(soudhar)* to dig wells and to buy seed and implements.

It seems that the famine began in 1334-35 and lasted for seven years. During this period, Muhammad bin Tughlaq found that the atmosphere of Delhi had become pestilential. Hence, the entire imperial camp moved to a place on the Ganges 80 kms away. This place was called Swargadwar ('Gateway to Heaven"), and the Sultan lived there for two years, food-grains being dispatched to him from Awadh. Many notable people from Delhi also moved to the areas where there was no famine.

After returning from Swarga-dwar, Muhammad Tughlaq conceived of a grand design to extend and improve cultivation. A Diwan called *'Diwan-i-Amir-i-Kohi'* was set up to take charge of a territory 30 *kroh* by 30 *kroh* (roughly: 100 Kms). He planned lo extend cultivation in the area so that "one span of land would not remain uncultivated." The intention was to bring barren *(banjar)* land under cultivation, not uncultivable *(usar)* land, as Barani asserts. Simultaneously, whatever was being cultivated would be improved.

In the words of Barani, "thus wheat would be sown instead of barley, and sugarcane instead of wheat", and "grape and date would be planted instead of sugarcane." Thus, the scheme had two aspects; one, to extend cultivation, and second, to improve the crops. Both would have led to the realisation of higher landrevenue. To implement the scheme, 100 *shiqadar* were appointed. They were honoured, and given horses, and large sums of money for giving agricultural loans *(sondhar).* We are told that in this way, 70 lakh tankas and more were advanced by way of *sondhar.* Afif, who wrote in the time of Firoz Tughlaq, puts this figure still higher, at two crores. Barani says that the entire scheme failed, and during three years, not a thousandth or hundredth part of wasteland was brought under cultivation. He ascribes this to the fact that the persons chosen to implement the scheme were incompetent. He calls them "greedy, impecunious men, without hope of salvation." Apparently, they had no understanding of local conditions, and spent the money meant on loans for their own expenses and needs.

If Muhammad bin Tughlaq had come back from his Gujarat expedition after suppressing the rebellion there, these men would have had to pay a heavy price. However, Muhammad bin Tughlaq died, and his successor, Firoz Tughlaq, wrote off the loans. Nevertheless, the scheme cannot be called a total failure. The idea of extending and improving cultivation with the help of agricultural loans became a standard practice with later sultans, and became a part of the agricultural policy of the Mughals. Thus, both Alauddin Khalji and Muhammad bin Tughlaq helped in the evolution of an agrarian policy which matured fully under the Mughals.

DOMESTIC POLICIES OF MUHAMMAD BIN TUGHLAQ

Muhammad Bin Tughlaq was an ambitious ruler and adopted several innovations in domestic affairs. Different measures were taken in the field of administration such as revenue reforms, taxation in Doab, improvement of agriculture, transfer of the capital and the introduction of token currency. Though these policies were attempted with best intentions but it adversely affected the fortune of the empire.

Muhammad Tughlaq carried out many measures for the improvement of the administration of revenue. One of these measures was preparation of a register in which income and expenditure of all the princes were recorded. The main motive of the Sultan was to introduce a uniform standard of land revenue all through his empire and to see that no village remained unassessed. However, nothing is known about the advantages of this system. In the beginning of his reign, the Sultan increased taxation in the Doab.

According to Barani, the taxation was raised by ten to twenty times more. Taxes were increased and at a time when there had been a famine in the Doab owing to the failure of rains. Therefore, the peasants, instead of paying the taxes, abandoned their lands and adopted highway robbery. The tax collectors continued to collect taxes by tyranny which resulted in widespread revolts. This policy of the Sultan proved to be a perfect failure. Even the usual revenue could not be collected from the Doab. Besides, the Sultan became unpopular among his subjects.

Muhammad Bin Tughlaq established a separate department of agriculture and appointed a minister Amir-i-kohi, to look after it. The main purpose of this department was to increase the land under cultivation. Nearly, seventy lakh rupees, was spent by the government in three years yet the experiment failed and the scheme was abandoned after three years. The corruption of the officer, poor quality of land chosen for farming and indifference of cultivators who were assigned land under government supervision were responsible for the failure of the scheme.

Muhammad Tughlaq's attempt to transfer the capital from Delhi to Daultabad was another futile measures adopted by him. Several reasons can be citied for him to take this step. The empire of the Sultan had extended far and wide within the territories of India and Daultabad was in fee centre and more strategically placed as compared to Delhi. The administration and consolidation of south India required more attention as compared to the north, the desire to keep the capital a safe distance from invasions of the Mongols or, on the contrary, be absence of danger from invasions of the Mongols, the temptation of wealth of the south, and, probably, the desire of the Sultan to spread Muslim culture in the south were different reasons of the Sultan to transfer the capital to Daultabad.

The common masses were neither prepared to shift themselves to a distant place nor was there any necessity of it. This scheme of the Sultan failed completely. Various types of coins were introduced by Muhammad Bin Tughlaq during his reign. The note worthy feature of the coinage system was the introduction of token currency and issue of copper and brass coins. The Sultan made these token coins legal tenders and kept their value at par with gold and silver coins. Previously, the copper coin was Jital (Paisa). Now, the Sultan issued Tanka (rupee), a silver coin, also that of copper. This scheme of the Sultan also failed miserably. Many historians blamed the Sultan for the failure of the scheme.

It was a blunder on the part of the Sultan that he did not take proper precaution to check imitation of coins issued by royal mints. Those coins, therefore, could be imitated by moderately skilled artisans. Therefore, the citizens began to mint token coins in their houses. In fact, both the Sultan and his subjects were responsible for the failure of this scheme.

Thus Muhammad Bin Tughlaq failed to carry any of the schemes to success. It can be said in favour of the sultan that his measures were ahead of his time; his subjects and officials failed to understand worth of his schemes and, therefore, did not cooperate with him to bring them to success. The Sultan himself was also responsible for the failure of his schemes to a large extent. The Sultan possessed an artistic mind but lacked practical wisdom. He, therefore, could formulate new schemes which, probably, were sound in principles but he failed to devise practical measures to bring them to success. The Sultan lacked patience also. He desired quick success; even minor failure enraged him and when desired results could not be achieved speedily, he abandoned his scheme in haste. All these weaknesses participated in failure of his domestic policies.

EXTENSION OF EMPIRE BY MUHAMMAD BIN TUGHLAQ

Muhammad Bin Tughlaq like his father pursued the policy of annexation. Whatever territories he conquered, he annexed them to the Delhi Sultanate and, thus extended its territories to the extent which no other Sultan of Delhi had even attempted. The Sultan conquered Peshawar and Kalanor after the return of the Mongols. The fort of Nagarkot was in Kangra district in Punjab. No Muslim ruler had conquered it by then and it was in the hands of a Hindu king. Muhammad Tughlaq conquered it though he restored it back to its ruler after his acceptance of suzerainty of Delhi. His plan to conquer Khurasan and Iraq failed miserably. His greatest achievement was in the south. He set out to end Hindu rule in south. He tried to enlist the service of 'Ulema', the Muslim clerics. Muhammad Tughlaq captured Kondhana or Singharh from Nag Nayak.

It was in the vicinity of Devagiri. Therefore, its conquest was necessary for the Sultan. Muhammad Tughlaq, thus, conquered greater part of south India and annexed it to the Delhi Sultanate. Muhammad failed to get any success in Rajasthan. He largely succeeded in carrying out his series of conquests. Of course, he failed at few places, yet his Empire was more extensive than any other Sultan of Delhi. The authority of the Sultan was acknowledged all over India, save Kashmir, Orissa, Rajasthan and a strip of Malabar Coast, and he established an effective system of administration over this vast empire.

CONQUESTS OF MUHAMMAD BIN TUGHLAQ

Conquest of Muhammad Bin Tughlaq was widespread. He extended his territories to the extent which no other Sultan of Delhi had even attempted. During early years of his reign, Muhammad Tughlaq planned to conquer Khurasan and Iraq. The unstable political condition of Central Asia inspired the Sultan to undertake this project. The Sultan raised a huge army of three lakh and seventy thousand soldiers for this purpose. But very soon the condition of Central Asia changed and the Sultan realised the futility of his scheme. Therefore, he abandoned the scheme and the army was dispersed.

The fort of Nagarkot was in Kangra district in Punjab. No Muslim ruler had conquered it by then and it was in the hands of a Hindu king. Muhammad Tughlaq conquered it though he restored it back to its ruler after his acceptance of suzerainty of Delhi. In south India, Ghiyas-ud-din Tughlaq had annexed Telingana and a large part of Malabar Coast. Muhammad Tughlaq made fresh annexations in the south. Muhammad Tughlaq captured Kondhana or Singharh from Nag Nayak. Muhammad Tughlaq, thus, conquered greater part of south India and annexed it to the Delhi Sultanate. Muhammad failed to get any success in Rajasthan, but largely succeeded in carrying out his series of conquests. Of course, he failed at few places, yet his Empire was more extensive than any other Sultan of Delhi. The authority of the Sultan was acknowledged over India, save Kashmir, Orissa, Rajasthan and a strip of Malabar Coast, and he established an effective system of administration over this vast empire.

REVOLT IN TUGHLAQ DYNASTY, MUHAMMAD BIN TUGHLAQ

Many revolts took place under the reign of Muhammad Bin Tughlaq. A few of them were attempted by his ambitious nobles but most of them were either the results of his oppressive policy or because of his failure to keep the state affairs under his control. A few of them succeeded and eventually led to the disintegration of the Empire.

The first revolt was that of Bha–ud–din Gurshasp in 1326 A.D. He was defeated and ultimately captured in 1327 A.D. In 1327-28 A.D. Bahram Aiba alias Kishlu Khan, governor Uch, Sindh and Multan, revolted against the Sultan. He was the guardian of the northwestern frontier of the empire. Therefore, rebellion was a serious affair. He was a friend of the late Ghiyas-ud-din and even Sultan Muhammad respected him. But he refused to send his family to the new capital *viz.*, Daultabad and killed the messenger of the Sultan. The Sultan who was in Deccan at that time hurriedly advanced against him. Bahram Aiba fled away but was captured and killed. His head was hung up in the gate of the city as a warning to others.

There was a revolt in Bengal in 1327-1328 A.D. Ghiyas-ud-din Bahadur who was taken to Delhi as captive by the late Ghiyas-ud-din Tughlaq was released by Muhammad and sent back to Sonargaon to rule jointly with Bahram Khan but he revolted after three years.

However, he was defeated and killed by Bahram Khan. After the death of Bahram Khan, the officers in Bengal began to quarrel among themselves. One of the loyal nobles, Ali Mubarak captured Lekhnauti and requested the Sultan to send somebody as governor. But the Sultan neglected his request and eventually Bengal became independent by 1340-41 A.D.

Revolts occurred in Sunam, Samana, Kara, Bidar, Gulbarga and Multan as well. However, the Sultan was successful in suppressing them all. In 1334-35 A.D. Sayyid Ahsan Shah, governor of Malabar, declared himself as an independent ruler. The Sultan marched against him in person, but the news reached him that there was a revolt in Lahore. Therefore, he retraced back and Malabar became an independent kingdom. During the same time the Hindus succeeded in establishing an independent kingdom at Telingana and Kanchi and foundation of the strong kingdom of Vijayanagara was laid down by Harihara and Bukka in 1336 A.D.

In Gujarat, the revolt was led by the foreign nobles. It had resulted in revolts in Malwa, Berar and Daultabad. The first revolt in Gujarat was suppressed by naib vazir. But while the Sultan was in Daultabad, another widespread revolt broke out in Gujarat under Taghi who, probably, commanded the sympathy of the people. The sultan himself marched towards Gujarat to suppress the revolt. The Sultan brought about peace and order in Gujarat and then proceeded towards Sindh to suppress the revolt there. Thus there were a number of revolts which occurred under the reign of Muhammad Tughlaq. He was successful in suppressing few of them but these rebellions ultimately resulted in the downfall of his vast Empire.

RELIGIOUS POLICY OF MUHAMMAD BIN TUGHLAQ

Muhammad Bin Tughlaq took his own decision regarding the matters of religious policy. The Sultan did not even permit the Ulema class to interfere in his administration. During his reign the Ulema class enjoyed monopoly over administration of justice. Muhammad Bin Tughlaq broke up that monopoly and appointed Qazis outside this class of people.

During early period of his reign, he neither sought recognition of Khalifa nor inscribed his name on his coins. The Sultan did nothing against Islam nor did he desire to flout the principles of Islam but he was not prepared to accept the interference of religion or that of any religious class in his administration. He used to change the decisions of Qazis whenever he found them unjust and discriminating. If a religious man was found guilty of corruption or rebellion, he was punished like any other ordinary person. Thus nobody was above the laws of the land. This is the reason why the Ulema class became antagonistic to Muhammad Tughlaq and spread discontentment against him.

Muhammad Tughlaq had to compromise with the Ulema during later years of his reign. He inscribed the name of Khalifa on his coins, sought recognition of his office from him in 1340 A.D. and invited Ghiyas-ud-din Muhammad, one distant relative of the Khalifa of Egypt, to his court. Muhammad Tughlaq was tolerant towards his Hindu subjects. He was the first Sultan of Delhi who distributed respectable offices to the Indian Muslims and the Hindus. In this field, he was ahead of his time. With his entire liberal attitude, Muhammad Bin Tughlaq failed to get admiration and sympathy of his subjects. But the reason was not his attitude but the failure of his schemes and oppressive measures of his policies.

DOWNFALL OF TUGHLAQ EMPIRE

Though Muhammad Tughlaq succeeded in extending his empire he failed to keep it intact for long. A large part of it was lost by him during the later years of his reign. There were several reasons which led to the downfall of the Tughlaq Empire. One of the major reasons is the occurrence of quite a few revolts during the reign of Muhammad Bin Tughlaq. A few of them were attempted by his ambitious nobles. But, most of them were either the outcome of his tyrannical policy or because of his failure to keep state affairs under his power.

A few of the revolts succeeded and, thus, led to the disintegration of his empire. In 1327-28 A.D. Bahram Aiba alias Kishlu Khan, governor Uch, Sindh and Multan, revolted against the Sultan. There was a revolt in Bengal in 1327-1328 A.D. Revolts occurred in Sunam, Samana, Kara, Bidar, Gulbarga and Multan as well. No ruler in medieval India has aroused so much controversy concerning his character and policy as Muhammad Tughlaq. He was a well educated man and there was hardly any branch learning in which he had not achieved excellence such as literature, history, philosophy, poetry, logic, mathematics, medicine, astrology and calligraphy. He knew both Persian and Arabic languages, and was interested in fine arts particularly music and patronised arts. Muhammad Tughlaq was extremely generous and distributed rewards, gifts and presents with open heart to deserving individuals.

He was a capable commander and a daring soldier. He proved his military talents when he fought against the Mongols. Even when he became the Sultan, he himself participated in important battles of his reign and thus spent his life mostly in battle-fields. Muhammad Tughlaq himself was primarily responsible for the conquest of the south. He faced many rebellions at the time of his reign but wherever he went he largely succeeded in suppressing them.

As a ruler, Muhammad Tughlaq was devoted and extremely labourious. But, he proved a failure. He gained no success in any field of administration during twenty-six years of his rule. All his policies of internal reform failed and each of them taxed the resources of the empire, brought misery to his subjects and ruined his reputation among them. The failure of the Sultan as an able administrator is not only because of his own weaknesses but also because of certain circumstances and non-cooperation of his subjects who were backward and prejudiced against him. Muhammad died when campaigning in Sindh. He was succeeded by his cousin Firoz Shah Tughlaq.

FIRUZ SHAH TUGHLAQ

Firoz Shah Tughlaq, 1309-1388 in Delhi, was a Muslim ruler of the Tughlaq Dynasty from 1351 to 1388. He was the son of a Hindu Rajput princess of Dipalpur. His father's name was Razzab (the younger brother of Gazi Malik). Gazi Malik means Gayasuddin Tughlaq. He succeeded his cousin Muhammad bin Tughlaq following the later's death from a fatal illness, but due to widespread unrest Firuz's realm was much smaller than Muhammed's. Firuz was forced by rebellions to concede virtual independence to Bengal and other provinces. He was known as an iconoclast.

Biography

The "Tarikh-i-Firuz Shah" is a historical record written during his reign that attests to the systematic persecution of Hindus under his rule. In particular, it records atrocities on Hindu Brahmin priests who refused to convert to Islam:

> *"An order was accordingly given to the Brahman and was brought before Sultan. The true faith was declared to the Brahman and the right course pointed out. but he refused to accept it. A pile was raised*

on which the Kaffir with his hands and legs tied was thrown into and the wooden tablet on the top. The pile was lit at two places his head and his feet. The fire first reached him in the feet and drew from him a cry and then fire completely enveloped him. Behold Sultan for his strict adherence to law and rectitude."

Under his rule, Hindus who were forced to pay the mandatory Jizya tax were recorded as infidels, their communities monitored and, if they violated Imperial ordinance and built temples, these were destroyed. In particular, an incident in the village of Gohana in Haryana was recorded in the "Insha-i-Mahry" (another historical record written by Amud Din Abdullah bin Mahru) where Hindus had erected a deity and were arrested, brought to the palace and executed en-masse.

In 1230, the powerful Ganga Vanshi Hindu King of Orissa, Anangabhima III consolidated his rule and proclaimed that an attack on Orissa constituted an attack on the king's god. A sign of Anangabhima's determination to protect Hindu culture is the fact that he named his new capital in Cuttack "Abhinava Varanasi." His anxieties about further Muslim advances in Orissa proved to be well founded. In 1361, the Indian region of Orissa was conquered by the Delhi Sultan Firoz Shah and he destroyed the Jagannath temple and the stone deity of Krishna, but the indigenous wooden image of the deity was saved.

Firoz probably learnt many lessons from his cousin Muhammad's rule. He decided not to reconquer areas that had broken away. He decided to keep nobles and the Ulema happy so that they would allow him to rule his kingdom peacefully. In fact, there were hardly any rebellions during his rule. We come to know about him from a 32-page brochure he wrote. Firoz allowed a noble's son to succeed to his father's position and jagir after his death. The same was done in the army, where an old soldier could send his son, son-in-law or even his slave in his place. He won over the Ulemas by giving them grants of revenue, which gave him political power. He increased the salary of the nobles. He stopped all kinds of harsh punishments such as cutting off hands. Firoz also lowered the land taxes that Muhammad had raised. Firuz's reign has been described as the greatest age of corruption in medieval India. It can be imagined from the fact that Firuz once gave a golden tanka to a distraught soldier so that he could bribe the clerk to pass his sub standard horse. The case of Imadulmulk Bashir, the minister of war who began his career as an inherited slave of Firuz, in course of his service is said to have accumulated wealth to the tune of thirteen crores, when the state's yearly income was six crores and seventy-five lakh tankas.

He was the first Muslim ruler to think of the material welfare of his people. Many rest houses, gardens and tombs were built. A number of madrasas (Islamic schools which provided Koranic education) were opened to encourage literacy. He set up hospitals for the free treatment of the poor. He provided money for the marriage of girls belonging to poor families. He commissioned many public buildings in Delhi. He built over 300 villages and dug 5 major canals for irrigation bringing more land under cultivation for growing grain and fruit.

Hindu religious works were translated from Sanskrit to Persian. He had a large personal library of manuscripts in Persian, Arabic and other languages. He brought 2 Ashokan Pillars from Meerut and Topara, carefully wrapped in silk, to Delhi. He re-erected one of them in his palace at Firoz Shah Kotla.

He had about 180,000 slaves, who had been brought from all over the country, trained in various arts and crafts. They however turned out to be undependable. Transfer of capital was the highlight of his reign. When the Qutb Minar struck by lightning in 1368 AD, knocking off its top storey, it was replaced by the existing two floors by Firoz Shah Tughlaq, faced with white marble. Firoz Shah's death led to many rebellions. His lenient attitude had weakened the sultan's position. His successor Ghiyas-ud-Din Tughlaq II could not control the slaves or the nobles. The army had become weak. Slowly the empire shrank in size. Ten years after his death, Timur's invasion devastated Delhi.

FIROZ'S CONCEPT OF BENEVOLENCE, AND PEOPLES' WELFARE

Firoz Tughlaq spells out his basic concept of benevolence in the Fatuhat-i-Firoz Shahi, a book which he is supposed to have written but of which only a portion is now available. Mentioning that in the past times, much "Muslim" blood had been shed, and varieties of tortures been used which he describes, such as cutting of hands, feet, ears and noses; plucking out the eyes, breaking bones, burning and flaying people alive etc., Firoz goes on to say that he had resolved that during his reign "no Muslim blood shall be shed without just cause or excuse, that there shall be no torture, and that no human beings shall be mutilated."

Firoz's orders in the matter covered both Muslims and non-Muslims, though Firoz prefaces his orders by saying that as a good Muslim, his concern was to prohibit all practices contrary to the Muslim holy law, the shara. The shara did, of course, sanction cut-ting off the hands and feet of robbers, and punishment for retalia-tion for a crime committed against an individual. We do not know if Firoz's prohibitions extended against such punishments. Perhaps, his orders were restricted to political, and in some cases, financial offences.

Firoz says that the purpose of giving drastic punishments in previous times was "to terrorise the people so that fear of the government gripped their hearts and the tasks of government were carried out (undisturbed)." Firoz asserts that the fear and prestige of the government did not decline by abrogating drastic punishments, In other words, people were drawn to the government without fear of punishment.

The basic concept of benevolence, that the state was to be based on the willing acceptance of the people, rather than fear or threats of violence, had wider implications, especially in a society where the large majority consisted of non-Muslims. As a part of his policy of conciliation, Firoz publicly destroyed the documents on the basis of which advance of money amounting to two crore tankas had been made to officials by Muhammad bin Tughlaq in order to expand and improve cultivation in the doab, but most of which had been misappropriated. In a somewhat childish manner, Firoz Tughlaq asked those who had been punished by Muhammad bin Tughlaq by their eyes, noses, hands and feet be-ing cut off, to write letters of goodwill which were put in a box and deposited at the head of Muhammad bin Tughlaq's tomb.

Likewise, no large scale punishments were given to those who had joined Ahmad Ayaz, the favourite of Muhammad bin Tughlaq, in putting up a rival prince on the throne at Delhi while Firoz was at Thatta. If Firoz had his way, he would have excused even Ahmad Ayaz, but his leading supporters would not permit it.

However, no attempt was made to recover the jewels and gold which Ahmad Ayaz had distributed to gather a following—a practice which was in sharp contrast to what Ghiyasuddin Tughlaq had done at the time of his accession, adopting harsh methods to disgorge funds from those who had benefited from the liberality of Khusrau Malik. Another step taken by Firoz Tughlaq was to restore the rent-free lands (inam, idrar) granted to theologians, the learned and the weaker sections but which had been resumed by the previous rulers and included in the royal crown-lands (khalisa). We are told that these grants were, in fact, increased.

It was due to these mild methods that in the exaggerated language of Barani, "the administration became stable, all the tasks of government became firm, and all men, high and low, were satisfied, and the subjects, Muslims and Hindus, made content, and everyone busied himself in his own persuits."

All contemporary writers refer to the general prosperity in Firoz Shah's long reign of 40 (lunar years), and the cheapness of commodities. Shams Siraj Afif, the biographer of Firoz, says that while food grains were cheap during the reign of Alauddin due to his strict regulations, there was all round cheapness in Firoz Shah's reign without any effort on his part! This prosperity was shared by everyone, including traders and artisans, because production and wages increased from year to year.

Referring obviously to previous practices, we are told that regulations had been made that "brocades, silks and goods required for the royal establishments were to be purchased at the market price, and the money paid."

Remarking that all homes were replete with grains, property, horses and furniture, and no women was without her ornaments, Afif goes on to say that there was such all round prosperity that even poor men could marry off their daughters at a young age! The obvious implication was that the girls were no longer needed to supplement the family income.

Regarding the peasants or the raiyat, Afif says that he was told that previously "it was the practice to leave the raiyat one cow and take the rest" Firoz tried to rectify this situation by abolishing all taxes not sanctioned by the shara, and by preparing a new valuation (jama) which was based on produce, not measurement. We shall discuss this when we take up Firoz Shah's administrative and agrarian reforms.

Firoz Shah's benevolent and humanitarian efforts extended to repairing and rehabilitating the mosques and the madrasas attached to them. The grants (idrar) of the teachers were raised from 100-200 tankas to 400 or 500, or 700 or even 1000 tankas.

EARLY CAREER OF FIROZ SHAH TUGHLAQ

As Muhammad-bin-Tughlaq had no son his cousin, Firoz. Shah Tughlaq succeeded him. He was the son of Ghiasuddin's younger brother Rajab and was born of a Rajput mother. Muhammad had no male heir but had, according to some accounts nominated his first cousin Firoz for the accession. At first Firoz was unwilling to take the seat of his terrible predecessor. All the chief men of the army, Muslims and Hindus alike offered the crown to him and pressed him to accept it in the interest of the kingdom. Firoz yielded and he was enthroned in the Camp on 23 March 1351. According to Havell, "The blood of Indo-Aryan royalty ran in the veins of Firoz Shah and it was at his Rajput mother's knee that he learnt the lesson of nobleness, oblige and the great traditions of Aryan policy which guided him in after life." Firoz Shah appears to have been greatly profited by the instruction of his uncle Muhammad Tughlaq in the affairs of state and by his education according to the strictest canons of Islam. He ruled for about 37 years upto 1388 A.D. During this period, he tried to bring peace and order in the country and did his best to save his empire from dismemberment.

Khwaja Jahan, the aged governor of Delhi, misled by a false report of Firoz's death, had set up as Sultan a child,'probably but not certainty' the son of Muhammad-bin-Tughlaq. When Firoz approached the Capital, Khwaja Jahan found resistance hopeless and surrendered. The Sultan wanted to spare him but unable to resist the pressure of his nobles, he had Khawaja Khan executed as a traitor and pretender.

PROMOTION OF INTERNAL TRADE BY FIROZ SHAH

To promote trade in the country Firoz removed some of the octroi duties which hampered inter-provincial circulation of commodities. He laid out numerous gardens in the vicinity of Delhi which besides beautifying the capital and satisfying aesthetic taste brought a rich income to the treasury.

ABOLITION OF ALL KINDS OF TORTURE

Firoz Tughlaq mitigated the severity of the criminal law by abolishing torture and mutilation as forms of punishment. He established a charitable hospital in Delhi. He also created an employment Bureau to meet the problem of unemployment. He provided pecuniary help for the marriage of Muslim girls of needy parents. He founded lot of cities and constructed canals and planted trees and made roads.

JAGIR SYSTEM

Firoz Tughlaq reintroduced the system of assigning 'Jagirs' or grants of land with its revenue to his military officers in lieu of cash salaries. This method of paying public servants had been abolished by Ala-ud-din Khilji who condemned it as tending to foster rebellion. He put the military organisation of his empire on a feudal basis. The Jagir system permitted the continuance of aged and uniform persons in their places with the privilege of sending their substitutes. The historians observe that the homes of the 'ryots' were full with grains, property, houses and furniture and everyone had plenty of gold and silver

Firoz Tughlaq organised the institution of slavery into a system. He instructed his officers to capture as many prisoners in war time as possible and to send the best to Delhi for the service of the court. He took special care to maintain and educate the slaves and utilised their services as soldiers, bodyguards and artisans. His object appears to have been two-fold viz, to prevent the inhuman massacre of the prisoners in war and to bring more infidels within the fall of Islam. Those chiefs who brought many slaves received the highest favour. When they were in excess, the Sultan sent them to Multun, Dipalpur, Hissar, Samana, Gujrat and other dependencies. Provision was made for their support on a liberal basis. They were provided for in the army. The institution of slavery took root and the Sultan looked upon its due regulation as one of his duties. The vast number of slaves hastened the disruption of the empire.

FINANCIAL POLICIES OF FIROZ SHAH TUGHLAQ

Firoz Shah's financial policies were aimed at the growth and prosperity of his state. He imposed only four types of tax on his subjects and abolished nearly twenty four taxes which were, undoubtedly, intense on the people. He abolished several internal trade taxes which resulted in lessening of prices of goods and improvement of trade. He also adopted measures for the development of quality of cultivation and better crops. Firoz increased salaries of his officers, gave them jagirs, abolished the practice of extorting truth by torture and also the practice of offering presents to the Sultan so that they might not pressurise the peasants. The peasants were freed from return of Taqavi given to them by the state. The measures of Firoz Shah were successful and resulted in the rising prosperity of both the subjects and the state. There was all round prosperity among people; and, there was no famine during the reign of Firoz Shah Tughlaq.

ADMINISTRATIVE POLICIES OF FIROZ SHAH TUGHLAQ

Firoz Shah's administrative policies of justice were based on the laws of Islam. This restored the privileges of the qazis. He was in favour of mild punishment and had his own court for administering justice. Firoz Shah had keen interest for the development of education in his state. He was a scholar himself and patronised several writers in his court. He established a fine library in the temple of Jwalamukhi which consisted of three hundred volumes of Sanskrit texts. A few of those texts were translated into Persian. The army organisation of Firoz Shah was comparatively weak. There was no standing army kept at the centre and the Sultan had to depend on the forces of the provincial governors at the time of war.

PUBLIC UTILITY WORKS OF FIROZ SHAH TUGHLAQ

Firoz Shah is attributed of founding three hundred towns which included those villages which were left desolated by the people but were again repopulated because of the facilities provided by the state during his reign. The important among them were Fatehbad, Hissar, Firozpur, Jaunpur and Firozabad. He generally lived in Firozabad, near Red fort of Delhi, which was his favourite city. He is also credited for the construction of many dams, colleges, palaces, caravan sarais, towns, hospitals, mausoleums, public baths, wells, bridges and several pleasure houses. He established a charitable hospital called Dar–ul–shafa near Delhi. Firoz Shah repaired many historical buildings such as the Jama Masjid of old Delhi, the mausoleums of Sultan Iltutmish and the Qutub Minar. Firoz Shah distributed a large quantity of wealth and land among saints and other religious people. An employment bureau was set up by Firoz shah, which arranged for the employment of the unemployed. He had set up a separate department which cared for the orphans and widows. Thus, Firoz Shah had done many works of public utility. Firoz Shah constructed five canals for the purpose of irrigation. The first one was one hundred and fifty miles long and carried the waters of the Yamuna River to Hissar. The second was ninety six miles long and carried water from Sutlej River to the Ghaghara. The third started from the Sirmaur hills and ran up to Hansi. The fourth ran from Ghaghara to Firozabad and the fifth ran from the Yamuna River to Firozabad.

He also built several tanks and dams to store water for irrigation. These irrigation facilities resulted in the extension of area under cultivation, enhancement of trade and also income of the state. Thus, though there were several flaws in the domestic policies adopted by Firoz Shah Tughlaq, but eventually he succeeded in achieving his aim of attaining peace and economic prosperity in his state and among his subjects.

RELIGIONS POLICIES OF FIROZ SHAH TUGHLAQ

Firoz Shah Tughlaq was the first Sultan of Delhi whose religious policies were based on the pre-eminence of Islamic laws. Other Sultans supported Islam and were prejudiced against the Hindus but none of them accepted Islamic laws as basic means of governing their administration. Firoz Shah Tughlaq proved an exception and accepted Islamic laws as basic principles in administering the state. Firoz Shah depended on the Ulema for interpretations and thus the religious policy remained intolerant towards people of every faith except the Sunnis. Firoz Shah was intolerant towards the Shiahs, the Sufis, the Ismaili group of Shias and also other sects. He remained fanatically intolerant towards the Hindus. He encouraged the Hindus for conversion. His biography gives a clear impression that regarded the rulers of the Muslims only. He destroyed the temple of Jvalamukhi in Kangra and one of the prime aims in attacking Puri was to destroy the Hindu temple so that, like Mahmud of Ghazni, he could claim to be an Idol breaker. He imposed Jizya on Brahmanas who were either left from this tax or neglected while collecting it by all previous Sultans.

Thus, Firoz Shah practiced severely intolerant policy towards the Hindus. Firoz got recognition of his title of Sultan from the Khalifa. He called himself the Naib of the Khalifa and inscribed his own coins. He did all this because he wanted to capture the loyalty of the Ulema and reactionary group of Muslims who all supported him in capturing the throne. The religious policy of Firoz was reactionary in principle and did positive harm to the state in practice. The Hindus who constituted the majority became disloyal to the state way, and his religious policy also participated in bringing about the disgrace of the Tughlaq Empire. Thus, the religious policies adopted by Firoz Shah were certainly the weak part of his administration which in a way resulted in the downfall of his empire.

CAUSES OF FALL OF TUGHLAQ EMPIRE

Firoz Tughlaq was a benevolent but a weak ruler. He lacked military abilities. He was not a good general which all rulers in those days were expected to be. His two long campaigns in Bengal were fruitless and the expedition to Sind though partially successful, led to no useful results. He made no attempt to recover the Deccan. His personal taste was not in the direction of military glory. He liked hunting. His revival of the jagir system was extremely unwise. It was a mistake which proved fatal to the empire under his weak successors. He retained in the army weak, old and infirm soldiers and officers no. longer fit for military service and allowed their sons and slaves to succeed them irrespective of their abilities and fitness.

This misplaced generosity seriously impaired the efficiency of the army which was the very basis of Muslim power in India. Another impolitic measure of Firoz was the abnormal development of the slave system. The huge number of slaves, whom he employed in his service, caused a heavy drain on the treasury. The loyalty of the slaves could not be counted upon.

They became a potential source of danger to the state. Thus the Sultan was to a great extent responsible for undermining the stability of the empire. His religious intolerance also contributed to the same result. The policy alienated the Hindus and a large number of non-Sunni Muslims (Shias) etc.

WEAK SUCCESSORS OF FIROZ SHAH

As he grew old Firoz left the affairs of the state to the hands of his ministers. In 1388 A.D. aged Sultan died having a good reputation behind him. After his death a number of rulers of the Tughlaq dynasty ruled upto 1412 A.D. But they were all weaklings and the Tughlaq empire soon fell under them. After Firoz his grandson Tughlaq Shah 11 (1388-89) succeeded, He was a debauch and when he had ruled hardly for few months he was beheaded by the Amirs.

Then his cousin Abu Bakar (1389-90) ascended the throne but he was not destined to enjoy a long reign. In August 1390, he was also dethroned and a younger son of Firoz Tughlaq ascended the throne with the title of Muhammad II (1390-94). He ruled for four years and died in 1394 because of his failing health. He was succeeded by his son Humayun (1394), who is also sometimes called Sikandar but he died the same year. Then came to the throne younger brother Mahmud (1394-95). But as the court was divided so another Tughlaq prince, a grandson of Firoz Tughlaq also began to rule as a ruler under the name of Nusrat Shah.

Thus from 1394-98 two Tughlaq rulers ruled side by side. Six successors came to the throne in the ten years following the death of

Firoz. They simply stood by and watched the empire fall to bits. Anarchy reigned supreme and civil war raged everywhere Taking advantage of the prevailing confusion the different provinces like Jaunpur, Gujrat, Malwa, Khandesh etc. became independent. In 1398 came the terrible news that the Mongols under Timur on the way to Delhi have crossed the Indus. Both Mahmud and Nusrat ran for their lives at the approach of Timur.

MUHAMMAD TUGHLAQ'S RESPONSIBILITY

His lack of common sense, hasty nature, hot temperament and whims, pride and obstinacy, harsh and cruel nature greatly led to the downfall of the Tughlaq Empire. Many provinces like Mabar Bengal, Warrangal, Dwarsamudra, Gujrat, Thatte etc. became independent during his reign.

WARS OF SUCCESSION

There was no definite law of succession among the Tughlaqs and consequently there were many wars of succession among then. In such wars they ruined them and invited many unnecessary troubles for them. The court had become the hot–bed of intrigues and conspiracies. This led to distntegeration of Delhi Sultanate.

THE VASTNESS OF THE EMPIRE

It was very difficult to control the distant provinces especially when the means of communications had not so developed. There were revolts in one or the other province. The governors were eager to assert their independence. There were rebellions in two different parts of such a vast empire, it was quite impossible to suppress them due to lack of rapid means of communication,

INTRIGUES OF THE AMIR AND MALIKS OF THE COURT

The Amirs and Maliks of the Tughlaq Court women of intriguing nature and greedy disposition. They were divided into hostile groups. Their mutual quarrels greatly undermined the prestige of the slate and ruined the Tughlaq empire.

THE JAGIRDARI SYSTEM

The jagirdari system which was abolished by Alauddin Khalji was revived by Firoz Tughlaq and the system continued after him throughout the Tughlaq period. It greatly encouraged the disruptive activities and weakened the Tughlaq Empire. Muhammad Tughlaq's visionary plans and Firoz Tughlaq's blind generosity had made the state bankrupt. It became very difficult for their successors to carry on the day-to-day administration properly.

REFERENCES

Bednorz, A. : *Moorish Architecture in Andalusia*, Cologne, London, 1992.

Bérinstain, Valérie : *India and the Mughal Dynasty*, New York: Abrams, 1998.

Hambly, G.: "*Cities of Mughal India*", New York: G. P. Putnam's Sons, 1968.

Heimann, Betty: *Facets of Indian Thought*, Geroge Allen & Unwin, London, 1964.

Ohlin Lloyd: *Delinquency and Opportunity: A Theory of Delinquent Gangs,* The Fress Press, Glencoe, Illionois, 1960.

Chapter 5

Timur Dynasty

INVASION OF TIMUR

The invasion of Timur in India took place in the year 1398 A.D. Timur's objective of attacking India was to fight against and destroy the rulers of India in order to plunder their wealth. Timur started his journey towards India from Samarqand in April 1398 A.D. He crossed the Sindh River in September and entered Punjab. The invasion of Timur led to the destruction of the power of the Delhi Sultanate and the Tughlaq dynasty. Prior to his invasion, his grandson Pir Muhammad, the governor of Kabul, had already sent an expeditionary force against India which had captured Uch and besieged Multan. Pir Muhammad joined Timur after the capture of Multan.

The governor of the fort of Bhatnir submitted after a brief resistance and the fort and the city were destroyed by Timur. Thereafter Timur proceeded towards Delhi massacring people and destroying everything which came in his way. Till then Sultan Nasir–ud–din of the Tughlaq dynasty had done nothing to resist the invader. When finally the Sultan and his wazir Mallu Iqbal attacked the army of Timur, they were easily defeated. Another battle took place between the Indian army and Timur in 1398 and the Indian army was completely routed. The Sultan and his wazir fled away from the capital. In Delhi, Timur first agreed to spare the citizens when requested by the Ulema, but when the citizens resisted the tyrannical behaviour of the soldiers of Timur, he ordered a general massacre and plunder. It continued for several days in which many people were killed, thousands were taken as slave and the entire wealth of the city was plundered. Timur stayed in Delhi for fifteen days and looted immense wealth. On his way back he plundered Firozabad, Meerut, Haridwar, Kangra and Jammu. He brought unparalled devastation in India. Wherever he went, he completely destroyed every thing. Thousands of villages were burnt, lakhs of people were massacred and all the cities were thoroughly plundered. Timur destroyed the Delhi Sultanate and also the dynasty of the Tughlaqs. Before Timur left India, he appointed Khizr Khan as governor of Multan, Lahore and Dipalpur.

TIMUR

Timur was a 14th-century conqueror of much of western and central Asia, and or Pirnazar founder of the Timurid Empire and Timurid dynasty (1370–1405) in Central Asia, which survived until 1857 as the Mughal Empire of India.

A descendant of Mongol conquerors, Timur-whose tribe had become Turkicized in identity and language and Persianized in culture and religion-aspired to recreate the empire of his ancestors. He was a military genius who loved to play chess in his spare time to improve his military tactics and skill. And although he wielded absolute power, he never called himself more than an emir.

Timur was in his lifetime a controversial figure, and remains so today. He sought to restore the Mongol Empire, yet his heaviest blow was against the Islamized Mongol Golden Horde. He was more at home in an urban environment than on the steppe. He styled himself a ghazi yet some Muslim states, e.g. the Ottoman Empire were impacted severely by his wars. A great patron of the arts, his campaigns also caused vast destruction. Timur told the qadis of Aleppo, during the sack of that newly-conquered city," I am not a man of blood; and God is my witness that in all my wars I have never been the aggressor, and that my enemies have always been the authors of their own calamity."

Name

His full name in the Arabic tradition of *ism, nasba, and nisbat* was *Timur bin Tara!ay Barlas*. *Timur* means "iron" in the Chagatai language and in Mongolian (compare *Temujin* "ironworker", the given name of Genghis Khan). The term *Temur* is ultimately derived from a Buddhist Hybrid Sanskrit word **eimara* ("iron").

At the point he reached adulthood he was better known and called as *Timur Gurkani*, *Gurkan* being the Persianized form of the original Mongolian word *kurugan*, "son-in-law", the title bestowed upon his ancestors due to the fact, that first person in Timur's ancestors who was by the name "kara-sharnoban", embraced Islam and married the daughter of Chagatai Khan, the son of Genghis Khan, thus became son-in-law of Chagatai Khan.

Various Persian sources use a byname, *Tîmûr-e Lang* which translates to "Timur the Lame", as he was lame after sustaining an injury to the leg in battle. During his lifetime his enemies used to tease him with it, much to Timur's discomfort. In the West, he is commonly known as *Tamerlane*, which derives from his Persian byname.

Timur was also the great grandfather of Babur, the founder of the Mughal Dynasty.

Early Life

Timur was born in Transoxiana, in City of Kesh (an area now better known as Shahrisabz, 'the green city,'), some 50 miles south of Samarkand in modern Uzbekistan. His father Taraqai was a little landowner and belonged to the Barlas, a nomadic Turkized Mongol tribe in the steppes of Central Asia. They were remnants of the original Mongol hordes of Genghis Khan, many of whom had embraced Turkic or Iranian languages and customs. Timur was a Muslim, his official religious counsellor was the Hanafite scholar 'Abdul-Jabbar Khwarazmi. He also constructed one of his finest buildings at the tomb of Ahmed Yesevi, an influential Turkic Sufi saint who was spreading Sunni Islam among the nomads.

Military Leader

In about 1360 Timur gained prominence as a military leader whose troops were mostly Turkic tribesmen of the region.. He took part in campaigns in Transoxania with the Khan of Chagatai, a fellow descendant of Genghis Khan. His career for the next ten or eleven years may be thus briefly summarized from the *Memoirs*.

Allying himself both in cause and by family connection with Kurgan, the dethroner and destroyer of Volga Bulgaria, he was to invade Khorasan at the head of a thousand horsemen. This was the second military expedition which he led, and its success led to further operations, among them the subjection of Khwarizm and Urganj.

After the murder of Kurgan the disputes which arose among the many claimants to sovereign power were halted by the invasion of the energetic Jagataite Tughlugh Timur of Kashgar, another descendant of Genghis Khan. Timur was dispatched on a mission to the invader's camp, the result of which was his own appointment to the head of his own tribe, the Barlas, in place of its former leader, Hajji Beg.

The exigencies of Timur's quasi-sovereign position compelled him to have recourse to his formidable patron, whose reappearance on the banks of the Syr Darya created a consternation not easily allayed. The Barlas were taken from Timur and entrusted to a son of Tughluk, along with the rest of Mawarannahr; but he was defeated in battle by the bold warrior he had replaced at the head of a numerically far inferior force.

Rise to Power

Tughlugh's death facilitated the work of reconquest, and a few years of perseverance and energy sufficed for its accomplishment, as well as for the addition of a vast extent of territory. It was in this period that Timur reduced the Jagatai khans to the position of figureheads, who were deferred to in theory but in reality ignored, while Timur ruled in their name. During this period Timur and his brother-in-law Husayn, at first fellow fugitives and wanderers in joint adventures full of interest and romance, became rivals and antagonists. At the close of 1369 Husayn was assassinated and Timur, having been formally proclaimed sovereign at Balkh, mounted the throne at Samarkand, the capital of his dominions. This event was recorded by Marlowe in his famous work *Tamburlaine the Great*:

Then shall my native city, Samarcanda...

Be famous through the furthest continents,

For there my palace-royal shall be placed,

Whose shining turrets shall dismay the heavens,

And cast the fame of lion's tower to hell.

A legendary account of Timur's rise to leadership, recorded among the Tatar descendants of the Qypchaq Khanate in Tobol, goes as follows:

One day Aksak Temür spoke thusly:

"Khan Züdei (in China) rules over the city. We now number fifty to sixty men, so let us elect a leader." So they drove a stake into the ground and said: "We shall run thither and he who among us

is the first to reach the stake, may he become our leader". So they ran and Aksak Timur (since he was lame) lagged behind, but before the others reached the stake he threw his cap onto it. Those who arrived first said: "We are the leaders". (But) Aksak Timur said: "My head came in first, I am the leader". In the meanwhile an old man arrived and said: "The leadership should belong to Aksak Timur; your feet have arrived but, before then, his head reached the goal". So they made Aksak Timur their prince.

It is notable that Timur never claimed for himself the title of khan, styling himself amir and acting in the name of the Chagatai ruler of Transoxania. Timur was a military genius but sometimes lacking in political sense. He tended not to leave a government apparatus behind in lands he conquered, and was often faced with the need to conquer such lands again after inevitable rebellions.

Period of Expansion

Timur spent the next 35 years in various wars and expeditions. He not only consolidated his rule at home by the subjugation of his foes, but sought extension of territory by encroachments upon the lands of foreign potentates. His conquests to the west and northwest led him among the Mongols of the Caspian Sea and to the banks of the Ural and the Volga. Conquests in the south and south-West encompassed almost every province in Persia, including Baghdad, Karbala and Northern Iraq.

One of the most formidable of Timur's opponents was another Mongol ruler, a descendant of Genghis Khan named Tokhtamysh. After having been a refugee in Timur's court, Tokhtamysh became ruler both of the eastern Kipchak and the Golden Horde. After his accidence, he then quarreled with Timur over the possession of Khwarizm and Azerbaijan. However, Timur still supported him against the Russians and in 1382 Tokhtamysh invaded the Muscovite dominion and burned Moscow.

After the death of Abu Said, ruler of the Ilkhanid Dynasty, in 1335, there was a power vacuum in the Persian Empire. In 1383 Timur started the military conquest of Persia. He captured Herat, Khorasan and all eastern Persia by 1385 and captured almost all of Persia by 1387. These conquests were characterised by exceptional brutality. For example, when Isfahan surrendered to Timur in 1387, he initially treated it with relative mercy as he commonly did with cities that surrendered without resistance. However, after the city revolted against

Timur's punitive taxes by killing the tax collectors and some of Timur's soldiers, Timur ordered the complete massacre of the city, killing a reported 70,000 citizens. An eye-witness counted more than 28 towers, each constructed of about 1,500 heads.

In the meantime, Tokhtamysh, now khan of the Golden Horde, turned against his patron and invaded Azerbaijan in 1385. This action would cause a counter by Timur that would become the Tokhtamysh–Timur war. In the initial stage of the war, Timur won a victory at the Battle of the Kondurcha River, however Tokhtamysh and his army were allowed to escape. After Tokhtamysh's initial defeat, Timur then invaded Muscovy to the north of Tokhtamysh's holdings. Timur's army burned Raizan and advanced upon Moscow, only to be pulled away before reaching the Oka River by Tokhtamysh's renewed campaign in the south. In 1395, at the Battle of the Terek River, Tokhtamysh's power was finally broken concluding the titanic struggle between the two monarchs. In this Tokhtamysh–Timur war, Timur first led an army of over 100,000 men north for more than 700 miles into the uninhabited steppe, then west about 1000 miles, advancing in a front more than 10 miles wide. The Timurid army almost starved, and Timur organized a great hunt where the army encircled vast areas of steppe to get food. Tokhtamysh's army finally was cornered against the Volga River in the Orenburg region and destroyed. During this march, Timur's army got far enough north to be in a region of very long summer days, causing complaints by his Muslim soldiers about keeping a long schedule of prayers in such northern regions. Timur during the course of his campaign destroyed Sarai, the capital of the Golden Horde, and Astrakhan, subsequently wrecking the Golden Horde's economy based on Silk Road trade.

Indian Campaign

Timur began a trek starting in 1398 to invade the reigning Sultan Nasir-u Din Mehmud of the Tughlaq Dynasty in the north Indian city of Delhi. His campaign was politically pretexted that the Muslim Delhi Sultanate was too tolerant toward its Hindu subjects, but that could not mask the real reason being to amass the wealth of the Delhi Sultanate.

Timur crossed the Indus River at Attock (now Pakistan) on September 24, 1398, but Timur's invasion did not go unopposed and he did meet some resistance during his march to Delhi, by the Governor of Meerut. Timur was able to continue his relentless approach to Delhi, arriving in 1398 to combat the armies of Sultan Mehmud, already weakened by an internal battle for ascension within the royal family.

The Sultan's army was easily defeated on December 17, 1398. On this day the army of Sultan Mahmud Khan had prepared 120 war elephants armoured with chain mail. He had put poison on the tusks, which put fright into the Tatar lines. Timur took action and the Tatars dug out a trench in front of their positions. Timur then took his camels and placed all the wood and hay he could on their backs. When the war elephants charged he lit the camels on fire and then prodded them with iron sticks. They charged at the elephants howling in pain. Timur had understood that elephants were easy creatures of panic. Faced with the strange specter of the burning camels flying straight at them with flames leaping from their backs, the elephants turned around and stampeded back toward their own lines. Timur entered Delhi and the city was sacked, destroyed, and left in ruins. Before the battle for Delhi, Timur executed a large number of captives, mostly Hindus.

Timur himself recorded the invasions in his memoirs, collectively known as Tuzk-e-Taimuriy. In them, he vividly described the massacre at Delhi:

In a short space of time all the people in the Delhi fort were put to the sword, and in the course of one hour the heads of 10,000 infidels were cut off. The sword of Islam was washed in the blood of the infidels, and all the goods and effects, the treasure and the grain which for many a long year had been stored in the fort became the spoil of my soldiers. They set fire to the houses and reduced them to ashes, and they razed the buildings and the fort to the ground....All these infidel Hindus were slain. Their women and children and their property and goods became the spoil of the victors. I proclaimed throughout the camp that every man who had infidel prisoners should put them to death, and whoever neglected to do so should himself be executed and his property given to the informer. When this order became known to the ghazis of Islam, they drew their swords and put their prisoners to death. One hundred thousand infidels, impious idolaters, were on that day slain. Maulana Nasiruddin Umar, a counselor and man of learning, who, in all his life, had never killed a sparrow, now, in execution of my order, slew with his sword fifteen idolatrous Hindus, who were his captives....on the great day of battle these 100,000 prisoners could not be left with the baggage, and that it would be entirely opposed to the rules of war to set these idolaters and enemies of Islam at liberty... no other course remained but that of making them all food for the sword.

Timur further describes as below in Tuzk-e-Taimuriý how he and his army massacred the Hindus population of Delhi after conquering it.

The savage Turks fell to killing and plundering, while the Hindus set fire to their houses with their own hands, burned their wives and children in them and rushed in to fight and were killed... All day Thursday and throughout the night nearly 15,000 Turks were engaged in slaying, plundering and destroying. When Friday morning dawned, my entire army, no longer under control, went off to the city and thought of nothing but killing, plundering and making prisoners. The sack was general during the whole day, and continued throughout the whole day Saturday, the seventeenth (Dec 17), the spoil being so great that each man secured from fifty to a hundred prisoners, men, women and children, while no soldier took less than twenty. There was likewise an immense booty in rubies, diamonds, pearls and other gems; jewels of gold and silver... gold and silver ornaments of the Hindu women obtained in such quantities as to exceed all account. *Excepting the quarter of the Sayyids, the scholars, and the other Mussulmans, the whole city was sacked.*

As per Malfuzat-i-Timuri, Timur targeted Hindus. In his own words, "Excepting the quarter of the saiyids, the 'ulama and the other Musalmans , the whole city was sacked". In his descriptions of the Loni massacre he wrote, "Next day I gave orders that the Musalman prisoners should be separated and saved."

Timur explains his objective behind the Indian campaign as below in *Tuzk-e-Taimuri*

My object in the invasion of Hindustan to lead an expedition against the infidels... (so that) the army of Islam might gain something by plundering the wealth and valuables of the Hindus... we may convert to the true faith the people of that country, and purify the land from the filth of infidelity and polytheism; and that we may overthrow their temples and idols and become ghazis and mujahids before God.

Timur left Delhi in approximately January 1399. In April he had returned to his own capital beyond the Oxus (Amu Darya). Immense quantities of spoils were taken from India. According to Ruy Gonzales de Clavijo, 90 captured elephants were employed merely to carry precious stones looted from his conquest, so as to erect a mosque at Samarkand – what historians today believe is the enormous Bibi-Khanym Mosque.

Ironically, the mosque was constructed too quickly and suffered greatly from disrepair within a few decades of its construction.

Last Campaigns and Death

Before the end of 1399, Timur started a war with Bayezid I, sultan of the Ottoman Empire, and the Mamluk sultan of Egypt. Bayezid began annexing the territory of Turkmen and Muslim rulers in Anatolia. As Timur claimed sovereignty over the Turkmen rulers, they took refuge behind him. Timur invaded Syria, sacked Aleppo and captured Damascus after defeating the Mamluk army. The city's inhabitants were massacred, except for the artisans, who were deported to Samarkand. This led to Timur's being publicly declared an enemy of Islam.

In 1400 Timur invaded Armenia and Georgia. More than 60,000 people from the Caucasus were captured as slaves, and many districts were depopulated.

He invaded Baghdad in June 1401. After the capture of the city, 20,000 of its citizens including Muslims were massacred. Timur ordered that every soldier should return with at least two severed human heads to show him (many warriors were so scared they killed prisoners captured earlier in the campaign just to ensure they had heads to present to Timur). After years of insulting letters passed between Timur and Bayezid, Timur invaded Anatolia and defeated Bayezid in the Battle of Ankara on July 20, 1402. Bayezid was captured in battle and subsequently died in captivity, initiating the 12-year Ottoman Interregnum period. Timur's stated motivation for attacking Bayezid and the Ottoman Empire was the restoration of Seljuq authority. Timur saw the Seljuks as the rightful rulers of Anatolia as they had been granted rule by Mongol conquerors, illustrating again Timur's interest with Genghizid legitimacy.

Timur's army ravaged Western Anatolia, with Muslim writers complaining that the Timurid army acted more like a horde of savages than that of a civilized conqueror. After the Battle of Ankara, Timur did take the city of Smyrna, a stronghold of the Knights Hospitalers, thus he referred to himself as ghazi. Timur was furious at the Genoese and Venetians whose ships ferried the Ottoman army to safety in Thrace. As Lord Kinross reported in *The Ottoman Centuries*, the Italians preferred the enemy they knew to the one they did not.

By 1368, the Ming had driven the Mongols out of China. The first

Ming Emperor Hongwu demanded, and received, homage from many Central Asian states paid to China as the political heirs to the former House of Kublai. Although Timur more than once sent to the Ming Government tributes after he had imprisoned the Chinese envoys for several months, he wished to restore the Mongol Empire, and eventually planned to conquer China. To this end, Timur made an alliance with the Mongols of the Northern Yuan Dynasty and prepared all the way to Bukhara. The Mongol leader Enkhe Khan sent his grandson Oljei Temur, also known as Buyanshir Khan. In December 1404, Timur started military campaigns against the Ming Dynasty and detained the Ming envoy, but he was attacked by fever and plague when encamped on the farther side of the Sihon (Syr-Daria) and died at Atrar (Otrar) in mid-February 1405. His scouts explored Mongolia before his death, and the writing they carved on trees in Mongolia's mountains could still be seen even in the 20th century.

Although he preferred to fight his battles in the spring, Timur died enroute during an uncharacteristic winter campaign against the ruling Chinese Ming Dynasty. It was one of the bitterest winters on record; his troops are recorded as having to dig through five feet of ice to reach drinking water. Records indicate though, that for part of his life at least, he was a surreptitious Ming vassal and that his son Shah Rukh visited China in 1420. He ruled over an empire that, in modern times, extends from southeastern Turkey, Syria, Iraq, Kuwait and Iran, through Central Asia encompassing part of Kazakhstan, Afghanistan, Armenia, Azerbaijan, Georgia, Turkmenistan, Uzbekistan, Kyrgyzstan, Pakistan, North-Western India, and even approaches Kashgar in China.

Northern Iraq remained predominantly Assyrian Christian until attacked, looted, plundered and destroyed by Timur leaving its population decimated by systematic mass slaughter. All churches were destroyed and any survivors forcefully converted to Islam by the sword. Of Timur's four sons, two (Jahangir and Umar Shaykh) predeceased him.

His third son, Miran Shah, died soon after Timur, leaving the youngest son, Shah Rukh. Although his designated successor was his grandson Pir Muhammad b. Jahangir, Timur was ultimately succeeded in power by his son Shah Rukh. His most illustrious descendant Babur founded the Mughal Empire and ruled over most of Pakistan and North India. Babur's descendants Humayun, Akbar, Jahangir, Shah Jahan and Aurangzeb, expanded the Mughal Empire to most of the Indian subcontinent along with parts of modern Pakistan and Afghanistan.

Markham, in his introduction to the narrative of Clavijo's embassy, states that his body "was embalmed with musk and rose water, wrapped in linen, laid in an ebony coffin and sent to Samarkand, where it was buried." His tomb, the Gur-e Amir, still stands in Samarkand, though it has been heavily restored in recent years. Timur had carried his victorious arms on one side from the Irtish and the Volga to the Persian Gulf, and on the other from the Hellespont to the Ganges River.

Contributions to the Arts

Timur became widely known as a patron to the arts. Much of the architecture he commissioned still stands in Samarkand, now in present-day Uzbekistan. He was known to bring the most talented artisans from the lands he conquered back to Samarkand, and is credited with often giving them a wide latitude of artistic freedom to express themselves.

According to legend, Omar Aqta, Timur's court calligrapher, transcribed the Qur'an using letters so small that the entire text of the book fit on a signet ring. Omar also is said to have created a Qur'an so large that a wheelbarrow was required to transport it. Folios of what is probably this larger Qur'an have been found, written in gold lettering on huge pages.

Timur was also said to have created Tamerlane Chess, a variant of shatranj (also known as medieval chess) played on a larger board with several additional pieces and an original method of pawn promotion. These pieces included the camel, siege-weapon, giraffe, and several others as well as boasting a complicated system involving the ability to exchange pawns for certain pieces should they reach the other side of the board. Timur's mandating of Kurash wrestling for his soldiers ensured for it a lasting and legendary legacy. Kurash is now a popular international sport and part of the Asian Games.

Sayyid Dynasty

The Sayyid dynasty ruled Delhi sultanate in India from 1414 to 1451. They succeeded the Tughlaq dynasty and ruled that sultanate until they were displaced by the Lodi dynasty.

This family claimed to be Sayyids, or descendants of Prophet Muhammad. The central authority of the Delhi Sultanate had been fatally weakened by the succesive invasion of Timur (Tamerlane) and his sack of Delhi in 1398. After a period of chaos, when no central authority prevailed, the Sayyids gained power at Delhi. Their 37-year period of dominance witnessed the rule of four different members of the dynasty.

The dynasty was established by Khizr Khan, deputised by Timur to be the governor of Multan (Punjab). Khizr Khan took Delhi from Daulat Khan Lodi on May 28, 1414 and founded the Sayyid dynasty.

But he did not take up the title of king and nominally, continued to be a *Rayat-i-Ala* (vassal) of the Timurids, initially of Timur and after his death, his successor Shah Rukh, grandson of Timur. Khizer Khan was succeeded by his son Mubarrak Khan after his death on May 20, 1421, who styled himself as Muizz-ud-Din Mubarak Shah in his coins. A detailed account of his reign is available in the *Tarikh-i-Mubarak Shahi* written by Yahya-bin-Ahmad Sirhindi. After the death of Mubarak Khan, his nephew Muhammad Khan ascended the throne and styled himself as Sultan Muhammad Shah. Just before his death, he called his son Ala-ud-Din from Badaun and nominated him as his successor.

The last ruler of this dynasty, Ala-ud-Din Alam Shah voluntarily abdicated the throne of the Delhi sulatanate in favour of Bahlul Khan Lodi on April 19, 1451 and left for Badaun. He continued to live there till his death in 1478.

The claim of Khizr Khan, who founded the dynasty known as the Sayyids, to descent from the prophet of Arabia was dubious, and rested chiefly on its causal recognition by the famous saint Sayyid Jalaluddin of Bukhara. He assumed no title associated with royalty, but was content with the position of viceroy of Shah Rukh, Tlmur's fourth son and successor, to whom he is said to have remitted tribute, and with the title of Rdjdt-i-A'ld, or 'the Exalted Standards.' His success reunited the Punjab to Delhi, but the turbulent governors and fief-holders who had withheld their allegiance from a lawful master hesitated at first to acknowledge an upstart, until by degrees many of the old nobles of the late dynasty submitted to him and were permitted to retain their former offices and emoluments.

The Hindus of the Doab and Katehr with held payment of tribute, and in the year of his accession Khizr Khan found it necessary to send an army under Taj-ul-Mulk to reduce to obedience Har Singh, the rebellious raja of Katehr. The raja fled into the forests of Aonla, but a rigorous blockade compelled him to submit and to give an undertaking to pay tribute in future. Mahabat Khan, governor of Budaun, also made his submission, and Taj-ul-Mulk recrossed the Ganges and compelled the fief-holders and Hindu chieftains of the lower Doab, among them Hasan of Rapri, Raja Sarwar of Etawah, and the raja of Kampil, to own allegiance to their new master.

In Chandwar he restored Muslim supremacy, which had been subverted by the Hindus, and returned to Delhi with the tribute, or plunder, which he had collected in the course of his expedition. The chronicles of the Sayyid dynasty are chiefly a history of expeditions of this nature. Khizr Khan was the most powerful ruler of a house the influence and dignity of which decayed with an unvarying and unchecked rapidity seldom surpassed in the most ephemeral of eastern dynasties, and even in his reign military force was the normal means of collecting the revenue. Recalcitrants were not treated as rebels, and the only punishment inflicted was the exaction of the taxes due from them and of a promise, which they usually violated on the first opportunity, to make regular remittances in the future.

Thus, in July, 1416, a most inconvenient season for the collection of revenue, Taj-ul-Mulk was sent to Bayana and Gwalior, not with a view to the reduction of these fortresses but merely to recover, by plundering at random the unfortunate culti-vators, the equivalent of the tribute which should have been paid. With this, and with arrears of tribute which he collected from Kampila and Patiall, he returned to Delhi. In 1415, Malik Sadhu Nadira had been sent to Sirhind as the deputy of Khizr Khan's son Mubarak, on whom that district had been bestowed, and in the following year the Turkish landholders, kinsmen and dependants of Bairam Khan, the former governor, rose under the leadership of Malik Tughan, put him to death, and occupied the fortress.

Zirak Khan was sent against them and pursued them across the Sutlej and as far as the lower slopes of the, Himalaya, but did not venture to continue the pursuit into the mountains, and returned to Delhi. In the same year Khizr Khan himself took the field with the object of chastising Ahmad I of Gujarat who, by pursuing his rebellious uncles to Nagaur, which was nominally, at least subject to Delhi, had violated the fronties of the kingdom. Ahmad, on learning of his approach, fled into Gujarat, and Khizr Khan retired, receiving on his homeward march tribute from Iliyiis Khan, the Muslim governor of Jhaln, the raja of Gwalior, and his own former protector, Shams Khan Auhadi of Bayana, whom he might well have spared.

On his arrival at his capital he learnt that Tughan and his followers had returned to Sirhind and were besieging Malik Kamal Badhan, who had been appointed deputy of Mubarak in the place of the murdered Nadira. On this occasion Zirak Khan was more successful, for he overtook the fugitive Turks at Pael, where Malik Tughan submitted and surrendered his son as a hostage for his good behaviour, for which subservience he was rewarded with the fief of jullundur. Early in 1418 Har Singh of Katehr was again in revolt, and was on this occasion brought to pay and suffered a complete defeat at the hands of Taj-ul-Mulk. He fled, and was pursued into the hills of Kumaon, where Taj-ul-Mulk, unable to seize the object of his pursuit, contented himself with the ignoble but customary satisfaction of plundering the people amongst whom the rebel had found an asylum, and returned to the plains.

From Katehr he marched to Etawah, and there besieged Raja Sarwar, who was again in rebellion. Unable–to reduce the fortress, he plundered the inhabitants of the district and returned to Delhi in May, but his devastating progress, which had resembled rather the raid of a brigand chief than an expedition for the permanent establishment of order, had so exasperated the people of the region through which he had passed that before the end of the year Khizr Khan found it neces-sary to follow in the tracks of his lieutenant, and the record of his progress exhibits both the frailty of the bond between him and his subjects and the futility of the means which he employed for the establishment of his authority.

He was compelled to use force against the people of Koil, within eighty miles of his capital, and then, crossing the Ganges, laid waste the district of Sambhal. His proceedings so alarmed Mahabat Khan of Budaun, who was in his camp and was, perhaps, conscious of shortcomings in his administration or apprehensive of the discovery of his the rebels, that he fled and shut himself up in Budaun, which Khizr Khan besieged for six months without success.

For the history of this and the following reign the sole original authority is an encomiast of the Sayyids, and it is impossible to fathom the under-current of politics or to estimate the difficulties with which Khizr Khan was confronted, but Mahabat Khan was an old noble of the late dynasty, and there were in the royal camp several of his former comrades who had formally submitted to the new order of things, and in June, 1419, Khizr Khan discovered the existence among them of a conspiracy to which Mahabat Khan was doubtless a party, and, in order to separate his enemies, raised the siege and returned towards Delhi. On June 14 he halted on the banks of the Ganges and put the leading conspirators, Qavam-ul-Mulk and Ikhtiyar Khan, to death..

In the following year he was reminded of his early misfortunes by the appearance in Bajwiira, near Hoshiarpur, of an impostor who pretended to be that Sarang Khan who had expelled him from Multan. The real Sarang Khan had died in captivity shortly after his surrender to Pir Muhammad, and this fact must have been widely known, but interest may lead the intelligent, as ignorance leads the vulgar, to espouse the cause of a pretender; and the name of the man who had driven before him, as chaff before the wind, the occupant of the throne of Delhi was well chosen by the impostor. Khizr Khan was, however, well served.

A family of the Lodi clan of the great Ghilzai or Khaljl tribe had recently been domiciled in India, and its leader, Malik Sultan Shah Bahrain, subsequently styled Islam Khan, by which title he may now conveniently be known, had been appointed governor of Sirhind. He was dispatched against the pretender, who marched to the Sutlej to meet him but was defeated and compelled to retire. After the battle Islam Khan was joined by Zirak Khan of Saihana and Malik Tughan of Jullundur, and before their overwhelming force the impostor fled, by way of Rupar, which he had made his head-quarters, into the mountains.

He was ineffectually pursued but emerged and fell a victim to the perfidy of Malik Tughan, who inveighed him into his power and treacherously put him to death, being prompted to this act rather by cupidity than by loyalty, for the impostor had amassed great wealth. In the same year Taj-ul-Mulk was dispatched on another foray dignified by the name of an expedition against rebels, into the districts of Koil and Etawah.

Raja Sarwar was besieged in his fortress, but no important military success was gained. The wretched inhabitants of the country were, as usual, plundered and Sarwar purchased the retreat of the raiders by a contribution to the royal coffers and one of his oft-repeated promises to pay with more regularity in the future. On returning from Etawah Taj-ul-Mulk plundered Chandwar and invaded Katehr, where he compelled Mahabat Khan to pay the tribute due from him. In August news was received at the capital that Malik Tughan, whose resources had been replenished by the plunder of the pre-tender, was again in rebellion and had marched from Jullundur to Sirhind where, having plundered the country, he was besieging the fortress. Malik Khair-ud-dln was sent to its relief and, marching by way of Samana, was there joined by Zirak Khan. Tughan raised the siege of Sirhind and retreated, and Khair-ud-dln and Zirak Khan pursued him across the Sutlej and compelled him to seek refuge with Jasrat the Khokar, the son of that Shaikha who had established his independence in the reign of Mahmud Shah.

Jasrat had been carried off into captivity by Timur, with his father, but on the conqueror's death had regained his freedom and returned to his country, where having established for himself an independent principality of considerable extent, he had gained over the army of Kashmir a victory which fostered in his mind extravagant notions of his power and importance and inspired in him the belief that the throne of Delhi was within his reach. Tughan's fief of Jullundur was bestowed upon Zirak Khan. In 1421 Khizr Khan marched into Mewat to assert his authority in that province, captured and destroyed the former stronghold of Bahadur Nahir and received the submission of most of the inhabitants. He then turned to Gwalior, and on January 13, during his march thither, his faithful minister, Taj-ul-Mulk, died, and his office was bestowed upon his son, Malik Sikandar Tuhfa, who received the title of Malik-ush-Sharq.

The raja of Gwalior took refuge within his fortress and by means of the usual dole and the usual empty promise relieved his subjects from the depredations of the royal troops. Thence the king marched to Etawah, where Sarwar Singh had lately died and his son was prepared to purchase peace on the customary terms, and here he" fell sick and hastened back to Delhi, where he died on May 20, 1421, having designated his son Mubarak Khan his heir.

He is extolled as a charitable ruler but his charity was confined within the narrow limits of his territories and to the members of his own faith. Mubarak, beside whose weakness that of his father assumes the appearance of strength, found it no longer necessary to feign vassalage to any of the rulers who now governed the fragments of Timur's vast empire, and freely used the royal title of Shah, which his father had never assumed. On his coinage he was styled Mu'izz-ud-dln Mubarak Shah, and another unmistakable claim to complete independence was exhibited in his profession of allegiance to the puppet Caliph alone.

He confirmed most of the nobles in the fiefs and appointments which they had held during the late reign, but, conscious of his own weakness, pursued the fatuous policy of perpetually transferring them from one fief to another. He perhaps attained his object of preventing any one noble from acquiring a dangerous local influence in any district of the kingdom, but it was attained at the cost of efficient administration, and the discontent of the nobles harassed by these vexatious transfers, led finally to his downfall.

In pursuance of this policy Malik Rajab Nadira, son of the late Sadhu Nadira, was transferred from Flrflza-bad and HansI to Dlpalpur, to make room for the king's nephew, Malik Bada, who eventually succeeded him as Muhammad Shah. The early days of the reign were disturbed by the activity of Jasrat the Khokar, who, with the interests of the fugitive Tughan as a pretext and the throne of Delhi as a lure, crossed the Sutlej and attacked Rai Kamal-ud-dln, a vassal of Delhi, at Talwandl.

Rai Firoz, a neighbouring fief-holder, fled towards the Jumna, and Jasrat occupied Ludliiana, ravaged the country eastwards as far as Rupar, and returning across the Sutlej, besieged Zirak Khan in Jullundur, when a composition not very creditable to either party was effected. Zirak Khan betrayed the interests of his master by the surrender of the fortress add Jasrat betrayed his guest by sending his son to Delhi as an hostage for his father's good behaviour, and his former adversary, Zirak by seizing and imprisoning him With Jundur as a base Jasrat again crossed the Sutlej and on June 22 appeared before Sirhind, now held for Mubarak Shah by Islam Khan Lodl.

In July, although the rainy season was at its height's, Mubarak Shah marched to the relief of Sirhind, and as he approached Samana Jasrat, after releasing Zirak Khan, who rejoined his master, retreated to Ludhiana, whither Mubarak Shah followed him. Jasrat, having collected air available boats, crossed the flooded river and encamped in security on the opposite bank. As the rains abated Mubarak Shah retired, in real or feigned apprehension, along the bank of the river to Qabulpur, while Jasrat, who had failed to observe that a force had been dispatched up stream to search for a ford, followed him.

The two armies were still facing one another when Jasrat learnt that this force had crossed the river and, fearing lest his retreat should be cut off, retreated precipitately towards Jullundur, but was unable to rest there owing to the vigour of Mubarak's pursuit, during which the fugitives suffered heavy losses, and retired to the lower slopes of the Kashmir highlands. Bhim, raja of Jammu, guided the royal army to the principal stronghold of the Khokars, which was captured, with heavy loss to the defenders, and destroyed, but Jasrat escaped. From the hills Mubarak Shah marched to Lahore ruinous and deserted since its capture by Timur's troops and spent a month in replacing its once formidable defences by a mud fort.

On returning to Delhi he left Malik Mahmud Hasan, who had distinguished himself at the passage of the Sutlej and was henceforward the ablest and most active of his nobles, with a force of 2000 horse to hold the restored outpost of the kingdom. By May, 1422, Jasrat had reassembled his army, descended from the hills, and attempted to carry the new citadel by assault, but was repulsed and forced to retire. For more than a month he harassed Mahmud Hasan by desultory skirmishes, but, finding his labour vain, retired to Kalanaur, his principal place of residence in the plains. Here he met Raja Bhim of Jammu, who was marching to the assistance of Mahmud Hasan, and after one battle made peace with him and retired towards the Beas.

In the meantime Mubarak Shah had dispatched to the aid of Mahmud Hasan the minister, Sikandar Tuhfa, who crossed the Ravi, once more drove Jasrat into the hills and marched to Lahore, where he was welcomed by Mahmud Hasan on September 28. Malik Rajab Nadira of Dipalpur arrived at Lahore at the same time, and the three nobles marched to Kalanaur, where they were met by Raja Bhim, to punish Jasrat's presumption. They invaded the Khokar country, but Jasrat had escaped into the higher ranges, and after plundering the homes of his tribesmen the three nobles returned to Lahore.

During the absence of the minister, Sikandar Tuhfa, from the capital the governor of Delhi, Sarvar-ul-Mulk, induced the feeble king to order, for the benefit of himself and his son, a redistribution of various important offices. Sikandar Tuhfa was dismissed from the office of minister, to make way for Sarvar-ul-Mulk, who was succeeded as governor of Delhi by his son Yusuf. Sikandar Tuhfa received the fief of Lahore as compensation for the loss of the first post in the kingdom, but his transfer thither necessitated the removal of Mahmud Hasan, who was transferred to Jullundur, but was ordered for the time to wait on Mubarak Shah with the contingent maintained from his fief.

These changes bred much discontent; to which may be traced the assassination of Mubarak Shah which took place twelve years later. In 1423 Mubarak Shah once more invaded Katehr, collected tribute from the people in the usual fashion, and, crossing the Ganges, entered the lower Doab, where he treated the Rajputs with great severity and behaved as though he were in an enemy's country. Zirak Khan was left as governor of Kampil, but his ill-treatment of the Hindus so alarmed the son of Sarvar Singh that he fled from the camp to Etawah and successfully defended the town against Malik Khair-ud-din Tuhfa, brother of Sikandar Tuhfa, who was fain to raise the siege on receiving the usual nugatory promise of tribute. Recent successes encouraged Jasrat the Khokar again to invade the kingdom.

He had defeated, and slain in battle his old enemy, Raja Bhim of Jammu and now overran and plundered the districts of Dipalpur and Lahore. Sikandar Tuhfa marched against him, but retired before him leaving him free to prepare for more extensive aggressions. At about the same time it was reported that Ala-ul-Mulk, governor of Multan, had died and that Shaikh. All, the deputy in Kabul of Suyurghatmish, the fourth son of Shahrukb, who had succeeded to the greater part of Tlmur's empire, proposed to invade and ravage the western Punjab and Sind. Malik Mahmud Hasan was sent to Multan, and restored some degree of confidence to the people who had been plundered by Shaikh 'All's troops. Towards the end of the year Mubarak was obliged to march to the aid of Gwalior, which was besieged by Hushang Shah of Malwa.

Hushang, on learning that Mubarak was marching towards Dholpur, raised the siege and marched to the southern bank of the Ghambal, so that when Mubarak reached the northern bank he found most of the fords held by the troops of Malwa, but he discovered an unguarded ford, crossed the river, and permitted his advanced guard to attack some outlying parties of Hushang's army. A trivial advantage was gained and some prisoners and plunder were taken, but neither party desired a general engagement or a protracted campaign, and negotiations ended in the retreat of Hushang to Mandu. Mubarak returned to Delhi in June, 1424, and in the following cold weather marched to Katehr, extorted three years' arrears of tribute from the raja, Har Chand, plundered the country as far as the foot of the Kumaon hills, and, marching down the banks of the Ramganga, crossed the Ganges and entered the Doab. It had been his intention to remain in the neighbourhood of Kanauj, and to establish his authority to the south of that district, but the country had suffered from famine and would neither repay rapine nor support the troops, and he was compelled to return.

He turned aside with the object of crushing a rebellion in Mewat, but the rebels laid waste their villages in the plains and retired into their mountain fastnesses, and the king was obliged to retire, but returned in 1425, when the rebels under Jallu, or Jalal Khan, and Qaddu, or 'Abd-ul-Qadir repeated their tactics of the preceding year. Mubarak on this occasion followed them into the hills, drove them from one stronghold, and pursued them to Alwar, where they surrendered.

Jalal Khan escaped, but Qaddu was carried prisoner to Delhi. In 1426 Mubarak traversed Mewat, plundering the people, on his way to Bayana to attack Muhammad Khan, a rebellious member of the Auhadi family. Most of the rebel's men deserted to the royal standard and Muhammad Khan was sent, with all the members of his family, to Delhi, where he was interned in Jahannuma. The district of Bayana was divided into two fiefs. Bayana itself being granted to Muqbil Khan and Sikri, later to be known as Fathpur, to Khair-ud-din Tuhfa. Mubarak marched from Bayana to Gwalior and returned to Delhi, which he reached in March, 1427, by way of the eastern bank of the Jumna. Shortly after his arrival at Delhi Muhammad Khan Auhadi and his family escaped from the capital and took refuge in Mewat where many of his former followers assembled around him.

Muqbil was absent from Bayana on an expedition, and Khair-ud-din Tuhfa held the fortress with an inadequate garrison. Muhammad Khan was joined by all classes of the inhabitants and Khiar-ud-din was obliged to evacuate the fortress and retire to Delhi. Malik Mubariz was sent from Delhi to recover Bayana and besieged the place, but the garrison defended it obstinately while Muhammad Auhadi withdrew to Jaunpur to seek help of Ibrahim Shah. Mubarak Shah recalled Mubariz and marched in person to Bayana, but before he could form the siege was disturbed by an appeal from Qadir Khan of Kalpi, who implored his aid against Ibrahim Shah, who was marching on Kalpi with the intention of annexing it.

Mubarak abandoned for the time all intention of reducing Bayana and turned against Ibrahim, who having plundered the district of Bhongaon near Mainpurl, was preparing to march on Budaun. Mubarak crossed the Jumna, and on reaching Atraull, sixteen miles from Koil, learnt that Mukhtass Khan, Ibrahim's brother, was threatening Etawah. Mahmud Hasan was detached against him and forced htm to join forces with his brother, and the army of Jaunpur traversed the Doab and crossed the Jumna near Etawah with a view to supporting the garrison of Bayana. Mubarak crossed the river near Chandwar (now Firozabad) and Ibrahim, in February, 1428, marched towards Bayana and encamped on the banks of the Gambhir, while Mubarak encamped at a distance of ten miles from him. Neither was anxious to risk a battle and for some time the operations were confined to affair of outposts, but on April 2 Ibrahim drew up his army for battle, and Mubarak, who lacked even the ordinary merit of physical courage, deputed his nobles to lead his army into the field.

The two armies fought, with moderate zeal and without any decisive result, from midday until sunset, when each retired to its own camp, but on the following day Ibrahim retreated tawards Jaunpur. He was followed for some distance, but Mubarak would not permit the pursuit to be pressed, and ordered that it should be abandoned. His encomiast praises his forbearance towards fellow Muslims, but we may believe that he did not choose to provoke too far an adversary whose strength he had not fully gauged. Mubarak then marched to Gwalior on his usual errand, and, after collecting an instalment of tribute, returned towards Delhi by way of Banana, still held by Muhammad Auhadi, who, on May 11, evacuated the fortress and retired into Mewat.

Mahmud Hasan was invested with the fief of Bayana and Mubarak returned to Delhi, where he found that "his prisoner Qaddu, the grandson of Bahadur Nahir, had been in secret correspondence with Ibrahim during the late campaign. He was put to death and his execution led to a fresh rebellion in Mewat headed by his brother, Jalal Khan. Sarwar-ul-Mulk, the minister, who was appointed to suppress it, followed the rebels into the hills in which they had after their manner, taken refuge and returned to Delhi on their paying him the empty compliment of a formal submission to his master. Jasrat the Khokar was again active, and in August news was received that he was besieging Kalanaur and had driven back to Lahore Sikandar Tuhfa, who had attempted to relieve the beleaguered town. Emboldened by his success he attacked Jullundur, and though he failed to capture the town he plundered the district and carried off into slavery large numbers of its inhabitants.

Zirak Khan from Samana and Islam Khan Lodi from Sirhindmarched to support Sikandar Tuhfa at Lahore, but before they could reach him he had succeeded in effecting a junction with Rai Ghalib, the defender of Kalanur, and had defeated Jasrat, driven him into the hills, and recovered all his spoil. Mahmud Hasan, having restored the royal authority in Bayana, returned to Delhi, and thence to Hissar, his former fief, and Mubarak invaded the plains of Mewat, where Jalal Khan and other chieftains of the country presented their tribute and were received at court. In July, 1429, Rajab Nadira died at Multan and Mahmud Hasan received the title of 'Imad-ul-Mulk and was transferred to that province, the government of which he had formerly held.

In the cold weather Mubarak marched to Gwalior and thence against the contumacious raja of Athgath, who was defeated and compelled to take refuge in the hills of Mewat. His country was plundered and many of his people carried off into slavery, and Mubarak marched to Raprl, expelled the son of Hasan Khan, and bestowed the fief upon Malik Hamzah. On his way back to Delhi he learnt of the death, at Bhatinda, of Sayyid Salim, who had served his house for thirty years. Mubarak, who seems to have been unacquainted with the true character of the Sayyid, and was certainly ignorant of that of his offspring, rewarded the father's long service by bestowing on his elder son the title of Salim Khan and on the younger that of Shuja'-ul-mulk.

The Sayyid had been both rapacious and parsimonious, and during his long tenure of the lucrative fief of Bhatinda had amassed enormous wealth. The central situation of this district in the province of which Khizr Khan had enjoyed the virtual sovereignty for some time before his establishment on the throne of Delhi had secured it from attack from without and from demands for contributions to the defence of the frontiers. The customary law of Muhammadan states in India, which made the ruler the heir of his officials, was especially formidable to those who had defrauded their sovereign and oppressed his subjects, and Salim Khan and Shuja'-ul-Mulk, who were in the king's power, attempted to secure their wealth by instigating Fulad, a Turkish slave of their late father, to rebel in Bhatinda. Their complicity in the rebellion was discovered, they were thrown into prison, and Yusuf, son of Sarvar-ul-Mulk, and Rai Hansu Bhati were sent to treat with Fulad and to induce him to surrender the treasure, but Fulad, who had no intention of surrendering it either to the king or to his late master's heirs, amused the envoys for a time with fair words and promises and, having thrown them off their guard, made a sudden attack on their troops, defeated them and was further enriched by the plunder of their camp. Zirak Khan, Malik Kalu, and Islam Khan Lodi were then sent to besiege the rebel in Bhatinda. Fulad announced that he was prepared to consider terms of submission provided that negotiations were conducted through 'Imad-ul-Mulk of Multan, in whom he had confidence, and 'Imad-ul-Mulk was summoned and arrived at court in August, 1430.

He was sent to Bhatinda, but it was discovered that the rebel's offer to treat with him had been merely a device to gain time, the negotiations broke down, and he returned to Multan after urging the officers before Bhatinda to continue the siege. Fulad, after holding out for six months, sent a large sum of money to Shaikh 'All of Kabul and summoned him to his aid.

In January, 1431, he left Kabul and marched to Bhatinda, and on his arriving within twenty miles of the town Mubarak's nobles hurriedly raised the siege and fled to their fiefs. Fulad issued from the fortress to meet him, paid him 200,000 tangas as the price of his assistance, and entrusted his family to his care, in order that they might be removed to a place of safety. A passing remark of the historian of this reign throws much light on the position of affairs in the Punjab during Mubarak's futile attempts to establish his authority in the Doab, the trans-Gangetic region, and the south-eastern districts of his kingdpm. Sikandar Tuhfa paid to Shaikh 'All "the sum which he had been wont to pay him annually,' and thus induced him to refrain from molesting Lahore during his retreat. From the reference to the yearly payment of blackmail it is clear that the kingdom had been exposed, during ifs intestine troubles, to the danger of invasion from the direction of Lahore. In the direction of Multan the worthless Mubarak was better served, and when Shaikh 'All, during his retreat, attacked a fortress within the limits of that province. Imad-ul-Mulk marched to Talamba and forced him to relinquish his prey.

Unfortunately 'Imad-ul-Mulk received orders to retire to Multan, and Shaikh 'All, attributing his retreat to cowardice or a consciousness of weakness, crossed the "Ravi near Khatibpur, plundered the country along the banks of the Chenab, and marched to within twenty miles of Multan. 'Imad-ul-Mulk sent Islam Khan Lodi to stem his advance, but Islam Khan's force, while still on the march, came unexpectedly on the invaders and was defeated before it could form for attack or defence. Islam Khan was slain, and the remnant of his force fled back to Multan. Shaikh 'All advanced to Khairabad, near Multan, and encamped there on May 15, 1431.

On the following day he advanced to attack one of the gates, but his troops were repulsed by a sortie of the garrison, and he did not resume the offensive until June 8, when he made a second attempt to carry the place by assault, but was again repulsed with heavy loss, and thereafter contented himself with harassing the garrison in a series of skirmishes until the arrival of a strong relieving force which attacked him and drove him within his entrenched camp, where he fled across the Ravi. He was pursued, and numbers of his army perished in the river and by the swords of the pursuers, but he eventually threw himself into Shorkot, leaving all his horses, camels, and equipment in the hands of the victors.

'Imad-ul-Mulk and the army which had marched to his relief followed the fugitives to Shorkot and Shaikh 'All fled with a small force to Kabul; leaving his nephew, Amir Muzaffar, with the remainder of his army in Shorkot. Further operations were stayed by the receipt of orders from the king, recalling to Delhi the relieving force, and most imprudently removing from Multan the able and energetic 'Imad-ul-Mulk, who was relieved by Khair-ud-din Tuhfa. Misfortunes now fell thick and fast on Mubarak.

Jasrat the Khokar again rebelled and marched on Jullundur. Sikandar Tuhfa, marching against him, met him on the Dhauti Wain, but was defeated and taken alive, and Jasrat marched to Lahore and besieged the city, which was defended by Sayyid Najm-ud-din, Sikandar's lieutenant, and Malik Khushkhabar, his slave. Meanwhile Shaikh 'All of Kabul had again invaded the Multan province and on November 13 captured Talamba, occupied the citadel, threw the leading citizens into prison, and plundered all the surrounding country.

At the same time Fulad, who still held Bhatinda, led an expedition against Rai Flriiz, whose fief lay in the neighbourhood, slew him and plundered the district which he had governed. Mubarak, on receiving news of these calamities, acted with unusual vigour and decision, and, having dispatched Sarvar-ul-Mulk in advance, with a force sufficient to check, if not to crush, Fulad, left Delhi, in January, 1432, for Lahore. The sudden flight of his enemies occasioned a modification of his plans. Jasrat raised the siege of Lahore and fled into the mountains, carrying with him his captive, Sikandar Tuhfa, and Shaikh Ali evacuated Talamba and retreated to Shorkot. Mubarak advanced no further, but bestowed the fief of Lahore on Nusrat Khan Gurgandaz and sent Sarvar-ul-Mulk to Lahore to escort the family of Sikandar to Delhi.

In August Jasrat was again active. He issued from his strong-hold, plundered some districts in the plains, and attacked Gurgandaz in Lahore, but, being worsted by him, retired again into the mountains. Mubarak, who had marched as far as Panlpat on hearing of his renewed activity, returned to Delhi on learning of his retreat, and sent 'Imad-ul-Mulk into the districts of Bayana and Gwalior In September he again left the capital to quell some disturbances in the Samana district, but returned to Delhi on hearing of his mother's illness and arrived in time to be present at her obsequies. Having rejoined his army he sent Sarvar-ul-Mulk widi a large force against Fulad, and Sarvar-ul-Mulk, after completing all dispositions for the siege of Samana, left Zirak Khan in charge of the operations and returned to the royal camp at Panipat. Mubarak now abandoned his intention of taking the field in person, and sent Malik Ilubdad Lodi to supersede Gurgandaz in the fiefs of Lahore and Jullundur, but as he was approaching the latter town Jasrat fell upon him at Bajwara, near Hoshiarpur, defeated him, and drove him into the lower slopes of the mountains. In November Mubarak invaded Mewat, where Jalal Khan was again in revolt, and drove him from one stronghold to another, compelling him to purchase peace on the usual terms of a present payment and promise of amendment. He was joined by 'Imad-ul-Mulk on his return from his successful foray into the Bayana district and dispatched Kamal-ud-din and other officers on similar raids into the districts of Etawah and Gwalior, returning, in January, 1433, to Delhi, where he learnt that Shaikh Ali was again preparing to march to the relief of Bhatinda, and dispatched 'Imad-ul-Mulk with reinforcements for the besieging army.

This measure curtailed the extent of Shaikh Ali's activity, but he issued from Shorkot, plundered the villages on the banks of the Ravi, enslaved their inhabitants, and marched on Lahore, which was held for the king by Yusuf, son of Sarvar-ul-Mulik, and Malk Isma'Il. These two officers, after enduring a short siege, discovered that the fidelity of the citizens, which had been sorely tried by constant attacks against which the royal garrison, could ill protect them, was uncertain, and fled from the city with their troops.

During their flight they suffered heavy losses at the hands of a force dispatched in pursuit of them by Shaikh Ali, who plundered Lahore, placed a garrison of 10,000 horse in the city, marched to DIpalpur, where Yusuf had taken refuge, and besieged that town. 'Imad-ul-Mulk, who was still besieging Bhatinda sent his brother, Malik Ahmad, to the relief of Yusuf, and Shaikh 'AH raised the siege of DIpalpur, but occupied all the towns lying between that place and Lahore.

Mubarak at length perceived that affairs in the north-western provinces of his kingdom demanded his personal attention, and marched to Samana, where he was joined by Kamal-ud-din and the other officers who had been sent to Etawah and Gwalior, and advanced to Talwandi, where 'Imad-ul-Mulk joined him from Bhatinda. The officers who still remained before that town were summoned to the royal camp, and Mubarak advanced to the Ravi. Here Sikandar Tuhfa, who had escaped from Jasrat's custody, appeared before him and received the ill-deserved title of Shams-ul-Mulk and a grant of the fiefs of Lahore, Dipalpur, and Jullundur. In the meantime Shaikh 'AH had retreated across the Chenab, and, as Shams-ul-Mulk advanced to take possession of his new fiefs, fled precipitately, leaving most of his horses, and his baggage, camp equipage, and booty, which were already bestowed in boats for transport across the Chenab, in his enemy's hands. Mubarak crossed the Ravi at Talamba and besieged Shorkot, which, after the lapse of a month, was surrendered to him by Amir Muzaffar, Shaikh 'All's nephew, who secured his safety by large gifts, and by bestowing a daughter in marriage on Muhammad Khan, the nephew and adopted son of Mubarak. The king then retired towards Multan after dispatching Shams-ul-Mulk to Lahore, where the garrison left by Shaikh 'All purchased for itself a safe retreat by the surrender of the town and citadel. Mubarak, after retiring to Dipalpur, wisely removed Shams-ul-Mulk from the important fiefs which he had recently bestowed upon him to Baysna, and conferred Lahore, DIpalpur, and Jullundur on 'Imad-ul-Mulk.

On his return to Delhi he discovered that Sarvar-ul-Mulk had for some time past been remiss in the performance of his duties as minister of the kingdom, and appointed Kamal-ud-din as his co-adjutor in the hope that the two would work in harmony. He was disappointed, for the influence of the abler and more energetic Kamal-ud-din soon eclipsed that of Sarvar-ul-Mulk, who, resenting hb virtual suppression in office, formed a faction consisting of some discontented Khatrls, Miran Sadr, the deputy muster-master-general, Qazi 'Abd-us-Samad Khan, a royal chamberlain, and others, and conspired against the king's life. On November 1 the king founded Mubarakabad, on the Jumna, and while superintending the building of this town learnt that the protracted siege of Bhatinda had at length been brought to a successful conclusion.

The news was confirmed by the receipt of the head of the rebel, Fulad, which had been severed from his body after his capture by Miran Sadr. He marched to Bhatinda and, after extinguishing the smouldering embers of disaffection, learnt that a dispute had arisen between Ibrahim Shah of Jaunpur and Hushang Shah of Malwa regarding the town and district of Kalpi, which had ever been included, in name at least, in the dominions of Delhi, and that they were marching to decide the question by an appeal to arms. He could not but resent an insult so gross and returned to Delhi to assemble his forces. On his way to Kalpi he turned aside to visit Mubarakabad, and here, on February 19, 1434, Sarvar-ul-Mulk found the opportunity which he had been seeking.

Miran Sadr relieved the royal bodyguard with a force of his own troops, and while the king was preparing for prayers entered his apartment on the pretext of taking leave of him, posting Sidharan, one of the Khatrls, at the door to prevent the entrance of any person not privy to the plot. While he engaged the king in conversation Sidhu Pal, another Khatri, cut him down with his sword, and Ranu and other Hindus rushed in and completed the bloody work.

On the death of Mubarak Shah, who had left no son, the nobles at Delhi raised to the throne Muhammad, the son of his brother Farld. Sarvar-ul-Mulk's complicity in the murder of the late king could not be concealed, but as he held possession of the royal treasury, armoury, and elephants he was too powerful to be touched and though he was suspected of designs on the throne it was necessary, for the time, to confirm him in his office, and he received the title of Khanjahan, while his accomplice, Miran Sadr, received that of Mu'In-ul-Mulk.

Kamal-ud-din, whose appointment had been the cause of Sarvar-ul-Mulk's disaffection, and other of Mubarak's nobles were desirous of avenging his death, but were compelled to bide their time, and Sarvar-ul-Mulk, with a view to intimidating them executed one officer of high rank and imprisoned others, seized all the vacant fiefs in the kingdom and distributed them among his creatures. Bayana, Amroha, Narnaul, Guhram, and some districts in the Doab were granted to Sindharan, Sidhu Pal, and their relatives who had been personally concerned in the murder of the late king. Sidhu Pal sent his slave Rami, another assassin, to Bayana to collect the revenue, but Yusuf Khan Auhadi marched from Hindaun to meet him, and when Ranu attempted to take possession of the fort attacked, defeated, and slew him.

The nobles who still held their fiefs made preparations for overthrowing Sarvar-ul-Mulk. Malik Ilahdad Lodi, now governor of Sambhal and Ahar, Malik Cliaman of Budaun, Amir 'All Gujarat! Amir Kambal, and others agreed to stand or fall together and raised the standard of revolt. Sarvar-ul-Mulk assembled an army to crush them, and appointed to its command Kamal-ul-dln, who had dissembled his hostility, associating with him his own son Yusuf, Sayyid Khan, and Sidharan the Khatri. This force advanced from Delhi to Baran and Ilahdad Lodi retired, but halted at Ahar on learning that Kamal-ud-dln favoured his cause.

His hostility to the minister and sympathy with the faction in arms against him could no longer be concealed, and Sarvar-ul-Mulk sent from Delhi to the army his slave Hushyar, nominally as Kamal-ud-din's assistant, but in fact as a spy upon his actions and a coadjutor of Yusuf and Sidharan. Malik Ghaman of Budaun now joined Ilahdad Lodi at Ahar and Kamal-ud-dln's attitude became so menacing that Yusuf and Sidharan returned to Delhi.

On their departure Ilahdad and his allies joined Kamal-ud-din, marched with him on Delhi, defeated Sarvar-ul-Mulk's troops in a battle before the city, and besieged him for three months in Siri. Sarvar-ul-Mulk discovered, in the course of siege which lasted for three months, that the king was in sympathy with the besiegers, and attempted to slay him as he had slain his predecessor, but Muhammad was prepared for the attempt and his armed attendants slew Sarvar-ul-Mulk, and seizing the sons of Mlran Sadr, executed them on the spot. Kamal-ud-dln and the confederates were then summoned into the city and the remaining conspirators retired to their houses. Sidhu Pal imitated the Rajput custom ofjauhar, set fire to his house; immolated his family, and died fighting, but Sidharan and the other Khatrls were taken alive and put to death, and Hushyar the slave and Mubarak.

The confederates repeated the ceremony of enthroning Muhammad Shah had swore allegiance to him, and in the new distribution of offices and fiefs Kamal-ud-din became minister and received the title of Kamal Khan, Malik Ghaman was entitled Ghazi-ul-Mulk and was confirmed in the fiefs of Budaun and Am-roha, Uahdad Lodi, who would accept no title for himself, obtained that of Darya Khan for his brother, who succeeded him in Sambhal, Malik Kholraj retained Hissar, and Haji Shudani was entitled Hisam Khan and appointed governor of the capital. In October Muhammad Shah made a pilgrimage to Multan to visit the shrines of the saints, and in 1436 marched to Samana and dispatched thence an army which is said to have laid waste the country of the Khokars.

Muhammad had been, until the fall of Sarvar-ul-Mulk, the victim of factions and the sport of circumstances, but when he had an opportunity of displaying his fitness for rule he so abused it as to lose both the affection and the confidence of those who had freed him from his enemies. After his return to Delhi from Samana his counsellors were perturbed by the news of successive calamities. In Multan the Langahs, an Afghan tribe recently settled in the district, rebelled against Muhammad Shah's governor; in the opposite direction Ibrahim Shah of Jaunpur invaded and annexed some of the south-eastern districts of the kingdom; and to the south of Delhi the raja of Gwalior and other Hindu chieftains openly repudiated their liability to pay tribute. Even the forays undertaken in his uncle's reign would have been preferable to inaction, but Muhammad remained in his capital, sunk in indolence and pleasure, until his nobles, losing heart, clearly perceived that if the ancient prestige of Delhi were to be preserved they must seek another leader.

It was during this period that the commanding qualities of Malik Bahlul Lodi, nephew and adopted son of Islam Khan and now governor of Sirhind, first attracted attention. As the king's weakness and meanness of spirit became more apparent he gradually extented his influence over the whole of the Punjab, and began to withhold the revenue due to the royal treasury. The condition of the remnant of the kingdom of Delhi was deplorable. Muhammad's nominal authority did not extend beyond Panipat to the north; on the south and south-east the raja of Gwalior, who had during the previous reign periodically acknowledged the sovereignty of Delhi, no longer made any pretence of fealty, and the king of Jaunpur had invaded and annexed the districts bordering on his kingdom.

The Hindus of the Doab, always refractory, disregarded with impunity an authority which was never asserted, and the turbulent tribesmen of Mewat plundered the country to within a short distance of the wall of the city. The Nobles of Delhi, despairing of a king who was content to loiter in his palace while his kingdom dissolved, had recourse, in 1440-41, to Mahmud Shah Khaljl of Malwa, an active and warlike prince who had in 1436 seized the throne of that kingdom, and sent repeated messages to him representing the miserable plight of the once glorious kingdom and imploring him to march to Delhi for the purpose of restoring peace and order. Mahmud set out, and Muhammad Shah, roused at length from his disgraceful torpor, prepared to oppose him.

Assembling such troops as he could muster, he sent an appeal for help to Bahlul Lodi, whose readiness to respond had its origin not in loyalty to Muhammad, but in the resolve to preserve the kingdom for himself. He would not, however, lend his aid unconditionally, and demanded as its price the death of Hisam Khan, governor of the capital, in whom he recognised either a dangerous rival or too staunch and powerful a champion of hereditary right the condition was fulfilled, and Bahlul led his forces to the support of the king. Meanwhile Mahmud, marching from Malwa by way of Hindaiin, was there joined by Yusuf Khan Auhadi and continued his advance to Delhi. Muhammad inarched forth to meet him, and the two armies confronted one another between Tughlqabad and the city. Here Muhammad, who had already proved himself to be devoid of the qualities of a leader of men, sank to the lowest depths of contempt by showing that he lacked the mere physical courage expected of the humblest soldier.

He would not take the field in person, but entrusted the command of his troops nominally to his son 'Ala-ud-din, with whom he associated Sayyid Khan Darya Khan Lodi, Qutb Khan, and other officers. Like Muhammad, but for a different reason, Mahmud Khalji refrained from personally engaging in the conflict. His courage was never impugned, and he was, indeed, brave to rashness, but he would not deign to take the field against Muhammad's officers, and was resolved to show that his own subordinates were well able to cope with them. Retaining for the protection of his person a small force of picked cavalry he entrusted the command of the rest of his army to his two sons Ghiyas-ud-dln and Nusrat Khan. The battle began at noon and lasted, without any decisive advantage to either side, until nightfall, when each army returned to its own camp.

The pusillanimous Muhammad, dreading the alternative prospects of being obliged to take the field or falling into the hands of the enemy, hastened to make undignified proposals for peace, which might have been rejected with contempt, had not Mahmud received reports which necessitated an immediate return to his capital. A mob at Maudu had removed the royal umbrella suspended over the tomb of Hushang Shah and had raised it over the head of a pretender whom they had proclaimed king of Malwa as representative of the Ghuri family. Accordingly he welcomed the overtures for peace and on the following day began his retreat.

With flagrant disregard of the agreement between the two kings Bahlul Lodi followed and attacked the retreating army, and obtained a trivial advantage over its rearguard and some plunder. It need not be assumed that Muhammad was privy to this act of treachery, for

Bahlul was beyond his control, but he participated in its guilt by becoming, in legal phrase; an accessory after the fact. The perfidious Afghan was received on his return with extravagant demonstrations, his mean and petty triumph was magnified into a victory over the army of Malwa, and the king distinguished him by styling him his son, and conferred on him the title of Khan Khanan.

Bahlul now consulted his interest by feigning loyalty to Muhammad and in the following year the king marched to Samana and there formally bestowed on him, in addition to the fiefs which he already held by grant from the crown, Dipalpur and Lahore, which were no longer his to bestow. Bahlul deigned to accept a commission to attack Jasrat the Khokar, but, on discovering that Jasrat was inclined to favour his designs on the throne of Delhi, made peace with him on easy terms and withdrew to Sirhind, where he strengthened himself by annexing the districts adjoining those which he already held, and by enlisting large numbers of Afghans, especially of his own tribe, in his army. He picked a quarrel, on trivial grounds, with Muhammad Shah, marched to Delhi, and besieged it, but failed to capture it, or perhaps, for he returned unmolested to his own dominions, where he styled himself Sultan Bahlul, was bought off, or retired on realizing the magnitude of the task with which he would be confronted after taking the city.

After the siege of the capital the disorders of the kingdom increased daily, and when Muhammad Shah died, in 1444, no point on his frontier was more than forty miles distant from Delhi, and the kingdom inherited by his son 'Ala-ud-dln, who assumed the title of 'Alain Shah, consisted of the city and the neighbouring villages. The new king was even more feeble and vacillating than his father, and although Bahlul humoured the nobles of Delhi by formally acknowledging his accession he sedulously continued his preparations for seizing the throne when the time should be ripe. Shortly after his accession 'Alam Shah marched towards Samana, apparently with no other purpose than that of showing that a king of Delhi yet dared to leave his palace, but was recalled by a rumour that Mahmud Shah of Jaunpur was marching on the city.

The report, which he had not taken the trouble to verify, proved to be false, and an outspoken courtier incurred his displeasure by upbraiding him for his undignified and unnecessary retreat.

In 1447 he marched to Budaun, where he was received with respect, and found the city so attractive that he resolved to reside there rather than at Delhi. Having prepared a dwelling for himself he returned to

Delhi, where the same blunt courtier remonstrated with him on the folly of the step which he contemplated, but gained nothing but his own removal from office. The king appointed one of his wife's brother's governors of the capital and in 1448 retired permanently to Budaun, where he abandoned himself entirely to the pursuit of pleasure. It is now proper to examine the condition of the territories over which Khizr Khan had established his authority.

The province of Multan had elected a ruler of its own, who never recognized, even formally, the royal authority; and the rest of the Punjab, as far south as Panlpat and Hissar, was in the possession of Bahlul, whose relative, Darya Khan Lodi, held the district of Sambhal, the western limit of which he had pushed forward as far as the ford Khvaja Khizr, on the Jumna near Delhi. Ad–joining this petty state on the south, within the limits of the Doab, was the state of Koll, held by 'Isa Khan the Turk, and south of this state Hasan Khan, another Afghan, held Rapri.

The lower central Doab, including Bhongaon, Patiali, and Kampil, was held by the Rajput, Raja Partab and to the west of the Jumna Daud Khan Auhadi was independent in Bayana. All these rulers were partisans of Bahlul. Gwalior was an independent Hindu state, and such tracts of Mewat as did not acknowledge the rule of Daud. AuhadI were held by native chieftains whose power extended almost to the gates of Delhi. 'Alam Shah, on his way to Budaun, took counsel with Qutb Khan, cousin of Bahlul, 'Isa Khan, and Raja Partab, regarding the possibility of rehabilitating the royal power. Hamid Khan, who was now minister, was obnoxious to Raja Partab, for his father, Fath Khan, had formerly devastated Partab's fief and carried off his wife. The three courtiers promised to add to 'Alam Shah's small kingdom forty parganas on condition that he put Hamid Khan to death. He was imprisoned, but escaped and fled to Delhi. After the king's departure from the capital a quarrel broke out between his two brothers-in-law, one of whom had been left there as governor and the other as chief of the city police, and one of them had been killed in a fight between their factions. The mob, at the instigation of Hisam Khan, had risen against the survivor and put him to death, and Hisam Khan and Hamid Khan remained arbiters of the destinies of Delhi. The restoration of 'Alam Shah was out of the question, and both desired to find a substitute who would be content with no more than the royal title and would permit them to govern in his name. The claims of the kings of Jaunpur and Malwa were considered and rejected, for the former was connected by marriage with 'Alam Shah and might attempt to avenge his wrongs and the latter was so attached to his distant kingdom that it was improbable that he would transfer his affections to Delhi. Their choice fell ultimately upon Bahlul, though there was little probability of his becoming a pliable instrument in their hands, and he was invited to Delhi.

He responded with such alacrity that he arrived with a force insufficient to establish his authority, but he formally received from Hamid Khan, in exchange for conciliatory promises, the keys of the city, and wrote to 'Alam Shah a letter as masterly as it was insincere, in which he explained that he was actuated solely by jealous zeal for the royal authority, which he had seen set at naught. Bahlul seated himself on the throne on April 19, 1451, and set out at once to Dipalpur to collect the troops which in his haste he had left behind. His letter to 'Alam Shah elicited the desired reply. The mean-spirited King, content with the ease and freedom from care which his residence in Budaun afforded, replied that he had neither fruit nor profit of sovereignty, that his father had styled Bahlul his son and that he himself freely and cheerfully resigned his throne to Bahlul as to an elder brother. Thus Bahlul, on his return to Delhi, ascended the throne not merely as the creature of a successful faction, but as the heir designate of a king who had voluntarily abdicated. The contemptible 'Alam Shah remained contentedly in Biudaun, where the revenue of the small territory which he had been permitted to retain sufficed to defray the cost of his pleasures.

REFERENCES

Bernard, Jessie: *Social Problems at Midcentury: Role, Status and Stress in a Context of Abundance,* New York: Holt, Rinehart and Winston, 1957.

Borchert, Bruno: *Mysticism: Its History and Challenge,* Samuel Wiser, York Beach, 1994.

Hopkirk, Peter: *The Great Game: The Struggle for Empire in Central Asia*, Kodansha, 1992.

Ikram, S.M. : *Muslim Civilization in India*, New York:Columbia University Press, 1964.

Okada, Amina: *Indian Miniatures of the Mughal Court*, New York, Harry N. Abrahms, Inc. Publishers, 1992.

Chapter 6

Muslim Conquest in the Indian Subcontinent

Muslim conquests in the Indian subcontinent mainly took place from the 13th to the 16th centuries, though earlier Muslim conquests made limited inroads into modern North India and Pakistan as early as the time of the Rajput kingdoms in the 7th century.

Prior to the conquest of India by the British East India Company, the Muslim Moghul Empire was able to annex or subjugate most of India's Hindu kings. However, it was never able to conquer the Hindu kingdoms in upper reaches of the Himalayas such as the regions of today's Himachal Pradesh, Uttarakhand, Sikkim, Nepal and Bhutan and the extreme south of India such as Travancore.

BACKGROUND

Like other societies in history, South Asia has been attacked by nomadic tribes throughout its long history. In evaluating the impact of Islam on the sub-continent, one must also note that the sub-continent was a frequent target of tribes from Persia and Central Asia who arrived from the North West. With the fall of the Sassanids and the arrival of the Caliphate's domination of the region these tribes began to contest with the new power and were subsequently integrated into it giving rise to Muslim dynasties of Central Asian heritage, generally Turkic - Mongols. In that sense, the Muslim invasions of the 10th century onwards were not dissimilar to those of the earlier invasions in the History of Central Asia during the 1st through to the 6th century. What does however, make the Muslim invasions different is that unlike the preceding invaders who assimilated into the prevalent social system, the Muslim conquerors retained their Islamic identity and created new legal and administrative systems that challenged and usually superseded the existing systems of social conduct and ethics. They also introduced new cultural mores that in some ways were very different from the existing cultural codes. While this was often a source of friction and conflict, it should also be noted that there were also Muslim rulers, notably Akbar, who in much of their secular practice absorbed or accommodated local traditions.

The first incursion by the new Muslim successor states of the Persian Empire occurred around 664 CE during the Umayyad Caliphate, led by Al Muhallab ibn Abi Suffrah towards Multan in Southern Punjab, in modern day Pakistan. Muhallab's expeditions were not aimed at conquest, though they penetrated only as far as the capital of the Maili, he returned with wealth and prisoners of war. This was an Arab incursion and part of the early Umayyad push onwards from the Islamic conquest of Persia into Central Asia, and within the limits of the eastern borders of previous Persian empires. The last Arab push in the region would be towards the end of Umayyad reign under Muhammad bin Qasim, after whom the Arabs would be defeated by the Rajputs at the Battle of Rajasthan in 738, and Muslim incursions would only be resumed under later Turkic and Central Asian mongol dynasties with more local capitals, who supplanted the Caliphate and expanded their domains both northwards and eastwards.

It took several centuries for Islam to spread across India and how it did so is a topic of intense debate. Some quarters hold that it occurred through inter-marriage, conversions, economic integration, to escape caste structures, and through the influence of Sufi preachers.

Conversion Theories

Considerable controversy exists both in scholarly and public opinion about the conversions to Islam typically represented by the following schools of thought:

1. That the bulk of Muslims are descendants of migrants from the Iranian plateau or Arabs.
2. Conversion was a result of the actions of Sufi saints and involved a genuine change of heart

3. Conversion came from Buddhists and the en masse conversions of lower castes for social liberation and as a rejection of oppressive existent Hindu caste structures.
4. Was a combination, initially made under duress followed by a genuine change of heart
5. As a socio-cultural process of diffusion and integration over an extended period of time into the sphere of the dominant Muslim civilisation and global polity at large.
6. That Muslims sought conversion through *jihad* or political violence
7. A related view is that conversions occurred for non-religious reasons of pragmatism and patronage such as social mobility among the Muslim ruling elite or for relief from taxes

An estimate of the number of people killed, based on the Muslim chronicles and demographic calculations, was done by K.S. Lal in his book *Growth of Muslim Population in Medieval India*, who claimed that between 1000 CE and 1500 CE, the population of Hindus decreased by 80 million. His work has come under criticism by historians such as Simon Digby (School of Oriental and African Studies) and Irfan Habib for its agenda and lack of accurate data in pre-census times. Western Historians such as Will Durant contend that Islam spread through violence.

Sir Jadunath Sarkar contends that that several Muslim invaders were waging a systematic jihad against Hindus in India to the effect that "Every device short of massacre in cold blood was resorted to in order to convert heathen subjects." In particular the records kept by al-Utbi, Mahmud al-Ghazni's secretary, in the Tarikh-i-Yamini document several episodes of bloody military campaigns. Hindus who converted to Islam however were not completely immune to persecution due to the Caste system among South Asian Muslims in India established by Ziauddin al-Barani in the *Fatawa-i Jahandari.*, where they were regarded as an "Ajlaf" caste and subjected to discrimination by the "Ashraf" castes

Critics of the "Religion of the sword theory" point to the presence of the strong Muslim communities found in Southern India, modern day Bangladesh, Sri Lanka and western Burma, Indonesia and the Philippines coupled with the distinctive lack of equivalent Muslim communities around the heartland of historical Muslim empires in South Asia as refutation to the "conversion by the sword theory". The legacy of Muslim conquest of South Asia is a hotly debated issue even today. Not all Muslim invaders were simply raiders. Later rulers fought on to win kingdoms and stayed to create new ruling dynasties. The practices of these new rulers and their subsequent heirs (some of whom were borne of Hindu wives of Muslim rulers) varied considerably. While some were uniformly hated, others developed a popular following. According to the memoirs of Ibn Battuta who traveled through Delhi in the 14th century, one of the previous sultans had been especially brutal and was deeply hated by Delhi's population. His memoirs also indicate that Muslims from the Arab world, Persia and Turkey were often favored with important posts at the royal courts suggesting that locals may have played a somewhat subordinate role in the Delhi administration. The term "Turk" was commonly used to refer to their higher social status. However S.A.A. Rizvi points to Muhammad bin Tughlaq as not only encouraging locals but promoting artisan groups such as cooks, barbers and gardeners to high administrative posts. In his reign, it is likely that conversions to Islam took place as a means of seeking greater social mobility and improved social standing.

IMPACT OF ISLAM AND MUSLIMS IN INDIA

Expansion of Trade

Islam's impact was the most notable in the expansion of trade. The first contact of Muslims with India was the Arab attack on a nest of pirates near modern-day Bombay to safeguard their trade in the Arabian Sea. Around the same time many Arabs settled at Indian ports, giving rise to small Muslim communities. The growth of these communities was not only due to conversion but also the fact that many Hindu kings of south India (such as those from Cholas) hired Muslims as mercenaries.

A significant aspect of the Muslim period in world history was the emergence of Islamic Sharia courts capable of imposing a common commercial and legal system that extended from Morocco in the West to Mongolia in the North East and Indonesia in the South East. While southern India was already in trade with Arabs/Muslims, northern India found new opportunities. As the Hindu and Buddhist kingdoms of Asia were subjugated by Islam, and as Islam spread through Africa – it became a highly centralising force that facilitated in the creation of a common legal system that allowed letters of credit issued in say Egypt or Tunisia to be honoured in India or Indonesia (The Sharia has laws on the transaction of business with both Muslims and non-Muslims). In order to cement their rule, Muslim rulers initially promoted a system in which there was a revolving door between the clergy, the administrative nobility and the mercantile classes. The travels of explorer Muhammad Ibn-Abdullah Ibn-Batuta were eased because of this system. He served as an Imam in Delhi, as a judicial official in the Maldives, and as an envoy and trader in the Malabar. There was never a contradiction in any of his positions because each of these roles complemented the other. Islam created a compact under which political power, law and religion became fused in a manner so as to safeguard the interests of the mercantile class. This led world trade to expand to the maximum extent possible in the medieval world. Sher Shah Suri took initiatives in improvement of trade by abolishing all taxes which hindered progress of free trade. He built large networks of roads and constructed Grand Trunk Road (1540–1544), which connects Calcutta to Kabul. Parts of it are still in use today. The geographic regions add to the diversity of languages and politics.

Cultural influence

The divide and rule policies, two-nation theory, and subsequent partition of India in the wake of Independence from the British Empire has polarised the sub-continental psyche, making objective assessment hard in comparison to the other settled agricultural societies of India from the North West. Muslim rule differed from these others in the level of assimilation and syncretism that occurred. They retained their identity and introduced legal and administrative systems that superseded existing systems of social conduct and ethics. While this was a source of friction it resulted in a unique experience the legacy of which is a Muslim community strongly Islamic in character while at the same time distinctive and unique among its peers.

The impact of Islam on Indian culture has been inestimable. It permanently influenced the development of all areas of human endeavour – language, dress, cuisine, all the art forms, architecture and urban design, and social customs and values. Conversely, the languages of the Muslim invaders were modified by contact with local languages, to Urdu, which uses the Arabic script. This language was also known as Hindustani, an umbrella term used for the vernacular terminology of Hindi as well as Urdu, both major languages in South Asia today derived primarily from Sanskrit grammatical structures and vocabulary.

Muslim rule saw a greater urbanisation of India and the rise of many cities and their urban cultures. The biggest impact was upon trade resulting from a common commercial and legal system extending from Morocco to Indonesia. This change of emphasis on mercantilism and trade from the more strongly centralised governance systems further clashed with the agricultural based traditional economy and also provided fuel for social and political tensions.

A related development to the shifting economic conditions was the establishment of Karkhanas, or small factories and the import and dissemination of technology through India and the rest of the world. The use of ceramic tiles was adopted from architectural traditions of Iraq, Iran, and Central Asia. Rajasthan's blue pottery was a local variation of imported Chinese pottery. There is also the example of Sultan Abidin (1420–70) sending Kashmiri artisans to Samarqand to learn book-binding and paper making. Khurja and Siwan became renowned for pottery, Moradabad for brass ware, Mirzapur for carpets, Firozabad for glass wares, Farrukhabad for printing, Sahranpur and Nagina for wood-carving, Bidar and Lucknow for bidriware, Srinagar for papier-mache, Benaras for jewellery and textiles, and so on. On the flip-side encouraging such growth also resulted in higher taxes on the peasantry. Numerous Indian scientific and mathematical advances and the Hindu numerals were spread to the rest of the world and much of the scholarly work and advances in the sciences of the age under Muslim nations across the globe were imported by the liberal patronage of Arts and Sciences by the rulers. The languages brought by Islam were modified by contact with local languages leading to the creation of several new languages, such as Urdu, which uses the modified Arabic script, but with more Persian words. The influences of these languages exist in several dialects in India today.

Islamic and Mughal architecture and art is widely noticeable in India, examples being the Taj Mahal and Jama Masjid.

Early Muslim Communities

Several reasons existed for the desire of the rising Islamic Empire to gain a foothold in Makran and Sindh; ranging from the participation of armies from Sindh fighting alongside the Persians in battles such as Nehawand, Salasal, Qadisia and Makran, pirate raids on Arab shipping to the granting of refuge to rebel chiefs.

The Punjab and Sindh region had also been historically under considerable flux as Central Asian Kingdoms, the Persian Empire, Buddhist Kingdoms and Rajput Kingdoms vied for control prior to the arrival of the Muslim influence.

Islam in India existed in communities along the Arab trade routes in Sindh, Ceylon and southern India.

Arab Invasion of Sindh

In 711, the Umayyad Caliph in Damascus sent two failed expeditions to Balochistan (an arid region on the Iranian Plateau in Southwest Asia, presently split between Iran, Afghanistan, andPakistan) and Sindh.

According to Muslim historical accounts such as the Chach Nama, the nature of the expeditions was punitive, and in response to raids carried out by pirates on Arab shipping, operating around Debal. The allegation was made that the King of Sindh, Raja Dahir was the patron of these pirates. The third expedition was led by a 20-year-old Syrian chieftain named Muhammad bin Qasim. The expedition went as far North as Multan, then called the "City of Gold," that contained the extremely large Hindu temple of Sun god.

Bin Qasim invaded the sub-continent at the orders of Al-Hajjaj bin Yousef, the governor of Iraq. Qasim's armies defeated Raja Dahir at what is now Hyderabad in Sindh in 712. He then proceeded to subdue the lands from Karachi to Multan with an initial force of only six thousand Syrian tribesmen; thereby establishing the dominion of the Umayyad Caliphate from Lisbon in Portugal to theIndus Valley. Qasim's stay was brief as he was soon recalled to Iraq, and the Caliphates rule in South Asia shrank to Sindh and Southern Punjab in the form of Arab states, the principal of whom were Al Mansura and Multan.

Battle of Rajasthan

The Battle of Rajasthan is a battle (or series of battles) where the Hindu alliance of Gurjara-Pratiharas and Rajputs defeated the Arab invaders in 738 CE and removed the Arab invaders and pillagers from the area east of the Indus River. The final battle took place somewhere on the borders of modern Sindh-Rajasthan. Following their defeat the remnants of the Arab army fled to the other bank of the River Indus. The Muslim conquest of Persia by Arab forces in a short space of time contrasts sharply to the defeat of the Arab armies by the Hindus.

Communities in the North-West

Subsequent to Qasim's recall the Caliphates control in Sindh was extremely weak under governors who only nominally acknowledged Arab control and shared power with coexisting local Hindu,Jain and

Buddhist rulers. Ismaili missionaries found a receptive audience among both the Sunni and non-Muslim populations here. In 985, a group around Multan declared themselves an independent Ismaili Fatimid State.

Coastal trade and the presence of a colony in Sindh permitted significant cultural exchange and the introduction of Muslim teachers into the subcontinent. Considerable conversions took place, especially amongst the Buddhist majority. Multan became a centre of the Ismaili sect of Islam, which still has many adherents in Sindh today. This region under generous patronage of the arts provided a conduit for Arab scholars to absorb and expand on Indian sciences and pass them onwards to the West.

North of Multan, non-Muslim groups remained numerous. From this period, the conquered area was divided into two parts: the Northern region comprising the Punjab remained under the control of Hindu Rajas, while the Southern coastal areas comprising Balochistan, Sindh, and Multan came under Muslim control.

LATER MUSLIM INVASIONS

Ghaznavid Period

Under Sabuktigin, Ghazni found itself in conflict with the Shahi Raja Jayapala. When Sabuktigin died and his son Mahmud ascended the throne in 998, Ghazni was engaged in the North with the Qarakhanids when the Shahi Raja renewed hostilities.

In the early 11th century, Mahmud of Ghazni launched seventeen expeditions into South Asia. In 1001, Sultan Mahmud of Ghazni defeated Raja Jayapala of the Hindu Shahi Dynasty of Gandhara, the Battle of Peshawar and marched further into Peshawar and, in 1005, made it the centre for his forces.

The Ghaznavid conquests were initially directed against the Ismaili Fatimids of Multan, who were engaged in an on-going struggle with the Abbassid Caliphate in conjunction with their compatriots of the Fatimid Caliphate in North Africa and the Middle East; Mahmud apparently hoped to curry the favour of the Abbasids in this fashion. However, once this aim was accomplished, he moved onto the richness of the loot of wealthy temples and monasteries. By 1027, Mahmud had captured most of Northern India and obtained formal recognition of Ghazni's sovereignty from the Abbassid Caliph, al-Qadir Billah.

Ghaznavid rule in North India lasted over 175 years, from 1010 to 1187. It was during this period that Lahore assumed considerable importance apart from being the second capital, and later the only capital, of the Ghaznavid Empire.

At the end of his reign, Mahmud's empire extended from Kurdistan in the west to Samarkand in the Northeast, and from the Caspian Sea to the Punjab. Although his raids carried his forces across Northern and Western India, only Punjab came under his permanent rule; Kashmir, the Doab, Rajasthan, and Gujarat remained under the control of the local Rajput dynasties.

In 1030, Mahmud fell gravely ill and died at age 59. He had been a gifted military commander, and during his rule, universities were founded to study various subjects such as mathematics, religion, the humanities, and medicine.

As with the invaders of three centuries ago, Mahmud's armies looted temples in Varanasi, Mathura, Ujjain, Maheshwar, Jwalamukhi, Somnath and Dwarka.

Shahâb-ud-Din Muhammad Ghori

Muhammad Bin Sâm better known as Shahâb-ud-Din Muhammad Ghori was a Afghan conqueror from the region of Ghor in Afghanistan. Before 1160, the Ghaznavid Empire covered an area running from central Afghanistan east to the Punjab, with capitals at Ghazni on the banks of Ghazni river in present-day Afghanistan, and at Lahore in present-day Pakistan. In 1160, the Ghorids conquered Ghazni from the Ghaznavids, and in 1173 Muhammad Bin Sâm was made governor of Ghazni. He raided eastwards into the remaining Ghaznavid territory, and invaded Gujarat in the 1180s but was rebuffed by Gujarat's Solanki rulers . In 1186 and 1187 he conquered Lahore in alliance with a local Hindu ruler, ending the Ghaznavid empire and bringing the last of Ghaznavid territory under his control, and seemed to be the first Muslim ruler seriously interested in expanding his domain in the sub-continent, and like his predecessor Mahmud initially started off against the Ismaili kingdom of Multan that had regained independence during the Nizari conflicts, and then onto booty and power. In 1191, he invaded the territory of Prithviraj III of Ajmer, who ruled much of present-day Rajasthan and Punjab, but was defeated at Tarain by Govindraj of Delhi, Prithviraj's vassal. The following year, Muhammad assembled 120,000 horsemen and once again invaded India.

Muhammad's army met Prithviraj's army again at Tarain, and this time Muhammad Bin Sâm won; Govindraj was slain, Prithviraj captured and Muhammad Bin Sâm advanced onto Delhi. Within a year, Muhammad controlled Northern Rajasthan and Northern Ganges-Yamuna Doab. After these victories in India, and Muhammad's establishment of a capital in Delhi, Multan was also incorporated into his empire. Muhammad Bin Sâm then returned east to Ghazni to deal with the threat on his eastern frontiers from the Turks and Mongols, whiles his armies continued to advance through Northern India, raiding as far east as Bengal.

Muhammad returned to Lahore after 1200. In 1206, Muhammad Bin Sâm had to travel to Lahore to crush a revolt. On his way back to Ghazni, his caravan rested at Damik near Sohawa (which is near the city of Jhelum in the Punjab province of modern-day Pakistan). He was assassinated on 15 March 1206, while offering his evening prayers. The identity of Ghori's assassins is disputed, with some claiming that he was assassinated by local Hindu Gakhars and others claiming he was assassinated by Hindu Khokhars, both being different tribes.

The Khokhars were killed in large numbers, and the province was pacified. After settling the affairs in the Punjab. Muhammad Ghori marched back to Ghazni. While camping at Dhamayak in 1206 AD in the Jehlum district, the sultan was murdered by the Khokhars Hasan Nizami and Ferishta record the killing of Muhammad Ghori at the hands of the Gakhars. However, Ferishta may have confused the Ghakars with the Khokhars. Other historians have also blamed Shahabuddin Ghori's assassination *to a band of Hindu Khokhars.*

All the historians before the time of Ferishta agree that the Khokhars, not the Gakhars killed Muhammad Ghori. Some also claim that Muhammad Bin Sâm was assassinated by the Hashshashin, a radical Ismaili Muslim sect. According to his wishes, Muhammad Bin Sâm was buried where he fell, in Damik. Upon his death his most capable general, Qutb-ud-din Aybak, took control of Muhammad's Indian conquests and declared himself the first Sultan of Delhi.

The Delhi Sultanate

Muhammad's successors established the first dynasty of the Delhi Sultanate, while the Mamluk Dynasty in 1211 (however, the Delhi Sultanate is traditionally held to have been founded in 1206) seized the reins of the empire. *Mamluk* means "slave" and referred to the

Turkic slave soldiers who became rulers. The territory under control of the Muslim rulers in Delhi expanded rapidly. By mid-century, Bengal and much of central India was under the Delhi Sultanate. Several Turko-Afghan dynasties ruled from Delhi: the Mamluk (1211–1290), the Khalji (1290–1320), the Tughlaq(1320–1413), the Sayyid (1414–51), and the Lodhi (1451–1526). Muslim Kings extended their domains into Southern India, Kingdom of Vijayanagar resisted until falling to the Deccan Sultanate in 1565. Certain kingdoms remained independent of Delhi such as the larger kingdoms of Punjab, Rajasthan, parts of the Deccan, Gujarat, Malwa (central India), and Bengal, nevertheless all of the area in present-day Pakistan came under the rule of Delhi.

The Sultans of Delhi enjoyed cordial, if superficial, relations with Muslim rulers in the Near East but owed them no allegiance. They based their laws on the *Quran* and the *sharia* and permitted non-Muslim subjects to practice their religion only if they paid the *jizya* (poll tax). They ruled from urban centres, while military camps and trading posts provided the nuclei for towns that sprang up in the countryside.

Perhaps the most significant contribution of the Sultanate was its temporary success in insulating the subcontinent from the potential devastation of the Mongol invasion from Central Asia in the 13th century, which nonetheless led to the capture of Afghanistan and western Pakistan by the Mongols (see the Ilkhanate Dynasty). The Sultanate ushered in a period of Indian cultural renaissance, The resulting "Indo-Muslim" fusion left lasting monuments in architecture, music, literature, and religion. In addition it is surmised that the language of Urdu (literally meaning "horde" or "camp" in various Turkic dialects) was born during the Delhi Sultanate period as a result of the mingling of Sanskritic Hindi and the Persian, Turkish, Arabic favoured by the Muslim invaders of India .

The Sultanate suffered significantly from the sacking of Delhi in 1398 by Timur, but revived briefly under the Lodi Dynasty, the final dynasty of the Sultanate before it was conquered by Zahiruddin Babur in 1526, who subsequently founded the Mughal Dynasty that ruled from the 16th to the 18th centuries.

Timur

Tîmûr bin Taraghay Barlas, known in the West as Tamerlane or "Timur the lame", was a 14th century warlord of Turco-Mongol descent, conqueror of much of western and central Asia, and founder of the

Timurid Empire and Timurid dynasty (1370–1405) in Central Asia, which survived until 1857 as the Mughal dynasty of India.

Informed about civil war in South Asia, Timur began a trek starting in 1398 to invade the reigning Sultan Nasir-u Din Mehmud of the Tughlaq Dynasty in the north Indian city of Delhi. His campaign was politically pretexted that the Muslim Delhi Sultanate was too tolerant toward its Hindu subjects, but that could not mask the real reason being to amass the wealth of the Delhi Sultanate.

Timur crossed the Indus River at Attock (now Pakistan) on 24 September. The capture of towns and villages was often followed by the looting, massacre of their inhabitants and raping of their women, as well as pillaging to support his massive army. Timur wrote many times in his memoirs of his specific disdain for the 'idolatrous' Hindus

Timur's invasion did not go unopposed and he did meet some resistance during his march to Delhi, most notably with the Sarv Khap coalition in northern India, and the Governor of Meerut. Although impressed and momentarily stalled by the valour of Ilyaas Awan, Timur was able to continue his relentless approach to Delhi, arriving in 1398 to combat the armies of Sultan Mehmud, already weakened by an internal battle for ascension within the royal family.

The Sultan's army was easily defeated on 17 December 1398. Timur entered Delhi and the city was sacked, destroyed, and left in ruins. Before the battle for Delhi, Timur executed more than 100,000 Hindu captives.

Timur himself recorded the invasions in his memoirs, collectively known as *Tuzk-i-Timuri*. In them, he vividly described the massacre at Delhi:

In a short space of time all the people in the [New Delhi] fort were put to the sword, and in the course of one hour the heads of 10,000 infidels were cut off. The sword of Islam was washed in the blood of the infidels, and all the goods and effects, the treasure and the grain which for many a long year had been stored in the fort became the spoil of my soldiers. They set fire to the houses and reduced them to ashes, and they razed the buildings and the fort to the ground....All these infidel Hindus were slain, their women and children, and their property and goods became the spoil of the victors. I proclaimed throughout the camp that every man who had infidel prisoners should put them to death, and whoever neglected to do so should himself be executed and his property given to the informer. When this order became known to the ghazis of Islam, they drew their swords and put their prisoners to death.

One hundred thousand infidels, impious idolaters, were on that day slain. Maulana Nasiruddin Umar, a counselor and man of learning, who, in all his life, had never killed a sparrow, now, in execution of my order, slew with his sword fifteen idolatrous Hindus, who were his captives....on the great day of battle these 100,000 prisoners could not be left with the baggage, and that it would be entirely opposed to the rules of war to set these idolaters and enemies of Islam at liberty...no other course remained but that of making them all food for the sword.

As per Malfuzat-i-Timuri, Timur targeted Hindus. In his own words, "Excepting the quarter of the saiyids, the 'ulama and the other Musalmans , the whole city was sacked". In his descriptions of the Loni massacre he wrote, "..Next day I gave orders that the Musalman prisoners should be separated and saved." During the ransacking of Delhi, almost all inhabitants not killed were captured and enslaved. Timur's memoirs on his invasion of India describe in detail the massacre of Hindus, looting plundering and raping of their women and children, their forced conversions to Islam and the plunder of the wealth of Hindustan (Greater India). It gives details of how villages, towns and entire cities were rid of their Hindu male population through systematic mass slaughters and genocide and their women and children forcefully converted en masse to Islam from Hinduism.

Timur left Delhi in approximately January 1399. In April he had returned to his own capital beyond the Oxus (Amu Darya). Immense quantities of spoils were taken from India. According to Ruy Gonzáles de Clavijo, 90 captured elephants were employed merely to carry precious stones looted from his conquest, so as to to erect a mosque at Samarkand — what historians today believe is the enormous Bibi-Khanym Mosque. Ironically, the mosque was constructed too quickly and suffered greatly from disrepair within a few decades of its construction.

THE MUGHAL EMPIRE

India in the 16th century presented a fragmented picture of rulers, both Muslim and Hindu, who lacked concern for their subjects and failed to create a common body of laws or institutions. Outside developments also played a role in shaping events. The circumnavigation of Africa by the Portuguese explorer Vasco da Gama in 1498 allowed Europeans to challenge Arab control of the trading routes between Europe and Asia. In Central Asia and Afghanistan, shifts in power pushed Babur of Ferghana (in present-day Uzbekistan) southward, first to Kabul and then to India. The dynasty he founded endured for more than three centuries.

Babur

Claiming descent from both Genghis Khan and Timur, Babur combined strength and courage with a love of beauty, and military ability with cultivation. He concentrated on gaining control of Northwestern India, doing so in 1526 by defeating the last Lodhi Sultan at the First battle of Panipat, a town north of Delhi. Babur then turned to the tasks of persuading his Central Asian followers to stay on in India and of overcoming other contenders for power, mainly the Rajputs and the Afghans. He succeeded in both tasks but died shortly thereafter in 1530. The Mughal Empire was one of the largest centralised states in premodern history and was the precursor to the British Indian Empire.

Babur was followed by his great-grandson, Shah Jahan (r. 1628–58), builder of the Taj Mahal and other magnificent buildings. Two other towering figures of the Mughal era were Akbar (r. 1556–1605) and Aurangzeb (r. 1658–1707). Both rulers expanded the empire greatly and were able administrators. However, Akbar was known for his religious tolerance and administrative genius while Aurangzeb was a pious Muslim and fierce advocate of more orthodox Islam.

Aurangzeb

While some rulers were zealous in their spread of Islam, others were relatively liberal. Moghul emperor Akbar was relatively liberal and established a new religion, Din E Elahi, which included beliefs from different religions. He abolished the jizya for some time. In contrast, his great-grandson Aurangazeb was more zealous and ruthless ruler

.

In the century-and-a-half that followed the death of Aurangzeb, effective Muslim control weakened. Succession to imperial and even provincial power, which had often become hereditary, was subject to intrigue and force. The mansabdari system gave way to the zamindari system, in which high-ranking officials took on the appearance of hereditary landed aristocracy with powers of collecting rents. As Delhi's control waned, other contenders for power emerged and clashed, thus preparing the way for the eventual British takeover.

Durrani Empire

The decay of the Mughal power saw a series of invasions by the Persian adventurer, Nadir Shah, but no occupation per se. Following his death, his Royal Guardsman Ahmed Shah Abdali – aPashtun – embarked on an invasion of conquest. In the short space of just over a quarter of a century, he forged one of the largest Muslim empires of the 18th century. The high point of his conquests was his victory over the powerful Marathas in the third Battle of Panipat 1761. In South Asia his empire stretched from the Indus at Attock all the way to the outskirts of Delhi. Uninterested in long term of conquest or in replacing the Mughal Empire, he became increasingly pre occupied with revolts in Persia and by the Sikhs. His empire started to unravel not long after his death.

Decline of Muslim Rule in Indian Subcontinent

The decline of Islamic rule in the Indian Subcontinent (India, Pakistan and Bangladesh) started most notably after Chhatrapati Shivaji's rebellion against all foreign rule, both Muslim and European.

He declared "Hindu Swarajya" (Self Rule of Hindus) and started assaulting the mighty Mughal Empire. Such was the impact of Shivaji on the Mughal Empire's decline that he was called the "Attila The Hun Of South Asia" by many contemporary European accounts.

Lawlessness prevailed in the Mughal Empire. Shivaji sacked Surat, the richest port of the Mughal Empire, twice, in 1663 and 1674. While comparing the Mughal Emperor Akbar with Shivaji in terms of military capability, Vincent Arthur Smith noted that Shivaji was a great warrior while on the other hand Akbar was more of an administrator and like his great grandson Aurangzeb his presence would have not stopped the decline of the Mughal Empire.

The Maratha War of Independence proved disastrous for the Mughal Empire as well as for Aurangzeb. The long and futile war bankrupted one of the most powerful empires in the world. Mountstart Elphinstone termed this a demoralizing period for the Mussalmans as many of them lost the will to fight against the Maratha Empire.

The Maratha Empire started to extend its reach defeating the Mughal Empire in a number of battles. Peshwa Baji Rao I carried his raid as far as Delhi and in 1737 defeated the Mughal General Amir Khan in Delhi. The invasion of Nadir Shah on Delhi in 1739 came two years after the Maratha Invasion of Delhi in 1737 showing that the once powerful Mughal Empire was in complete shambles even before Nadir Shah invaded Delhi.

In the 1740s the Maratha Empire annexed Bengal, Bihar and Orissa. In 1758 the Maratha Empire after expelling Timur Shah Durrani, son of Ahmad Shah Durrani and his commander in chief Jahan Khan from Lahore, expanded their Empire all the way up to Peshawar. Ahmad Shah Abdali (Ahmad Shah Durrani) after assessing the power of the Marathas decided to make alliances with other Muslim Powers in order to confront the powerful Maratha Empire.

Acknowledging the might of the Maratha Empire extending into Afghanistan and into other Muslim countries, Durrani enlisted two major Muslim allies, Nawab Shuja-ud-daulah of Oudh and Afghan Rohilla Chief Najib-Ud-Daulah. On the other hand the Marathas were refused support by Hindu powers such as the Rajputs, Jats and Sikhs.

The defeat in the Third Battle of Panipat from the coalition forces of Durrani Empire, Rohillas and theNawab of Oudh was a major setback but it didn't demolish the Marathas. By 1770 the Maratha Empire once again regained control of Delhi, the imperial capital of Hindustan, and nominated their own nominee to the post of Mughal Emperor.

The Rohilla chief Najib-Ud-Daulah's son Zabita Khan accepted the Maratha Suzerainty. The Afghan raids were also put to n end after Ahmad Shah Abdali fell ill. For the next 30 years the Marathas ruled Delhi until their defeat at the hands of the British in the Second Anglo-Maratha War. The Maratha Army was defeated at Assaye, Aligarh, Farrukhabad and finally in Delhi and then in Patiala by the British. Hence by 1803 almost the whole of modern day India and Bangladesh came under the sway of the British Empire, though the Marathas ruled large parts of western India till 1818 when the Third Anglo-Maratha War was fought which ended the Maratha Empire completely.

In northwest India, in the Punjab, Sikhs developed themselves into a powerful force under the authority of twelve Misls. By 1801, Ranjit Singh capturedLahore and threw off the Afghan yoke from North West

India. In Afghanistan Zaman Shah Durrani was defeated by powerful Barakzai chief Fateh Khan who appointed Mahmud Shah Durrani as the new ruler of Afghanistan and appointed himself as Wazir of Afghanistan. Sikhs however were now superior to the Afghans and started to annex Afghan provinces.

The biggest victory of the Sikh Empire over the Durrani Empire came in the Battle of Attock fought in 1813 between Sikh commander-in-chief Dewan Mokham Chand who was a Hindu Khatri and was 70 years old at the time of battle, and Wazir of Afghanistan Fateh Khan and his younger brother Dost Mohammad Khan. The Afghans were routed by the Sikh army and the Afghans lost over 9,000 soldiers in this battle. Dost Mohammad was seriously injured whereas his brother Wazir Fateh Khan fled back to Kabul fearing that his brother was dead. In 1818 the famous Hindu general Misr Diwan Chand slaughtered Afghans and Muslims in trading city of Multan killing Afghan governor Nawab Muzzafar Khan and five of his sons in the Siege of Multan. In 1819 the last Indian Province of Kashmir was freed from Muslim rulers by Misr Diwan Chand who registered another crushing victory over weak Afghan General Jabbar Khan. The Koh-i-Noor diamond was also freed from Muslim control by Maharaja Ranjit Singh in 1814. In 1823 a Sikh Army led by Misr Diwan Chand routed Dost Mohammad Khan the Sultan of Afghanistan and his brother Azim Khan at Naushera (Near Peshawar). By 1834 the Sikh Empire extended up to the Khyber Pass thus recovering the whole of the Indian Subcontinent from Islamic Rule. Hari Singh Nalwa the Sikh general remained the governor of Khyber Agency till his death in 1837. He consolidated Sikh hold in tribal provinces. The northernmost Indian territories of Gilgit, Baltistan and Ladakh was annexed by Dogra Rajput General Zorawar Singh between 1831-1840.

Iconoclasm

Nalanda

In 1193, the Nalanda University complex was destroyed by Afghan Khilji-Ghilzai Muslims under Bakhtiyar Khalji; this event is seen as the final milestone in the decline of Buddhism in India. He also burned Nalanda's a major Buddhist library and Vikramshila University , as well as numerous Bhuddhist monasteries in India. When the Tibetan translator, Chag Lotsawa Dharmasvamin (Chag Lo-tsa-ba, 1197–1264), visited northern India in 1235, Nalanda was damaged, looted, and largely deserted, but still standing and functioning with seventy students. Mahabodhi, Sompura, Vajrasan and other important monasteries were found to be untouched. The Ghuri ravages only afflicted those monasteries that lay in the direct of their advance and were fortified in the manner of defensive forts.

By the end of the 12th century, following the Muslim conquest of the Buddhist stronghold in Bihar, Buddhism having already declined in the south declined in the North as well as survivors retreated to Nepal, Sikkim and Tibet or escaped to the South of the sub-continent.

Vijayanagara

The city flourished between the 14th century and 16th century, during the height of the Vijayanagar Empire. During this time, it was often in conflict with the kingdoms which rose in the Northern Deccan, and which are often collectively termed the Deccan Sultanates. The Vijaynagar Empire successfully resisted Muslim invasions for centuries. But in 1565, the empire's armies suffered a massive and catastrophic defeat at by an alliance of the Sultanates, and the capital was taken. The victorious armies then razed, depopulated and destroyed the city over several months. The empire continued in slow decline, but the original capital was not reoccupied or rebuilt.

Somanath

The first temple of Somnath existed before the beginning of the Christian era. The second temple, built by the Maitraka kings of Vallabhi in Gujarat, replaced the first one on the same site around 649. In 725 Junayad, the Arab governor of Sind, sent his armies to destroy the second temple.

The Pratihara king Nagabhata II constructed the third temple in 815, a large structure of red sandstone. Mahmud of Ghazni attacked this temple in 1026, looted its gems and precious stones, massacred the worshippers and burned it. It was then that the famous Shivalinga of the temple was entirely destroyed.

The fourth temple was built by the Paramara King Bhoj of Malwa and the Solanki king Bhimdev I of Gujarat (Anhilwara) between 1026 and 1042. The temple was razed in 1297 when the Sultanate of Delhi conquered Gujarat, and again in 1394. Mughal Emperor Aurangzeb destroyed the temple again in 1706.

REFERENCES

Bosworth, C.E., *The Ghaznavids*, Edinburgh University Press, Edinburgh, 1963.

Brend, Barbara : *The Emperor Akbar's Khamsa of Nizami*, London: British Library, 1995.

Joe R. Feagin: *Social Problems: A Critical Power-Conflict Perspective,* Englewood Cliffs, N.J.: Prentice-Hall, 1986.

Jonathan Bloom: *The Art and Architecture of Islam, 1250-1800,* Pelican History of Art. New Haven, 1994.

Oommen, T.K.: *Protest and Change: Studies in Social Movements*, New Delhi, Sage, 1990.

Chapter 7

Tribal Policy of the Mughals Period

By the time Akbar ascended the throne important changes had taken place in the influence and position of many of the tribes. It was most marked in the Peshawar Valley. The Khashi in conjunction with the Khalils had defeated the Umar Khel Dilzaks. Soon after the Khashi defeated their old ally Khalil and expelled them from Bajaur Gagiani and in their turn were defeated by the Dilzaks. The Victory of the Dilzaks aroused the fear and suspicion of the Khashi whose leader Malik Ahmad again defeated them in the battle of the Guzar Rud. The unfortunate Dilzak received another defeat at the hands of Khalil and Mohmand under the leadership of Kamran. The result of this defeat was disastrous for the Dilzaks who lost their possessions consisting of Khyber-Karappa passes. But the victors could not enjoy the fruits of their victory for long. The Khashi confederacy was not prepared to tolerate the rising power of any other tribe. Under the leadership of Khan Kaju it defeated the Khalil and Mohmand at Shaikh Tapur in 1549. As a result of this scramble for power the Khashi came out as the strongest tribe in the Peshawar valley. Next, to them stood the Mohmands. The Khalil Dilzak and Gagiani had lost practically all power and influence.

The Bangash region also witnessed very important changes. The combined armies of the Bangash and Khatala defeated Brakzais and forced them to take shelter in Tirah and became the absolute master of the whole Bangash region. The Turi, an Indian tribe, left its old habitat on the shore of the river Indus near Nilab and settled as neighbours of Bangash, Nilab, now became the home of the Khatak who originally inhabited Waziristan.

RELIGIOUS MOVEMENT

It was in the beginning of Akbar's reign that a new religious movement caught the imagination of many of these tribes. Its founder. Bayazid, the son of Shaikh Abdulla and was born at Jullundhar in the Punjab in 1525, His mother retired to Kaniguram, on the borders of Qandahar, where his lather was living. When he came of age, he assumed the style of Pir-i-roshan and began to preach his new doctrines. To meditate constantly on Almighty God, to place confidence in the instructions received...to view the nature of God with the eye of the heart and to see Him face to face in every mansion and on every side with the light of intellect, to cause no injury to the creatures of the All-just...to annihilate one's self before Deity-absolute and in God to be eternal and absolute, become one with the unity..." A number of Tribes joined the Pir. The religious fervour aroused by this movement made the tribes fanatical and they began to fight the imperial army caring little for their lives or blood.

Till 1585, the tribes were Mirza Hakim's concern because he was in occupation of Kabul. Bayazid had established his sect in 1542 and was gathering followers round himself. He said that he had received the Divine command for the destruction of those who knew no God. He began sending out his men from Hashtnagar on raiding expeditions. This aroused Mirza's Government into action. Bayazid was arrested and produced before a tribunal of Ulemas at Kabul. He saved his life through the intercession of some influential men and returned to Tirah. Here he expelled the Tirahis from Tirah because he suspected them of apostacy from his doctrines and of intriguing with the Mughals. He treacherously murdered 300 of them. Others fled to Nangrahar. Bayazid attacked the latter place but was beated back with great slaughter by Muhsin Khan. He escaped with difficulty to Kalpani where he died soon after from fatigue of his flight. In 1585 Kabul was incorporated into the Mughal empire and the tribes became the direct concern of the State. Akbar was not satisfied with their behaviour. Their plundering raids and reluctance to recognise any suzerain power was intolerable to him. But more obnoxious than anything else were their intrigues with the Uzbegs. It appears that the tribal leaders were in the pay of the latter who incited them to rebellion. They knew that Akbar had designs on Transoxiana. The Tribes would serve the very useful purpose of harassing the Mughal army in the rear if it marched to the land of the Oxus. Indeed, the Uzbeg intrigues made the war against the tribes more determined and bloody.

AKBAR'S TRIBAL POLICY

Akbar's tribal policy was the same as that of his grandfather with one difference. The emperor never exacted tribute from them. They were only asked to remain peaceful and faithful. If they yield they were to be treated benevolently and generously. If they resisted they were to be severely punished. To keep watch over them a number of forts were built and troops were stationed at strategic places. A local militia was also raised from among the tribes. It formed a part of the royal army which was sent to punish the refractory tribes.

This change in policy, though apparently not very important, was a move in the right direction. One of the causes of tribal rebellion was the latters poverty. Babar had been forced to levy tribute because of the scarcity of money. Akbar suffered from no such disadvantage and His treasury could not be much enriched by the tribute from the tribes. He gave it up in the interest of the general policy.

On assuming control of Kabul in December 1585 Akbar drew up a comprehensive plan to punish the Yusufzais who were causing trouble under their leader Kalu. Zain Khan Kokaltash was sent to subdue them in Bajaur. It was derided to send another army to the plains east of Buner. As the result of a tie Birbal was given preference over Abul Fadl to lead this army. Hakim Abul Fath was ordered to accompany Birbal. The aim of these expeditions, writes Abul Fadl was that the "crooked tribe might be guided a right and that the black hearted ones who did not accept council should be punished."

The Kokaltash entered Bajaur from the west. There were 300 Yusufzai householders in that region. They were severely punished. Brought to bay, Ghazi Khan, Mirza Ali, Taus Khan, Nazir and other leaders submitted. The Kokaltash now proceeded to Sawad. Here lived 40,000 Yusufzai families. They were defeated and fled into the mountains. The Mughal general laid the foundation of a fort, Chakadara, in the mart of Sawad and started punishing them. Twenty-three times did he score victory against the enemy and destroyed seven of their stockades. The whole region with the exception of Karakar defiles and Buner was subdued by him. He sent word to Birbal that the Afghans were assembled in the Karakar Pass between Sawad and Buner and demanded reinforcement.

Birbal had swept through the plains and was marching towards Buner. At this time reached the letter of Zain Khan and also a farman from the emperor directing him to march *via* the Malkand Pass and join the Kokaltash. He gave up his old plan and marched to meet Kokaltash.

The three generals assembled at Chakadara. A council of war was held. Birbal refused to recognise Zain Khan as superior. Nor could he pull on with Hakim Abul-Fath. The Raja and the Hakim came from hard language to mutual abuse. The Kokaltash pacified them. He suggested that Chakadara should be held by one of the armies, and the other two should reduce the tribesmen by punitive expeditions. The Raja and the Hakim disagreed with him. They insisted that all of them should march back and punish the tribes in the way. Zain Khan had to give in. His other suggestion that the withdrawal should be effected through Malkand Pass was also ignored. His colleagues resolve to retire through Karakar and Malandari Passes.

The army began to cross the Karakar Pass. The Afghans attacked it, they were repulsed they succeeded in driving away the camels and the bullocks carrying on the baggage of the imperialists. Zain Khan again sounded a note of warning. He placed three suggestions before the Raja: either they should erect a fort to serve as source of safety and from there send raiding parties among the Afghans; or as they held the enemy's families and poverty as hostages they may write conciliatory letters to the tribal leaders and take from them the promise of obedience; or again they, should halt and send a report to the court requesting the emperor to send an army which might be stationed to guard the tops of the defile through which they would have to pass. These plans were also rejected by Birbal and on 16th February. 1556 the army began to cross the Malandari Pass. Little heed was said to marching regulations. The Afghans pelted at, the imperialists arms and stones with the result that a large number of soldiers and officers including Birbal were killed Hakim Abul-Fath and Zain Khan escaped with difficulty. The shattered force joined Akbar at Attock in the same month. The emperor was stricken with grief at the loss of his dearest friend.

He censured the Hakim and the Kokaltash. But, in fact, the

responsibility for the disaster lay partly on him as he had sent Birbal and the Hakim who had hardly any knowledge of the military art. It may equally be attribute to the folly of these inexperienced generals. If the suggestions of the Kokaltash had been carried out, it would have been possible to avert it. Now the emperor decided to send a larger army under a number of experierced generals. In the beginning prince Murad and Todermal were sent. They were to be assisted by Zain Khan and Hakim Abul Fath. When prince Murad was recalled. Man Singh was sent to take his place. He was further reinforced by Raja Bhagwan Das. Akbar had become vindicative and was bent upon revenge. On earlier occasions, the generals had been instructed to have the life of as many tribesmen as possible and when the prisoners were sent to the court, they were awarded gold asharfis and robes of honour, and released. Now the emperor issued orders that no mercy should be shown to the enemy.

These generals did their job well. Man Singh established his camp near Chind on the bank of the Indus and erected a fort there. Todar Mal established his camp near Lungar hill in Sawad. Thus the two outlets for the Yusufzais were close. They were hemmed in and punished. Many were killed and a large number of them were taken prisoner to be sold in Turan and Persia. The condition of the Yusufzai deteriorated further if the vindictiveness of the imperial army was not enough to ruin them they were overtaken by famine and pestilence. Kalu. Sultan Qoraish, Bustan, etc. submitted to Ismail Quli. It was settled that when they came out from the hill country they would be forgiven.

EMPEROR'S VINDICTIVE POLICY

This agreement demonstrates that the emperor's vindictive policy did not hold the field for long. He must have realised the futility of this method. The Afghans could not be changed to loyalty thus. Saner judgment had the better of anger and the emperor was ready to forgive enemies if they repented.

Inspite of the dire punishment meted out to them, the Yusfzais did not give up their old habits. When the Ghoria tribes took up the cause of Jalal and tried to close the passage of Mohammad Sulaiman, the Yusufzais assisted them. Again when Jalal, son of Bayazid, was forced to leave the company of the Afridi and the Orakzai, who submitted to the imperialists, he was sheltered by the Yusufzais. Zain Khan was ordered to go to Sawad and Ismail Quli Khan to Hashtnagar so that Jalal might not be able to reurn to Tirah. But he succeeded in making good his escape. The imperial generals received instructions to punish the Yusufzais for the shelter they had afforded to Jalal. Zain Khan erected a number of forts at strategic places. One was built on the bank of Penjkora, another in Chakadara, a third at Malakand and a fourth near at Sarobi. His object was to overawe the tribes through the soldiers stationed in these forts, and if necessary punish them with their help.

This new technique frightened the Afghans. They thought that their freedom was in danger. The Yusufzais of Demghar again chose Kalu, who had previously submitted to the Mughals, as their leader, and retired to the hills of Mahro to start the fight, against the Mughals. Mohammad Bahri and Malik Asghar also joined Kalu. Fighting went on for eight months. Kalu despatched Mohammad Bahri and Malik Asghar to invade the fort of Sarobi. But they were beaten back with huge losses. At last the Yusfzais were driven to bay. By 1589, Kalu's position had so much deteriorated that he sought shelter with the imperial officers, and was sent to the court. Akbar ordered him imprisonment. Shaikh Ismail, who was respected and honoured by the pious and believed to possess the power of performing miracles tendered his submission and came to the court. The purpose of his visit was to secure forgiveness for the Afghans. For the time being, the Yusufzais became quiet.

But in 1592, they started the trouble again. In concert with the Gagiani, they attacked Mohammad Quli Turkoman, the Mughal officer in Bigram. Upon the advance of Zain Khan and Shahbaz Khan, the rebels withdrew and the latter conquered Buner. During the remaining years of Akbar's reign we do not hear of any major operation against the Yusufzais.

Abul Fadl time and again refers to the outbreak of the Yusufzais and their suppression, which conclusively proves that they in their heart of hearts never accepted the suzerainty of the emperor. Their obedience varied with the pressure of the royal army on them. When the troops withdrew they gave up all the pretence of friendship.

Another tribe which caused serious trouble was the Tariki or Ghoria. They had 10,000 households in Peshawar. When Man Singh was going to Kabul in 1585, he had been instructed to chastise them and make the roads safe. But he did not do it.

The necessity for a major operation against the Tarikis arose in 1586. Sayyid Hamid Bokhari, the fiefholder of Peshawar was negligent in his duties. He passed his time in the fort of Bigram leaving the administration in the hand of one Musa. The latter despoiled the property and the honour of the Tarikis. They, therefore, joined hands with Jalal and rebelled in Bigram and invaded the fort. In the melee Sayyid Hamid was killed, but his son Sayyid Khan defended the fort. On receiving this the emperor sent Zain Khan to the relief of the besiege.

Meanwhile, Mohammad Sulaiman arrived at Kabul about the middle of September 1586. Raja Man Singh decided to escort him to the court. When the Tarikis learnt of it they raised the siege of Bigram. With Jalal as their leader, they hid themselves on either side of the Khyber between Peshawar and Tirah and waited for the coming of the imperialists. Man Singh got an inkling of their designs. He did not consider it safe to escort Sulaiman in these circumstances. Leaving him in Pesh Bulaq near Jalalabad, Man Singh marched ahead of him. He chastised the Afridis in Tirah and crossed the Khyber. On his way to Peshawar, Jalal did not attack him in the defile and Man Singh arrived at Ali Masjid. Here he was joined by the army of Madho Singh which Raja Bhagwan Das had sent. Jalal now opened the attack but he was defeated and put to flight. Man Singh recrossed the Khyber and brought Mirza Sulaiman to Peshawar.

The army sent by Akbar under Zain Khan also arrived at Peshawar. It assisted Man Singh to "punish the Tarikis. He planted a number of outposts between Kabul and the Indus and manned them with soldiers. The Tarikis were now frightened and repented. They were given lands to settle firstly near Jalalabad and then near Peshawar. But in 1596 the Tarikis rose into rebellion again, the reason being the murder of the Mughal Governor Qasim Khan, by Zaman Mirja. The Khyber route became unsafe. Qulich khan and Zain Khan were sent to punish the rebels. They built forts at strategic points and garrisoned them adequately. The Tarikis retreated into the ravines and their leaders hid themselves in the Koh Safed.

Like the Yusufzais, the Tarikis also could not be fully and effectively suppressed. Their obedience was fitful and mostly depended upon the presence of the royal army. The Afridis, the Orakzais and the Tirah also defied the royal authority. They had given shelter to Bayazid and on the latter's death to his son Jalal. The Afridis had leagued themselves with the Tarikis when they attacked Man Singh. In 1587 Man Singh and Muttalib Khan marched to Tirah to punish them. Jalal was defeated near Dar Samand. He was pursued and his house was burnt. Upon this the Afridis and the Orakzais tendered their submission. They gave hostages for good conduct. The royal army returned to Bangash.

Jalal who had fled to the Yusufzais returned again, and revived the trouble. Sadiq Khan was sent to punish him. He did not think it advisable to enter the defiles and appointed his men to keep watch on every side. He conciliated the tribes with the result that they gave up Jalal. In 1588 the Orakzais surrendered Jalal's family to the imperial army. Besides, they gave hostages and undertook to preserve peace in Khyber. Jalal now fled to Turan. But he again returned to Tirah in 1591.

Abul Fadl says that he could get no assistance in Turan. This does not appear to be plausible: because the Uzbegs were financially assisting these tribes to prevent Akbar's design on Transoxiana taking shape. The Afridis and the Orakzais again extended protection to Jalal Qasim Khan was sent to punish them. The hilly country was closely invaded and the Afghans begged for peace. They represented that they had turned away Jalal Upon this Qasim Khan was ordered to return to Kabul.

In 1592 Jalal appeared in Tirah again. Qasim Khan followed him close at his heels. A number of Afridi leaders and tribesmen were killed and the remaining gave hostages. Jalal left Tirah and went to the Kafirs. He was ousted from Kafiristan as well. He made one more attempt to find shelter in Tirah but the inhabitants turned their backs on him and he fled to Kaniguram.

The murder of Qasim Khan by Zaman Mirza again encouraged the people of Tirah and in conjunction with the Tarikis they unfurled the banner of revolt in 1596 Qulich Khan was sent to punish them. Some of the Afridi leaders renewed their oath of loyalty Others should, have been chastised but Qulich Khan did not dare enter the defiles. His attitude was approved by the emperor and in 1598 he was replaced by Zain Khan. The latter routed the Afghans with skill and courage.

Jalal was killed in 1600 among the Hazaras. In 1602 his brother Ahdad stirred up strife in Tirah. The Afridis, the Pani, the Orakzai and Suri joined him. Takhta Beg was sent to punish them. The influence of Ahdad declined and he fled to Cauhana. Later in 1604 when Takhta Beg was returning to India from Kabul his passage was bloked by the Alizai section of the Orakzai Afghan. But they were given a sound beating. Thus unrest among the tribes of Tirah lasted till the end of the reign of Akbar.

The Kafirs did not take any conspicuous part in the tribal strife. In 1592 Jalal sent his associate Wahdat Ali to capture Kafiristan and prepare a refuge for him there. Wahdat Ali conquered the fort of Kaushan; but Zain Khan defeated him and forced him to submit and surrender Kaushan. The country upto Kashghar and Badakhshan was reduced to subjection. Zain Khan encouraged the Kafir chiefs to settle down and develop the country. The Kakar tribe harassed the weak, and closed the road to Qandhar. In 1595 Shah Beg Khan was sent to chastise the miscreants.. Many of them were killed, some took to flight and the remaining submitted.

In 1600 the Lohani tribe sought the assistance of Jalal in its fight against the Hazaras who were, allies of the emperor; But they were defeated and Jalal was forced to fly to the hill of Rabat. Murad Beg came with the imperial army to assist the Hazaras to further harass the enemy. During the fight Jalal was killed by some unknown person.

The Hazaras always remained peaceful. In 1537 Shadman Hazara submitted and was given Ghazni in fief. In 1539 M. Sanjar, M. Bashi, Shadman and other Hazara leaders visited the court. Favours were conferred upon them and the daughter of Mirza was given in marriage to the Prince Royal.

The policy of Akbar towards the Balochis was in general the same as towards other tribes. Conciliation was employed with ultimate recourse to force if conciliation failed. There remained, however, one important difference. Balochistan never drew so much attention of the emperor as the Afghanistan region. With few raids at long intervals the Balochis were left free to behave as they liked. This can be attributed to the comparative strategical as well as economic insignificance of Balochistan. In 1577 Shah Quli was sent to chastise the Balochis for their plundering habits. Instructions were given to him to the effect that he should first try conciliation, if he failed, he should punish them. The advance of the imperial army struck the Balochis with terror and they sent their representatives and begged for pardon which was granted.

In 1576 when Akbar crossed the Sutlej, the Balochi chief like Haji Khan and others fled from the neighbouring regions. They feed that they would have to take service with imperial government. Man Singh and others were sent to arrest them. They, however, failed in their attempt. It was reported in 1586 that the Balochis had reverted to their old habit of plundering and blackmail. Ismail Quli Khan and Rai Singh were sent against them. They brought the Balochi chiefs, Ghazi Khan,

Bahadur Khan, etc., to the court. They were pardoned and their country was restored to them. Henceforward the Balochis did not rebel in the reign of Akbar.

Inspite of the persistent efforts of Akbar, the tribes continued restive throughout the last 20 years of his reign. One army was sent after the other, the whole region was devastated, a large number of people were wounded and killed; but all this did not bring the emperor nearer the goal. He bequeathed to his successors the same problems which he had inherited from his forefathers.

Various reasons can be assigned for this failure. The rise of the Roshanid sect was the most important of them. It gave the struggle a religious colour and gave the tribesmen the zeal and determination of a fanatic. Another reason was the interference of the Uzbeg rulers in the tribal conflict. Akbar realised the implications of this intrigues and made determined efforts to root out the rebels finally, the death of Birbal made both the parties more bitter and the conflict still more bloody and ferocious.

It is really very unfortunate that Akbar who started with such noble ideas failed so miserably. It really goes to the credit of the emperor that in the very beginning he took up the threads of Babar's policy and made further improvements upon it. Non-imposition of tribute "on the tribes was a very wise move. If the things had gone on well, the illustrious emperor would have moved further and contributed largely to the settlement of the problem.

When Jahangir ascended the throne in 1605 the condition of the tribal area was as unsatisfactory as ever. But a change occurred in the attitude of different tribes. Under Akbar the Yusufzai and the Ghoria Khel were the most rebellious but during his son's rule the Bangash raised the flag of revolt. The reason appears to be that Yusufzai and the Ghoria had been weakened by constant fighting against the Mughals and wanted time to recover. The Bangash, on the other hand, had not taken a very conspicuous part in the rebellion in the reign of Akbar and therefore they retained enough strength to defy the imperial power.

The new sovereign attempted to follow the policy of his predecessor though conciliation was not so much practised as repression. Another change was the revival of the system of imposition of tribute which Akbar had abolished to conciliate the tribes. The Governor of Kabul was charged with the responsibility of maintaining peace. In addition, troops were sent from time to time to Bangash to meet any special emergency. But the relation between the officers commanding these troops and the Governor were not defined and led to much bickering in the future. In the early years of Jahangirs' reign. Khan Dauran was the Governor of Kabul. Ahamad Beg, Taus Khan and Qazi Izzatullah were sent one after another to bring the people of Bangash to obedience. The Afghans remained on the defensive.

But in 1611 they started trouble under Ahdad. Khan Dauran was in the interior of the province and Mu'izzulmulk alone was in Kabul. Ahdad attacked the city. But the inhabitants led by Nad' Ali and Mu'izzulmulk put up a brave resistance. Also the neighbouring population rose against the besiegers and threatened to close their line of retreat. Ahdad broke up his camp and fled. Nad' Ali pursued him for a short distance and then returned. When the report about Ahdad's adventure reached the court Khan Dauran was degraded and Qulich Khan was commissioned to punish the tribes in Bangash.

Dissensions among the Mughal officers and the death of Qulich Khan came to Ahdad as a heaven sent opportunity and he again took the offensive in 1614. At this time Motaqid Khan was in Peshawar and Khan Dauran in Kabul. They attempted to close the way upon Ahdad. But he made a surprise attack on Tirah and killed and captured many a royal soldiers. He then turned his attention to Jalalabad and Pish Bulaq. But Mu'taqid Khan overtook him and put to death a large number of his followers. Ahdad fled to Gharkh where Khan Dauran besieged him. In the struggle which ensued 300 Afghans were killed and 100 taken prisoner. Gharkh was burnt and Ahdad was forced to fly to Qandhar.

When in 1617 Mahabat Khan replaced Khan Dauran, the dead Governor of Kabul, the task of subduing Bangash as also the power of directing the Bangash army were entrusted to him. Thus the chance of disagreement between the Governor of Kabul and the commander of the Bangash army almost disappeared. Allahadad, the son of Ahdad who had come to the court was given the title of Rashid Khan and sent with the imperial army. Mahabat was Instructed to support his cause as against Ahdad and thus create dissension among the Afghans. Allahdad's son and brother were detained at court as hostages. After his arrival at Kabul Mahabat Khan sent Allahdad with an army to Bangash. But he deserted and joined the enemy. Thereupon his son and brother were imprisoned in Gwalior. Soon Allahdad repented and submitted. He was pardoned and sent back to the court. His brother was also released from the prison.

In 1619 when THE season for collection of the revenue arrived, Mahabat Khan sent a force under Izzat Khan to ravage and plunder the hill country. Izzat Khan lost his life in the action. Thereupon Mahabat Khan sent another force which severely chastised the tribes. Three years later Mahabat was recalled and Bangash relapsed to its former unsettled condition.

Zafar Khan was sent to replace Mahabat It was at this time that Yalangtosh, the Uzbeg officer of Nazr Muhammad attacked Ghazni. Incited by him Ahdad came to Tirah and created trouble.. Yalangtosh made peace with Zafar Khan and retreated but Ahdad was surrounded the mountains and killed.

Other tribes, on the whole, did not give much trouble to the imperial government. About 8000 families of Khaturs and Dilzaks lived near Amrohi. They committed oppression—and robbery. In 1607 Zafar Khan, the son of Keka was sent to capture the headmen of Khatur and escort the Dilzaks to Lahore. Zafar Khan successfully carried out the instructions.

In the year 1607 Ahmad Beg, Jagirdar of Peshawar came with the Maliks of the Yusufzai and the Ghoria Khel and waited upon the emperor in Kabul. The sons of Mirza Sanjar of Hazara together with Mashi and Shadman the chief leaders of Hazara came to the court. These suppliants were rewarded by the emperor and sent back to their own country.

Jahangir initiated no new policy to cope with the situation created by the tribes. He generally followed the policy of fire and sword. The reason why the tribal risings were not more serious was that they were exhausted and also that, comparatively speaking, they were possessed of a lesser religious fervour and excitement.

Before entering into the history of the relation of the tribes with the last two great emperors of the Mughal dynasty it will be proper to narrate the changes which had occurred in their position during the last fifty years. When Akbar came to the throne most of them had settled down in their new homes; but there still remained a few who were moving from place to place. They established themselves in their new abodes after the accession of Shahjahan.

The Khataks in their eastward expansion had moved far as Sakesar.

Bhira arid Khushab and occupied Makhad. In Akbar's reign the Khatak chief, Malik Akor had become a vassal of the emperor and in 1587 founded Akora on the south bank of the Kabul. His son Yehya seized the territory of the Mandar Pathans which lay nearest to that river. This tract became known as Tari Bulaq. But as he failed to expel the entire Mandar tribe, he was able to establish only one foothold on the northern bank of the Kabul opposite Akora.

The Turis who had settled as neighbours of the Bangash were supplanting the latter. The Bangash were getting weaker because of internecine warfare amongst themselves. The Turis on the other hand, were getting fresh accession of strength due to new arrivals from their original place of habitation. The result was that in course of time they supplanted the Bangash in their possessions and only two villages Shalozan and Zeran remained in the hands of the latter.

In the tribal policy, Shahjahan followed the precedent set up by his father. This was mainly due to the fact that the tribal risings were neither so frequent nor so serious. Besides, his attention was engrossed up by more important affairs.

The rebellion of Khan Jahan Lodi afforded to the tribes the opportunity to rise against the Mughal government. Khan Jahan, after his defeat in the Deccan, intended to go to the north-west frontier in the hope that his Afghan brethren would extend to him protection and second his efforts against the imperial government. He succeeded in instigating Kamaluddin, a royal officer in the north-west to turn a traitor. But holding out false promises to the Muhammadzai, the Khalil, the Mohmand, the Daudzai, the Yusufzai, the Barklani, the Khatak, the Imaq, the Haji and the Turi, Kamaluddin enlisted their support for Khan Jahan's cause. He sent for Abdul Qadir, son of Ahdad and tempted him with the hand of his daughter in marriage. He also won over Karimdad son of Jalal and Muhammad Zaman, a relative of Ahdad. In 1630 the Afghan tribesmen collected under his banner at Yulum ford and threatened to attack Peshawar.

The situation tended to be grave and the emperor sent Abdulla Khan and Sayyid Muzaffar to intercept Khan Jahan. They succeeded in their project. Khan Jahan had to give up his idea of going to the Afghans and turned towards Bundelkhand. The task of subduing the Afghans was given to Said Khan who was posted in Kohat.

When Said learnt of the threatened tribal attack on Peshawar he came to that city. His councillors suggested to him to try conciliation by persuading Kamaluddin to give up this treacherous move. He acted accordingly and sent a message to the rebel leader. The latter pretended to have been much impressed by the goodwill of Said Khan and even made a show of loyalty. But in reality he was completing his preparations for the attack and, when he had done it, he appeared before the city and invaded the citadel. The number of soldiers at the disposal of Said Khan being inadequate, he could not afford to leave some of them in the city and attack the enemy with the rest. So he decided to stand a siege. The Afghans were unable to take the fort by storm and despairing of success, they retreated. Said Khan pursued them and captured and killed as many of them as he could. Lashkar Khan was at the time the Governor of Kabul. He being a Shia, the Qatan, a Sunni group, resented his presence. Besides this Shah Jahan wanted to post an abler man in Kabul. Therefore Said Khan was appointed in place of Lashkar Khan. Raja Jagat Singh was sent as thanedar of Bangash. Both these officers were ordered to root out the unrest in the Kabul province.

Said Khan first tried conciliation. In 1637 he sent to court Muhammad *Zaman* and Sahib Dad—two sons-in-law of Ahdad, Qadir Dad, a grandson of Ahdad, Alai, wife of Ahdad. Abdul Qadir, and Rashid Khan. The emperor gave a robe of honour and a horse to each Muhammad *Zaman* and Sahib Dad; and sent Rashid Khan, the cousin of Ahdad as Governor to Tilangana.

In the year 1633 a rebellion broke out in Naghz. Karim Dad, an uncle of Ahdad was invited by some Afghans to lead them in their struggle with the imperial government. They were supported by the Tirha, the Orakzai and the Shah Beg Afridi clans. A brother of Karim Dad, at the instigation of Nazr Muhammad also joined the rebels. They threatened to capture Tur. When Said Khan came to know of this tribal confederacy and its objects, he despatched Raja Jagat Singh and Yaqub with a strong force to suppress it. When the imperial army arrived near Naghz the insurgents retreated. The inhabitants of Naghz made common cause with the Mughals; and Karim Dad with many of his followers fled into the mountains. The houses of the insurgents were given up to plunder. Rain and hailstorm completed the picture of their misery. They were attacked from the base of the mountains. Unable to continue resistance Karim Dad surrendered with his entire family. The army now returned to Peshawar, and the information about the successful conclusion of the campaign was sent to the court. The emperor ordered that Karim Dad should be executed; and this was done. By the year 1639 Said Khan had established peace in that region.

This very year, the emperor went on a visit to Kabul. When Yalangtosh, an officer of Nazr Muhammad, had besieged that city, certain Hazara tribes who were formerly under the government of Kabul, transferred their allegiance to the invader. Said Khan was now ordered to bring them back to their former obedience. Those who accepted the Mughal suzerainty were to be protected; others were to be plundered and killed. Khan Dauran Nusrat Jung was also asked to assist Said Khan. The two generals were instructed to attack the Hazaras from two sides. Their plan succeeded to the satisfaction of the emperor. Said Khan brought 27 Hazara chiefs to the court. They were pardoned and conciliated with award of gifts and presents. In this way, peace was restored in the province of Kabul.

Shahjahan did not pay any serious attention to the affairs of the Balochis. But Aurangzeb who was the Governor of Multan and Sindh from 1648 to 1652 threw himself into the task of bringing them under control. The Hot Baloch had a number of strongholds in Sindh and the Punjab. One section of them held the upper Derajet for two centuries with Dera Ismail Khan and Us jurisdiction included Daryakhan and Bakkar east of the Indus. Its leader Ismail Khan sent presents to Shahjahan and made Dara his patron. Taking advantage of his position on the boundary between the two provinces, Lahore and Multan, he now claimed to be subject to Dara, the Governor of Lahore and refused to admit the jurisdiction of the Governor of Multan. On the basis of this plea, he refused to see Aurangzeb when summoned by the latter. The prince secured the permission of the emperor and forced him to pay respects to himself.

Another Baloch tribe, the Nuhani occupied the country adjacent to that of the Hots on the route to Qandhar. Their leader was Alam Aurangzeb wrote a conciliatory letter to him, asking him to come and wait upon him. He refused, whereupon the royal army expelled him from his territory.

Nahardi and Jukia tribes inhabited Kirthar and Lakhi hills which separate Sindh from Balochistan. They had built forts in Bela and Kahra from where they occasionally came out and plundered the imperial territory. Aurangzeb sent Malik Hussain against them. For ten days he marched along the border of the lower Sindh, exacted promises of submission and tribute from Harun. Khartratal (Nahmordi chiefs) and Murid (Headman of Jukias) and the name of the emperor resounded in the hills of southern Afghanistan.

The above account should not lead any one to believe that the spirit of insurgence was for all time rooted out of the Balochis. Aurangzeb was able to restore only a truce. The moment his strong arm was removed from that region, the tribes reverted to their old habits.

Of the first six Mughal emperors, the reign of Shahjahan is remarkable for the peace which prevailed among the tribes. Their outbreaks being not very serious, there was little improvement in the traditional policy. But the calm did not arise out of the goodwill and loyalty of the Afghans. It was due to the frequency of the passage of the imperial army to and from Transoxiana and Qandhar. This period may be said to mark the lull before the terrible storm which was to burst out in the next reign, necessitating the despatch of many an experienced general, large armies and even the presence of the emperor to quell it The repressive measures of Jahangir and Shahjahan had conclusively proved that the Afghans could not be suppressed by sword.

No sooner did Aurangzeb ascend the throne than the first rumblings of the coming storm became audible Bhagu assumed the leadership of a band of Yusulzais and crowned a child. Muhammad Shah as their ruler. He gave a religious sanction to his authority by securing the support of Mulla Chalak who was held in high honour by the Afghans. A large number of other tribesmen rallied to his standard and he crossed the Indus in 1667 and invaded Bakhli. The invaders seized the fort, of Chhachal and other Mughal outposts fell into their hands. This was the signal for a general rising. Other Yusufzai bands began to plunder the Mughal territory near Attock and Nilab. The Mughal officers of these outposts sent out urgent requisitions to Delhi and Peshawar for speedy assistance.

The emperor made preparations for an all-out offensive against the Yusufzais. Kamil Khan, the faujdar of Attock was ordered to collect all thc Mughal officers and soldiers and proceeded to the tribal area. Amir Khan, the subedar of Kabul was asked to send Shamshir Khan to assist him. A third army under Amin Khan was despatched from the court.

Kamil Khan was the first to arrive on the battlefield Abdul Rahim Khan of Peshawar sent reinforcements to him under Murad Quli. Thc imperial army marched towards the ferry of Harun in order to cross the Indus and enter the Yusufzai country. But the Afghans forestalled the imperialists by crossing the river themselves. They entrenched themselves near the ferry to dispute the passage. A bloody battle occurred in which the Mughals were victorious. Large number of Afghans were captured. Some were drowned in the river, but the majority of them crossed to the other side and fled. Thus the imperial territory to the east of the Indus was cleared of the enemy. As Kamil Khan did not have a sufficient number of men and material to cross the river and enter the Yusufzai territory, he waited for Shamshir Khan.

When the latter arrived the task of subduing the Afghans was entrusted to him. He crossed the Indus and attacked the Yusufzais in their own country. Their property was plundered, their houses razed to the ground and their farms burnt. While these operations were going on a report came that a strong force of the Yusufzai had assembled near Mansur. Shamshir Khan marched to that place. Now another report was received that the rebels had massed together at Bunj air whither the royal army made its way. The Yusufzais were defeated and fled to the hills from where they began to shower bullets and arrows killing a number of royal soldiers. The conflagration spread to other tribes and the Malizais of Sawad and Tirah flocked to the assistance of the Yusufzais. They assembled together at Mansur. Shamshir Khan launched a vigorous attack against them. They were defeated and they fled into the mountains. The Mughal soldiers pursued them hotly. Many Afghans were slain or drowned in the Sawad.

Muhammad Amin Khan who had been sent from the court arrived upon the scene of action in August 1667. He crossed the Kabul river at Nari and took over the supreme command from Shamshir. It was reported that the Sherpa Afghan clan was still carrying on plundering activities and that the Bajauris had also risen in revolt. Asghar Khan who was sent to punish them plundered Shahbazgarhi and gave it to fire. Muhammad Amin Khan himself entered the Sawad valley, punished the Afghans and returned to Chind in October. As he had been summoned to court, he left the place leaving Shamshir Khan the task of keeping the tribes in peace. During the next 5 years; *i.e.* till 1672 no tribal rising occurred. But from this it should not be inferred that the Afghans had been thoroughly crushed. As they had received a terrible hammering they could not raise their head. They wanted time to recover.

In 1672 started another conflagration. Some indiscretion of the faujdar of Jalalabad incited the tribes to take up arms. The Afridis rose under their chieftain Akmal Khan. He crowned himself king, struck coins in his name and proclaimed war against the Mughals. At this time

Muhammad Amin Khan, the Viceroy of Afghanistan was at Peshawar. In the spring he left for Kabul. It was reported to him that the Afridis were blocking the Khyber Pass. Being haughty and rash he paid no heed to the warning of his friends and advanced to Ali Masjid where he entrenched himself. The Afghans opened the attack from the heights and rolled down huge stones upon the Mughal army. Panic and disorder seized the imperialists. The Afghans, now descended from the hills and attacked the enemy from close quarters. A large number of imperial soldiers and officers, including Amin Khan's son Mir Abdulla and his son-in-law Mirza Sultan were killed, while thousands were captured and turned into slaves. Amin Khan was so deeply struck with shame that he thought of dying fighting. But his attendants forcibly led him out of the battle field and he came to Peshawar.

This victory raised the prestige of Akmal Khan in the eyes of the Afghans. A large number of tribesmen including Khushhal Khan joined him. The father of the latter Shahbaz Khan was an ally of the Mughals. In 1659 Khushhal Khan succeeded his father in the chieftainship of the clan. He was employed by the Mughals in an expedition against the Afridis and the Orakzais of Tirah whence he returned in 1660. When Auangzeb was firmly established on the throne Khushhal fell into disgrace and was imprisoned in Ranthambhor by the emperor. He was released in 1666 after more than two years' captivity, and was sent with Muhammad Amin Khan to participate in the war against the tribes. Another cause of friction arose when the emperor assigned the fief of Tari Bulaq to Sher Muhammad Bangash in preference to Khushhal who had been holding it for a considerable time. This so much disgusted Khushhal that he threw his lot with Akmal Khan.

The emperor was not slow to realise the gravity, of the situation and took immediate steps to meet it. Amin Khan was degraded and Fidai Khan, the Governor of Lahore was sent to Peshawar to guard against the tribal attack. Besides this Mahabat Khan was recalled from the Deccan and entrusted with the task of finishing the Afghans. But he failed to make much headway and arrived at Kabul leaving the Khyber Pass blocked as before.

The emperor was highly displeased and sent Shuja'et Khan with Jaswant Singh to replace Mahabat. In February 1674 Shuja'et entered Karappa Pass in the north-east of Kabul river. That night there was a heavy downpour of rain and snow. The Afghans assembled on the hills on either sides of the pass and hurled stones and shot arrows and bullets from above. A large number of imperial troopers were killed and the rest sought refuge in a sale place. When the day dawned, the tribesmen came down and hand to hand fight ensued. Shuja'et Khan died fighting like a soldier. A band of Rajput soldiers sent by Jaswant Singh succeeded in rescuing a part of the Mughal army and bringing it back to a safe place.

This second disaster further alarmed Aurangzeb and he came to the conclusion that his personal presence was necessary to quell the outbreak. Huge preparations were made and the emperor started from the capital. He reached Hasan Abdal in June 1674 and stayed there for 1½ years to guide the campaign. Fidai Khan was ordered to replace Mahabat Khan as Viceroy of Afghanistan. Asghar was called from the Deccan and sent to clear the Khyber region. Prince Akbar was directed to march to Kabul by way of Kohat.

But the emperor was not satisfied by sending armies only. He began to apply the art of diplomacy. Many Afghan tribes were won over by the grant of presents, pensions and Jagir. The Bangash tribe joined the emperor and sent contingents of troops to assist him. The Dudzai, the Tarakzai and the Tirah tribes followed the example of their brethren when they realised the anger arising out of non-submission. Muhammad Ashraf, the son of Khushhal entered the imperial services. The son of Bhagu wrote to the emperor that he was ready to wait upon him if he was given promise of safety. The followers of Darya Khan Afridi intimated that they were ready to bring the head of Akmal if they were forgiven their past activities.

Military strategy was proceeding simultaneously. Asghar Khan defeated the Mohmand when they made a night attack on him near Peshawar. They suffered heavy losses, a number of them being killed and a large number having been taken prisoners. They blocked the Khyber route. Asghar Khan took upon himself the task of clearing the passage and escorting Fidai Khan to Jalalabad. A tribal battle occurred near Ali Masjid in which either side suffered heavy losses. Asghar Khan himself was severely wounded but he managed to put the enemy to flight. But the Afghans rallied together again and closed the pass further ahead. So Asghar Khan was forced to escort Fidai Khan to Jalalabad by way of Bazarak and Seh Chuba

Next Asghar Khan occupied Nangrahar, punished the Ghilzais and cleared the Jagadalak Pass of the army. While he was staying at

Gandamak, 30 to 40 thousand Afghans attacked him but they were put to flight. The name of Asghar Khan became an object of terror among the Afghans and their women used to hush their children to sleep by uttering it.

Prince Akbar had till now done nothing. He passed a short time at Kabul and then returned to Hasan Abdal leaving Fidai Khan in command. In the spring of 1675 while the latter was returning from Kabul to Peshawar the Afghans attacked him in the Jagdalak Pass. Fidai Khan's van was defeated but he succeeded in saving the centre. The report of the tragedy reached Asghar Khan at Gandamak and he came to the rescue of Fidai Khan and defeated the enemy.

This was followed by a serious defeat of the imperialists. Mukarram Khan was fighting the Afghans in Kotal Khapush in the Bajaur country. He had plundered their villages and killed many of them. One day two Afghan contingents surprised him and outnumbered him. Mukarram's brother Shamshir Khan and brother-in-law Mir Azizullah were killed. Mukarram saved his life by flying to Bajaur. Prompt measures were taken to cow down the Afghans. Sarbulend Khan was sent with 9000 men and a vast quantity of material against the enemy. Asghar Khan was posted at Jalalabad, Hizabr Khan in the Jagdalak Pass, Firaq Khan in Lemghant. Ilahidad in Gharibkhana and Khanjar Khan in Bangash. But even these precautions could not save the imperial army from two more reverses. Hizabr Khan was slain with his son Abdulla and the thanedar of Barangab was driven out of his post.

Inspite of these reverses, the emperor left Hasan Abdal towards the end of 1675 and returned to Delhi. Prof. Jadunath Sarkar, basing his views upon Ishwar Das, suggests that the situation had sufficiently improved to enable the emperor to leave Hasan Abdal and return to Delhi. But Manucci and Khushhal Khan state that the emperor returned on account of failure. In this case it is difficult to agree with Ishwardas. We have seen how even a few months before the emperor had left, one Mughal general had been killed and another expelled from his outpost. Akmal Khan had not been arrested, Khushhal Khan was still inciting the tribes to fight against the Mughals. In the circumstances it cannot be accepted that the position of the imperialists had reasonably improved.

The reasons why Aurangzeb left Hasan Abdal were quite different. More important problems, like the subjugation of the Deccan and Rajputana were pressing upon his attention. It was no use wasting time in the north-west. The task of subduing the Afghans could rather be left in the hands of a prince.

In October 1676 Prince Muazzam was appointed Viceroy of Afghanistan with the title of Shah-i-alam. He arrived in Kabul in August 1677 and after a few months' stay there returned to Delhi. On his recommendation Amir Khan was appointed to officiate for him. He assumed charge in 1678 and continued to govern Afghanistan with signal ability till his death 20 years later.

Unfortunately the period of Amir Khan's viceroyalty has not been given the importance which it deserves. Khafi Khan and Mustaid Khan have given a detailed description of the activities of the Mughal army in the period preceding the viceroyalty of Amir Khan, though the fact of the matter is that it failed to achieve anything substantial. The presence of the emperor did no doubt cow down the rebels, but there was no guarantee that they could not raise their heads, the moment the royal arm was removed from amongst them. It was Amir Khan who by his wise and judicious policy accomplished what the Mughal soldiery failed to do. It does signal credit to him that during the long period of his stewardship no serious rising occurred in Afghanistan.

POLICY OF AMIR KHAN

To fully appreciate Amir Khan's achievements it is necessary to study the situation when he took the reins of office in his hands. The conflagration which had started in 1672 had continued with unabated fury. The emperor had come to Hasan Abdal and gone back but the Afghans had not been suppressed. They had suffered huge losses but their spirit was still undaunted. Their leaders like Khushhal Khan and Akmal Khan were touring the hilly regions preaching revolt and revenge, and infusing a new spirit among the tribesmen.

Amir Khan first tried the method of the sword. But on realising its futility he resorted to conciliation. He so drew by noose of kindness the Afghan leaders who had held their heads and neck higher than heavens that they become obedient and he so captured by sincerity and friendship of those savages that they voluntarily bound themselves to the saddle strap of obedience. By the magic of his right thinking the leaders of that tribe spread out mutual dissensions and fell down upon one another: stranger still, every one of them sought to improve his affairs by taking the advice of Amir Khan. The Afghans left their shy and unsocial manners and began to visit him without any suspicion. Further he kept many of the hillmen usefully employed by enlisting them in the imperial service and profusely bribed the clans out of the imperial coffers, his own income and his illegal exactions.

The above remark brings out clearly the policy followed by Amir Khan. It had a three-fold aspect, economic, social and diplomatic. He paid regular subsidies to the clansmen: he established social contacts with them and won their confidence to the extent of encouraging them to discuss their domestic matters with him; he raised a tribal militia; and finally, by diplomacy he pitted one tribe against the other. The Ma'athirul'umara gives a very interesting example. On one occasion almost all the tribes recognised Akmal Khan as their leader. Amir Khan realised the seriousness of the situation and induced Abdulla Khan Khawazgi to write a letter to the chief of every tribe. We for a long time were waiting .. that sovereignty may be transferred to the Afghans. But we are unacquainted with the disposition of the person who is to be raised to the throne. In reply they dilated upon Akmal Khan's qualities and recommended his name for Kingship. Abdulla Khan again wrote: These qualities are excellent but the finest that a ruler should possess is justice and consideration for the subjects of every class. In order to test him be good enough to take the trouble to enquire how he will divide the territory among the tribes if it came into his possession. If he be timid or partial it will at once become evident. The heads of the tribes enquired of Akmal Khan but he could not decide as to how to divide such a small country among so many people. The result was schism. To avoid it, he was compelled to begin division. When he favoured some, others raised a hue and cry and went off their own country.

The result of this wise policy was that peace prevailed for 20 years in the hills. The Afridis came to terms with the Mughals. Khushhal Khan's attempts to incite the tribes to rebellion ended in smoke. His own son and grandson joined the Mughals, and the former betrayed him into the enemy's hand. In 1681 Khushhal Khan died in captivity.

In 1701 Amir Khan also died. His wife Sahibji was a prudent lady. She took an active part in political and financial matters and to her must be attributed a large measure of Amir Khan's success. To prevent disorder she kept back the news of her husband's death informing only the emperor of it. The latter wrote to her to conduct affairs until the arrival of Shah Alam. Sahibji got hold of a person who resembled Amir Khan. He would sit in a palanquin and pose as the late Viceroy. On the arrival of Bahadur Shah she handed over the charge of the Administration to him and left the country. When in 1702 Shah Alam was returning to Peshawar *via* Bannu he entered the Isa Khail country intending to reach his destination by Kalabagh. A tribe of the Khataks reduced him to narrow straits. But Afdal Khan, the grand son of Khushhal rescued him and escorted him to Lakki.

Now turning to the Balochis, we hear very little about them in this region. In the early part of it a report came from Gujarat that a Boloch imposter was parading as Dara-Shikoh and was causing trouble. Mahabat Khan, the Subedar of that place turned him out. In 1698 another report was received from Multan that Hati had been punished.

REGARD TO THE POLICY OF AURANGZEB

To sum up, the reign of Aurangzeb can be divided in two periods, in regard to the policy followed towards the tribes. The first 1667-78 was marked by a resort to arms but it did not bring much success. It was during the succeeding two decades *viz.* the period of the stewardship of Amir Khan that the Afghans were made into sincere friends. To understand the causes of this change, it is necessary to find out why the Afghans, defied the Mughal authority. In the first place they were very poor and had no other alternative but to take recourse to plunder to make both ends meet. This meant breach of law and order. Secondly, they were lovers of freedom. If the slightest doubt arose in their mind that the Mughal Government wanted to encroach upon it, they put everything at stake to ward off this danger. Thirdly, the Afghans had an abundant amount of energy. Not being directed into the right channel, it expressed itself in plunder and robbery. The previous Mughal emperors had tried to meet the second and third demands by a partial policy of conciliation and of enlistment of the tribes in the army. Amir Khan made an advance on the policy and gave a complete solution to the whole problem. He started the method of regularly subsiding the tribal leaders. Thus the question of poverty was generally solved. By establishing direct contact with the Afghans, he succeeded in removing their suspicions. And by enlisting them in the army he gave an outlet for their energy.

It will not be out of place to examine at this stage the effect of tribal affairs upon the internal and foreign policy of the Mughals. Their insurgence lasted throughout the 150 years of the Mughal rule with occasional breaks in between, which entailed huge losses in men, material and money.

Time and again, the imperialists suffered major disasters. The massacre of Birbal with nearly his entire army in the reign of Akbar, of Izzat Khan and murder of Shuja'et Khan in the reign of Aurangzeb are the points in case. Besides, even when the Mughals won, they had to pay heavily in men and money. These losses necessarily affected the internal administration. These soldiers and money could have been usefully employed in other parts of the empire. To quote a few examples, Akbar could have used them in the Deccan.

About Aurangzeb, Sarkar's remarks are worth quoting. It relieved the pressure on Shivaji by draining the Deccan of the best Mughal troops for service on the north-west frontier. The Maratha chief took advantage of this diversion of his enemy's strength to sweep in a dazzling succession of triumphs through Golkunda to the Karnatak and back again through Mysore and Bijapur to Raigarh, during the fifteen months following December 1676. It was the climax of his career, but the Afridis and the Khataks made its unbroken success possible.

On foreign policy also the effect was not inconsiderable. From the very beginning, the tribes put impediments in the path of the Mughal rulers in the realisation of their dream regarding Transoxiana. Babar, while a ruler in Kabul, could not afford to start for Samarqand before bringing these ever-rebellious tribes to submission.

Humayun's invasion of that country failed because of the disturbances created by Kamran who, in his turn was assisted by the tribes. From the beginning of the reign of Akbar, the Uzbeg rulers started the practice of supporting financially the tribal leaders who could serve the useful purpose of harassing the Mughal army from the rear if it proceeded to attack Transoxiana. This continued in the reign of Jahangir. It is, however, worth noticing that in the reign of Shah Jahan, when the Mughal army actually invaded Transoxiana, the Afghans were so much terrified that they dared not raise their heads even once.

THE POLICE SYSTEM

Akbar's police administration was well organized and efficient. 'The police may be divided into three categories of urban, district and village police. In all the cities and towns of the empire there were kotwals charged with the duty of maintaining public order and decency. The kotwal's functions have already been enumerated. He was both the head of the city police and committing and trying magistrate. He had to apprehend thieves, robbers and other petty criminals and to punish them. His main duty was to see that the life of the city continued undisturbed. Besides, he had to examine weights and measures, keep an eye on the currency and to enforce Akbar's social legislation. He was held personally responsible for the value of the property stolen in case he failed to discover the thief. He was authorised to inflict on offenders punishment which included torture, mutilation of limbs and flogging. He was, however, not empowered to inflict the penalty of death. In short, the kotwal's duties were quite comprehensive and his powers wide and despotic. In the district, law and order was maintained by the faujdar who was assisted in this work by the amils and other revenue officers of the parganas. Of course, the faujdar had a kotwal at the district headquarters to take charge of the police duty of the city. The faujdar's main duties were the policing of roads of the district and suppressing disorders of all kinds. Like the kotwal he was responsible for producing the stolen property, if he failed to trace the thief. He possessed the power of dealing summarily with disturbances, and in normal times he successfully maintained peace and tranquillity. There were more than one *thana* or police station in a pargana. As for the police administration of the villages, Akbar, following the immemorial custom of the country, established the principle of local responsibility. The village headman was required to discover the thieves and robbers within a specified time. In the event of his failure, he had to make good the loss from his own pocket. If a crime occurred on the boundary of more than one village, the headmen of the villages concerned were held responsible for it. Usually the entire village was answerable for every crime and was laid under contribution for making good the loss. There was, however, a chaukidar for every village for normal police work.

The police arrangement under Akbar was fairly efficient and maintained a high standard of public order and tranquillity. It will, however, be idle to imagine that there were no cases of theft, immorality, cheating or disturbances of public peace. There were professional thieves and robbers in the hills and the jungles who descended to the plains to ply their trade whenever there was lack of vigilance on the part of the local police. Though they are exaggerated in some particulars, the accounts of contemporary European travellers yield a fairly accurate picture of the state of the country in the second half of the sixteenth century. But in view of the law abidingness and high morality of the people and the severity of the penal law the standard of public security was not lower than it is in our time.

Education

In the sixteenth century no government in any country in the world considered it to be its duty to educate the public. Even England recognised this duty as late as 1870. Akbar was, however, far in advance of his age and made an attempt to raise the intellectual level of the people. Although he did not establish a net work of schools and colleges all over the country for the benefit of the school-going population and did not allocate a fixed percentage of the state revenue for expenditure on education, yet he encouraged education in diverse ways. There were in his empire primary and secondary schools, and even colleges. Some of them were established and maintained by government, while others depended upon private philanthropy. There was *a maktab* or primary school attached to every mosque where elementary reading, writing, arithmetic, besides the Quran, were taught. In addition to these, there were madarsas which may be called secondary schools or colleges. Akbar established colleges at Fatehpur Sikri, Agra, Delhi and other places, and richly endowed them. His example was followed by his courtiers. Quite early in his reign Maham Anaga had built a madarsa near the western gate of *Purana Qila* at Delhi. Khwaja Muin established a college at Delhi. There were many such colleges in all important towns with a sufficiently large Muslim population. In these colleges Islamic theology, jurisprudence, philosophy, logic and astronomy were taught by distinguished teachers, some of whom had received education outside India. There were schools and higher centres of learning for the Hindus in every part of the country. In spite of the destruction wrought by the iconoclastic zeal of the early Turkish invaders, Hindu centres of learning had not completely disappeared. There was a remarkable revival, of our ancient learning during the age of Akbar.

There was a school in every village and in fact a school attached to every temple where reading, writing and arithmetic and religious books were taught. In higher centres of learning, Hindu theology, Sanskrit grammar, philosophy, literature, logic, astronomy, higher mathematics and other sciences were studied. Akbar made an attempt to revise the curriculum and to include certain important subjects in the courses of study meant for grown up boys at schools and colleges.

These subjects were science of morals and social behaviour, arithmetic, notations peculiar to arithmetic, agriculture, mensuration, geometry, astronomy, physiognomy and fore-telling, household economy, public administration, medicine, logic, and *tabi,* the *riyazi* and the *illahi* sciences and history. Students of Sanskrit were required to study grammar, philology, logic, Vedanta and Patanjali. These were to be studied gradually. The teacher was only to assist the pupils to learn.

Students were particularly advised to commit moral precepts and sayings to memory, and no one was to neglect "those things which the present time required". Probably colleges were required to specialise in some of the above subjects. It is unlikely that every institution was required to teach all the above subjects. Another reform introduced was to open the madarsas to Hindus. For the first time in medieval India, Hindus and Musalmans received their education in common schools and read the same books. The reform was necessitated by the fact that Akbar had made Persian compulsory for all the state officials and by his desire to create a common nationality.

V.A. Smith erroneously supposes that the reform had no relation to facts and was, therefore, unreal and useless. The system produced remarkable men in every walk of life who contributed to the success of the later days of Akbar and of the reigns of Jahangir and Shah Jahan and were able enough to shed lustre on any age and in any country. This is enough to show that the reform had proved efficacious. Akbar's court was a centre of learning and art. The emperor, his courtiers and officials were liberal patrons of letters. The age consequently witnessed a cultural renaissance of a high order. Works of high literary value were produced in various subjects, particularly on historiography. The Hindi poetry of Akbar's age is unrivalled and has become classical for all time. Such high production would have been impossible without proper educational organization and atmosphere.

The court played a very important part in the emperor's scheme of the propagation of education and culture. Akbar encouraged men of letters and arts to produce standard scientific and literary works on a variety of subjects. Books on religion, philosophy, literature, biography, history, mathematics, astronomy, medicine and other subjects were brought out in large numbers. Poetry was not neglected. Fine arts like architecture, music and painting were also encouraged. Inspired by the laudable ambition of creating a common culture, Akbar established a Translation Department and had outstanding works in Sanskrit, Arabic and Turki rendered into Persian, so as to enable the Hindus and Muslims to know the best in each other's religion and culture. For the above purpose the services of high-ranking scholars in the country were requisitioned.

Many famous scholars from outside India were also invited to assist the indigenous talent in the above work. Many a Sanskrit treatise, including the Vedas and the Ramayana and the Mahabharata, was rendered into Persian. Arabic works of repute on Muslim theology and arts were also translated into Persian. A school of Indian historiography was founded and a large number of histories were written by eminent historians. Libraries were opened. The royal library in the palace was one of the most wonderful institutions of the kind in the world. It consisted of many thousand books all of which were manuscripts, sumptuously bound and beautifully illustrated. The books were classified according to their subject-matter and the language in which they were written. There were Sanskrit, Persian, Greek, Kashmiri and Arabic works.

Hindi, which was coming into prominence, was patronised. Although the education as planned by Akbar was through the medium of Persian which was the court language and compulsory for state servants, schools attached to temples and private institutions founded and maintained by the Hindus must have imparted knowledge through the medium of Hindi. The measures undertaken by the emperor indicated a desire on his part to raise the moral and intellectual standard of the people. It must, however, be admitted that the scheme was meant mainly for the upper and middle class people.

Religious Policy

The inquisitive Akbar made a scientific examination of various religions then known in India and that his enquiry led him to the conclusion that there was truth in every religion. He thought it undesirable, therefore, that a comparatively young religion like Islam should be considered to possess the monopoly of Truth and continue as the religion of the State. Hence he abolished Islam as the religion of the State and established in its place, a religion of his own choice known as the Din-i-Ilahi. This, new religion, which has been compared to the theosophical order of our time, was an eclectic faith and consisted of good principles culled from every religion. It was based on "reason" and not the "authority of any man". It was Akbar's policy not to impose his religion by force on his subjects. It was, therefore, confined to the court circle and had just a few thousand followers. Even after the establishment of the Din-i-Ilahi, Akbar pursued the policy of giving full religious toleration to his people. It was but natural for a monarch who believed that there was truth in every religion and that there was the same God everywhere, whether He be worshipped in a church, a mosque, a temple, or a synagogue, to treat all religions alike and to give the followers of every faith complete freedom of conscience and worship. Contrary to the practice which had existed since the advent of Islam in the country, Hindus were permitted to perform public worship and to preach their religion. Those Hindu men, women and children who were forcibly converted to Islam were allowed to go back to their ancestral religion, if any liked. Christians were allowed to build churches and proselytise Hindus and Muslims to Christianity. No kind of disability was imposed on any one on account of his faith. State employment was open to all people irrespective of their race, caste or religious belief. These religious reforms appeared revolutionary in as much as they brought down Islam from its position of dominance which it had enjoyed for centuries, to one of equality with other religions. Its important followers, particularly the *Ulema* who had hitherto presumed to guide the State and shape its religious policy, were greatly disturbed at the change. They levelled charges of irreligiosity and even apostacy against Akbar and instigated the Muslim public to rebel against him. Early in 1580 Mullah Muhammad Yazdi, the Qazi of Jaunpur, issued a *fatwa* to the effect that the emperor had ceased to be a Muslim and rebellion against him was lawful. About this very time Akbar had introduced certain administrative reforms, such as, conversion of jagir lands into *khalsa* (reserve) land and cutting down of allowances of imperial officers. The discontent caused by these reforms persuaded some of the high imperial officers in Bihar and Bangal to join hands with the disaffected and humiliated Muslim theologians and they broke out into a fearful rebellion. The immediate political effect of Akbar's policy of religious toleration was not good and involved the country in a civil war; but the emperor was not to be cowed down into surrender and abandonment of the statesman-like policy of treating all religions alike. He put down the rebellion and *severely chastised* the malcontents. The policy of absolute religious toleration stood the test and continued throughout his reign and with some modification down to the time of Aurangzeb.

Some modern scholars, notably V.A. Smith and Woolseley Haig, have held that, while Akbar gave complete religious toleration to other faiths, he persecuted Islam. This view is based on the statements of the Jesuit missionaries and of the historian Badayuni. The former, in their anxiety to show to their superiors in Goa and Lisbon the success of their mission and that the emperor was well on the way to embrace Christianity, sent highly exaggerated and even false reports to them. They informed the credulous Christians of Europe that he had not only abandoned Islam but was persecuting it. Badayuni was a bigoted mullah in whose eyes justice and fairness shown to other religions was tantamount to injustice to and persecution of Islam. As has been mentioned, the very fact that Islam had ceased to be the state religion gave moral offence to its orthodox followers. They denounced as persecution of Islam such unexceptionable measures as the giving of equal privileges to every faith for the propagation of its principles and the allowing of freedom to the converts to revert to their original religions, if they liked. Badayuni gives a long list of the so-called measures of persecution. They are:—

(1) Akbar made it obligatory to wear silk dresses and ornaments at prayer time.

(2) He forbade Islamic prayers.

(3) He stopped the call to prayer in the Assembly Hall.

(4) He prohibited Muslim fasts.

(5) Pilgrimage to Mecca was prohibited.

(6) Muslim festivals were discontinued.

(7) No one was allowed to give the name of Muhammad and Ahmad to his children.

(8) Mosques were plundered and converted into stables.

(9) Shaving of beards was allowed.

(10) Flesh of wild boars, pigs and tigers was permitted.

(11) Study of Arabic was discouraged.

(12) Those who killed cows and other animals on prohibited days were punished, sometimes with capital punishment.

A critical examination of the charges makes it clear that most of them were groundless. If Akbar had forbidden Islamic prayers, it was Superfluous to order silk dresses and ornaments to be put on at the prayer time. We know from Badayuni's own book and from the writings of the Jesuit missionaries that Muslim call to prayer and five daily prayers were common enough throughout Akbar's reign. It is ridiculous to imagine that the masses should have been ordered not to keep the fast of Ramzan. Similarly, pilgrimage to Mecca continued to be undertaken as before. We know it from several sources, including the Jesuit missionaries, that as late as 1585 many men and women were permitted to proceed to Mecca. The celebration of Muslim festivals and the naming of Muhammad and Ahmad were common-place things throughout Akbar's reign, as is clear from the statement of many a contemporary writers. There is no concrete instance to show that mosques were plundered or converted into stables. Unlike Hindu temples, mosques possess no articles of value and as such, they are not worth plundering. It may be that at the time of war a mosque might have been utilised for military purposes. In view of our knowledge that hundreds of mosques remained and were utilized as places of worship, it seems too much to believe that any general order for their conversion into stables could have been given. We know from many paintings of the later days of Akbar's reign that the emperor's nobles and courtiers continued to grow beards. If Akbar shaved his beard and his example was followed by some of his courtiers, it should not be taken to be an instance of the persecution of Islam. Similarly, flesh of boars was not forced on any one. Probably those who ate it were not hated or punished. Akbar emphasised the study of Persian and patronised Sanskrit and Hindi. No order was issued banning Arabic. The fanatics like Badayuni thought that the encouragement of Sanskrit amounted to a ban on Arabic. It is, thus, clear that Akbar made no attempt to persecute the religion of his ancestors. What he really did was to bring it down to the level of other religions and to look upon Muhammad as a prophet and not the Prophet so far as he personally was concerned.

Public Services

The Mughul imperial service, which conducted the administration so efficiently and made Akbar's reign brilliant, cannot be called national. It was mostly foreign in personnel and consisted of Turks, Mongols, Uzbegs, Persians, Arabs and Afghans, with a little sprinkling of Indian Muham-madans and Hindus. According to Blochmann, 70 percent of Akbar's senior officials were foreigners, who had either come from Central Asia for service or had settled in this country for one or two generations. Most of them had accompanied Babur and Humayun to our land and attached themselves to the ruling family. Akbar had thrown open the higher services to the Hindus; but the number of Hindus holding high civil and military posts was comparatively very small. Nor was the proportion of Indian Muhammadans in any way high. Among the Hindus who held high posts Rajputs predominated. Inspite of Akbar's policy of "India for the Indians" the Mughul imperial service remained a heterogeneous institution, mainly foreign in personnel, till the end of his reign.

Admission to the service was. based on merit and fitness. Race, caste and creed played little part in the recruitment of its members. Sometimes political considerations obliged the emperor to appoint certain men to high posts in the imperial service. But even these men were not promoted to the higher rank unless they had shown themselves competent by approved service and loyalty. All the members of the imperial service were given the designation of mansabdars and their rank, position and emoluments were determined by the mansabs which they held.

Promotion depended upon approved service and not on seniority or pay. The emperor reserved to himself the right of promoting or degrading the highest officers including the ministers at will. Even the prime-minister could be degraded to the post of governor or even to a lesser rank. Raja Todar Mal, after having served as prime-minister, was, subsequently, transferred to the post of a governor. Such examples were by no means rare. It was not necessary that an officer holding a small post should pass through various stages before his appointment to the highest post in a particular branch of service. In all cases continuance in a high post or promotion was not possible without approved service and unflinching loyalty.

The imperial service was organised on bureaucratic principles. It was military in organisation and outlook. As has been shown in connection with an account of the army, every official was the holder of a mansab or official appointment of rank and profit. He was required to maintain a contingent of troops and auxiliaries and furnish the same for the service of the State whenever called upon to do so. The members of the service, called "mansabdars", were classified into 33 grades which ranged from the mansab of 10 to that of 10,000. Thus the imperial service was organised on definite military lines and its members were expected to perform military duties in addition to their main work, administrative or judicial. Like all bureaucracies, it was highly efficient and loyal.

There was little specialisation of appointments. Services were not clearly demarcated as administrative, revenue or judicial. In fact, there was no distinction between civil and military services even. Any officer was at any time liable to be transferred to an altogether new form of employment. For example, Raja Todar Mal, who was essentially a financier of the highest ability, was transferred more than once to act as a governor and even as a military commander. Abul Fazl, the eminent scholar and historian, was sent on a diplomatic mission and also had to conduct a military expedition in the Deccan. Raja Birbal, who was no more than a court wit, was ordered to lead an expedition against the tribal Pathans. There was no separate educational or medical service, though teachers and physicians were employed as imperial servants.

Generally speaking, the officials were divided into two, broad divisions, namely (1) those who served the emperor at court, and (2) the others who held definite appointments, whether at the capital or in the provinces. The names of both kinds of officers were recorded in separate registers and the officers who were required to attend at court were expected to keep themselves in readiness to carry out any orders that the emperor might give. They had their own troops which, too, were kept ready for service. The officials whose names were recorded in another register held various kinds of appointments, such as, governorship or other positions in the provinces and districts, or posts in the imperial secretariat or household department.

The officials were either paid by grant of jagirs or in cash from the royal treasury, Akbar preferred the latter mode of payment; but as payment by grant of jagirs had come down from the past, he could not abolish the system altogether. But the number of officers who were paid their salaries by assignment of land was, however, very small towards the end of his reign. The salaries and allowances of the officials were enormous. A first grade mansabdar of live thousand was paid Rs. 30,000 a month, a second grade mansabdar of the same class received Rs. 29,000 a month, and a third grade official of that rank got Rs. 28,000 a month. The officials were, however, required to pay out of their salaries the cost of their military establishments. If the cost of the establishment were deducted from their salaries, the emoluments of a mansabdar of five thousand would, on a rough estimate, be Rs. 18,000, that of one thousand Rs. 5,000, and that of 500, Rs. 1,000 a month. In Akbar's time the payments were made for all the twelve months of the year.

The Mughul public service, though well-organised, suffered from certain drawbacks. In the first place, there were no regular rules of appointment, promotion or dismissal. Secondly, fixity of tenure was not guaranteed. This led to intrigues and sometimes to neglect of duty. It was the emperor's pleasure to appoint or promote any one he liked. Akbar, who possessed the never failing quality of judging human character at sight, almost invariably chose right kind of officers and promoted only those who deserved it. But under his successors, who were less gifted rulers the imperial service began to deteriorate. Thirdly, the cost of maintaining the fixed quota of troops and auxiliaries was very heavy. On account of the tradition of a luxuriously high standard of living and their own position in life, imperial officials of the upper grades were required to be extravagant and there was, therefore, no incentive to thrift. The average officer spent large sums on luxuries, banquets and presents, and was obliged to exploit poor people. In spite of these drawbacks the Mughul imperial service under Akbar was one of the most highly organised, talented, loyal and efficient services then known to the world. It carried out the imperial policy expeditiously and made Akbar's reign successful and brilliant.

NATIONAL POLICY ON TRIBALS

For the first time after the country became Independent, the Government of India is proposing the formulation of a National Policy on Scheduled Tribes.

The policy seeks to bring Scheduled Tribes into the mainstream of society through a multi-pronged approach for their all-round development without disturbing their distinct culture. There are 67.8 million Scheduled Tribe people, constituting 8.08 per cent of India's population. There are 698 Scheduled Tribes spread all over the country barring States and Union Territories like Chandigarh, Delhi, Haryana, Pondicherry and Punjab. Orissa has the largest number – 68—of Scheduled Tribes.

Scheduled Tribes are those, which are notified as such by the President of India under Article 342 of the Constitution. The first notification was issued in 1950. The President considers characteristics like the tribes' primitive traits, distinctive culture, shyness with the public at large, geographical isolation and social and economic backwardness before notifying them as a Scheduled Tribe. Seventy five of the 698 Scheduled Tribes are identified as Primitive Tribal Groups considering they are more backward than Scheduled Tribes. They continue to live in a pre-agricultural stage of economy and have very low literacy rates. Their populations are stagnant or even declining.

The Constitution through several Articles has provided for the socio-economic development and empowerment of Scheduled Tribes. (You may list the provisions here, if necessary). But there has been no national policy, which could have helped translate the constitutional provisions into a reality. Five principles spelt out in 1952, known as

Nehruvian Panchasheel, have been guiding the administration of tribal affairs. They are:

1. Tribals should be allowed to develop according to their own genius
2. Tribals' rights in land and forest should be respected
3. Tribal teams should be trained to undertake administration and development without too many outsiders being inducted
4. Tribal development should be undertaken without disturbing tribal social and cultural institutions
5. The index of tribal development should be the quality of their life and not the money spent.

Realising that the Nehruvian Panchasheel was long on generalities and short on specifics, the Government of India formed a Ministry of Tribal Affairs for the first time in October 1999 to accelerate tribal development. The Ministry of Tribal Affairs is now coming out with the draft National Policy on Tribals. Based on the feedback from tribal leaders, the concerned States, individuals, organisations in the public and the private sectors, and NGOs, the Ministry will finalise the policy.

The National Policy recognises that a majority of Scheduled Tribes continue to live below the poverty line, have poor literacy rates, suffer from malnutrition and disease and are vulnerable to displacement. It also acknowledges that Scheduled Tribes in general are repositories of indigenous knowledge and wisdom in certain aspects.

The National Policy aims at addressing each of these problems in a concrete way. It also lists out measures to be taken to preserve and promote tribals' cultural heritage.

FORMAL EDUCATION

Formal education is the key to all-round human development. Despite several campaigns to promote formal education ever since Independence, the literacy rate among Scheduled Tribes is only 29.60 per cent compared to 52.21 per cent for the country as a whole (1991 Census). The female literacy rate is only 18.19 per cent compared to the national female literacy rate of 39.29 per cent. Alienation from the society, lack of adequate infrastructure like schools, hostels and teachers, abject poverty and apathy towards irrelevant curriculum have stood in the way of tribals getting formal education.

To achieve the objective of reaching the benefit of education to tribals, the National Policy will ensure that:

- Tribals are included in the national programme of Sarva Shiksha Abhiyan run by the Ministry of Human Resource Development.
- Schools and hostels are opened in areas where no such facilities exist.
- At least one model residential school is located in each tribal concentration area
- Education is linked with provision of supplementary nutrition.
- Special incentives like financial assistance, pocket allowance, free distribution of textbooks and school uniforms are provided
- Teaching is imparted in tribals' mother tongue at least up to the primary level. Educated tribal youth are given employment as teachers, wherever possible. (This will obviate the need to employ teachers belonging to far-off places who find commuting is as difficult as staying in a village with no basic amenities.
- Pedagogy is made relevant so that tribals do not find it as alien.
- Curriculum and cocurriculum include aspects of meta skill upgradation of tribal children.
- Curricula for meta skill upgradation are to include aspects of tribal games and sports, archery, identification of plants of medicinal value, crafts art and culture, folk dance and folk songs, folk paintings etc.
- Emphasis is laid on vocational/professional education. Polytechnics are set up for studies in subjects like forestry, horticulture, dairying, veterinary sciences, polytechnics.

TRADITIONAL WISDOM

Dwelling amidst hills, forests, coastal areas, deserts, tribals over the centuries have gained precious and vast experience in combating environmental hardships and leading sustainable livelihoods. Their wisdom is reflected in their water harvesting techniques, indigenously developed irrigation channels, construction of canc bridges in hills, adaptation to desert life, utilisation of forest species like herbs, shrubs for medicinal purposes, meteorological assessment etc.

Such invaluable knowledge of theirs needs to be properly documented and preserved lest it should get lost in the wake of modernisation and passage of time.

The National Policy seeks to:

- Preserve and promote such traditional knowledge and wisdom and document it

- Establish a centre to train tribal youth in areas of traditional wisdom
- Disseminate such through models and and exhibits at appropriate places
- Transfer such knowledge to non-tribal areas.

HEALTH

Although tribal people live usually close to nature, a majority of them need health care on account of malnutrition, lack of safe drinking water, poor hygiene and environmental sanitation and above all poverty.

Lack of awareness and apathy to utilise the available health services also affect their health status. In wake of the opening of tribal areas with highways industrialization, and communication facilities, diseases have spread to tribal areas. Endemics like malaria, deficiency diseases, venereal diseases including AIDS are not uncommon among tribal populations.

However, lack of safe drinking water and malnutrition are well-recognised major health hazards. Tribals suffer from a deficiency of calcium, vitamin A, vitamin C, riboflavin and animal protein in their diets.

Malnutrition and undernutrition are common among Primitive Tribal Groups who largely depend upon food they either gather or raise by using simple methods. The poor nutritional status of tribal women directly influences their reproductive performance and their infants' survival, growth and development. Tribal people, who are self reliant and self-sufficient, have over the centuries developed their own medicine system based on herbs and other items collected from the nature and processed locally. They have also their own system of diagnosis and cure of diseases. They believe in taboos, spiritual powers and faith healing. There are wide variations among tribals in their health status and willingness to access and utilise health services, depending on their culture, level of contact with other cultures and degree of adaptability.

Against this background, the National Policy seeks to promote the modern health care system and also a synthesis of the Indian systems of medicine like ayurveda and siddha with the tribal system.

The National Policy seeks to:

- Strengthen the allopathy system of medicine in tribal areas with the extension of the three-tier system of village health workers, auxiliary nurse mid-wife and primary health centres.

- ❖ Expand the number of hospitals in tune with tribal population
- ❖ Validate identified tribal remedies (folk claims) used in different tribal areas
- ❖ Encourage, document and patent tribals' traditional medicines
- ❖ Promote cultivation of medicinal plants related value addition strategies through imparting training to youth
- ❖ Encourage qualified doctors from tribal communities to serve tribal areas
- ❖ Promote the formation of a strong force of tribal village health guides through regular training-cum-orientation courses
- ❖ Formulate area-specific strategies to improve access to and utilisation of health services
- ❖ Strengthen research into diseases affecting tribals and initiate action programmes
- ❖ Eradicate endemic diseases on a war footing.

DISPLACEMENT AND RESETTLEMENT

Displacement of people from traditional habitations causes much trauma to the affected people. Compulsory acquisition of land for construction of dams and roads, quarrying and mining operations, location of industries and reservation of forests for National Parks and environmental reasons forces tribal people to leave their traditional abodes and land – their chief means of livelihood. Nearly 85.39 lakh tribals had been displaced until 1990 on account of some mega project or the other, reservation of forests as National Parks etc. Tribals constitute at least 55.16 percent of the total displaced people in the country. Cash payment does not really compensate the tribals for the difficulties they experience in their living style and ethos.

Displacement of tribals from their land amounts to violation of the Fifth Schedule of the Constitution as it deprives them of control and ownership of natural resources and land essential for their way of life. The National Policy for Tribals, therefore, stipulates that displacement of tribal people is kept to the minimum and undertaken only after possibilities of non-displacement and least displacement have been exhausted.

When it becomes absolutely necessary to displace Scheduled Tribe people in the larger interest, the displaced should be provided a better standard of living.

The National Policy, therefore, mandates that the following guidelines be followed when tribals are resettled:

- When displacement becomes inevitable, each scheduled tribe family having land in the earlier settlement shall be given land against land. A minimum of two hectares of cultivable land is considered necessary and viable for a family (comprising man, his wife and unmarried children).
- Tribal families having fishing rights in their original habitat shall be granted fishing rights in the new reservoir or at any other alternative place
- Reservation benefits enjoyed at the original settlement shall be continued at the the resettlement area.
- Additional financial assistance equivalent to nearly one and a half year's minimum agricultural wages for loss of customary rights and usufructory rights of forest produce shall be given.
- Tribals are to be resettled close to their natural habitat by treating all the people so displaced as one group to let them retain their ethnic, linguistic and socio-cultural identity and the network of kinship and mutual obligations
- Free land is to be provided for social and religious congregations.
- If resettlement is possible only away from the district/taluka, then substantively higher benefits in monetary terms shall be given.
- When tribal families are resettled en masse, all basic minimum amenities shall be provided at the new sites. They include roads and passages, electricity, drainage and sanitation, safe drinking water, educational and health care facilities, fair price shops, a community hall and a panchayat office.

FOREST VILLAGES

Tribal's age-old symbiotic relationship with forests is well known. Recognising this fact, even the National Forest Policy committed itself to the close association of tribals with the protection, preservation and development of forests and envisaged their customary rights in forests.

It is, however, a matter of serious concern that about 5000 forest villages do not have minimum basic living conditions and face a constant threat of eviction.

The National Policy suggests that any forceful displacement should be avoided. Human beings move on their own to places with better opportunities. The forest villages may be converted into revenue villages or forest villages may be developed on par with revenue villages to enable the forest villagers enjoy at least the minimum amenities and services that are available in revenue villages.

The National Policy, therefore, mandates that;

- Educational and medical facilities, electricity and communication, approach roads and such other basic amenities be provided to forest villagers.
- Public Distribution System (PDS) and Grain Banks be established to prevent food problems.
- Advanced agriculture and animal husbandry technologies be introduced so that forest villagers raise their production, incomes and economic standards.
- Bank and other institutional loans be made available for entrepreneurs with viable projects of income generation
- Tribals be given opportunities to partake in joint forest management and encouraged to form cooperatives and corporations for major forest related operations
- Integrated area development programmes be taken up in and around forest areas
- Tribals' rights in protection, regeneration and collection of minor forest produce (MFP) be recognised and institutional arrangements made for marketing such produce
- Efforts be made to eliminate exploitation by middlemen in cooperatives like Tribal Development Cooperative Corporations (TDCCs), Large Sized Multi Purpose Societies (LAMPS) and Forest Development Cooperatives by introducing minimum support prices for non agricultural produce on the lines of minimum support prices for agricultural produce.

Shifting Cultivation

In the evolution of human civilisation, shifting cultivation preceded agriculture as we know it today. In shifting cultivation, tribals do not use any mechanized tools or undertake even ploughing. A digging stick and a sickle are the usual tools. It is widely practised in whole of North-Eastern region besides the States of Andhra Pradesh, Orissa, Tamil Nadu and to some extent in Chhattisgarh and Jharkhand. Though the practice is hazardous to environment, it forms basis of life for tribals. Traditionally, shifting cultivation has been in vogue in hilly terrains where tribals have had the right on land either individually or on community basis. Because of poor yields, crops do not meet their food requirement for more than four months or so in a year.

The tribals involved in shifting cultivation do not seem to have any emotional attachment to the land as an asset or property needing care and attention as in non-tribal areas. In shifting cultivation lands, no attention is paid to the replenishment of soil fertility. Tribals merely believe in harvesting crops without putting in efforts or investments. Land is just left to nature to recoup on its own.

To handle the problem of shifting cultivation, the National Policy will focus on the following aspects:

- Land tenure system will be rationalised giving tribals right to land ownership so that they will invest their energy and resources in checking soil erosion and fertility – which have hitherto been neglected as land belonged to no one but was subject to exploitation by every one.
- Agricultural scientists will be asked to focus on shifting cultivation and evolve suitable technologies to improve production.
- The shifting cultivators will be ensured sufficient food supply through the public distribution system and grain banks. Tribals will be encouraged to raise cash crops and horticultural plantations.
- Training and extension programmes will be organised to sensitise tribals about alternative economic strategies so that they can come out of shifting cultivation.

Land Alienation

Scheduled Tribes being simple folk are often exploited to forgo their foremost important resource – land – to non-tribals. Although States have protective laws to check the trend, dispossessed tribals are yet to get back their lands. Yet, another form of land alienation takes place when States promote development projects like hydro-electric power stations and mining and industries. These developmental activities, which do not confer any benefit on tribals directly, render them landless.

The National Policy for Tribals seeks to tackle tribal land alienation by stipulating that;

- Tribals have access to village land records
- Land records be displayed at the panchayat
- Oral evidence be considered in the absence of records in the disposal of tribals' land disputes
- States prohibit transfer of lands from tribals to non-tribals

- Tribals and their representatives be associated with land surveys
- Forest tribal villagers be assigned pattas for the land under their tillage since ages
- States launching development projects take adequate care to keep tribal lands intact and when not possible, allot land even before a project takes off.

Intellectual Property Rights

Scheduled Tribes are known for their knowledge and wisdom of ethnic origin. There is, however, no legal and/or institutional framework to safeguard their intellectual property rights.

The National Policy, therefore, will aim at making legal and institutional arrangements to protect their intellectual property rights and curtailing the rights of corporate and other agencies to access and exploit their resource base.

Tribal Languages

The languages spoken by tribals-tribal languages-are treated as unscheduled languages. In the wake of changing educational scenario, many of the tribal languages are facing the threat of extinction. The loss of language may adversely affect tribal culture, especially their folklore.

The National Policy aims at preserving and documenting tribal languages. Education in the mother tongue at the primary level needs be encouraged. Books and other publications in tribal languages will be promoted.

Primitive Tribal Groups (PTGs)

Primitive Tribal Groups (PTGs) are Scheduled Tribes known for their declining or stagnant population, low levels of literacy, pre-agricultural technology, primarily belonging to the hunting and gathering stage, and extreme backwardness. They were considered as a special category for support for the first time in 1979. There are 75 Primitive Tribal Groups spread over 15 States and Union Territories. The 25 lakh PTG population constitutes nearly 3.6 per cent of the tribal population and 0.3 per cent of the country's population. PTGs have not benefited from developmental activities. They face continuous threats of eviction from their homes and lands. They live with food insecurity and a host of diseases like sickle cell anaemia and malaria. The National Policy envisages the following steps to tackle PTGs' problems:

- To boost PTGs' social image, their being stigmatized as 'primitive' shall be halted.
- Efforts shall be made to bring them on par with other Scheduled Tribes in a definite time frame. Developmental efforts should be tribe-specific and suit the local environment.
- Effective preventive and curative health systems shall be introduced.
- PTGs' traditional methods of prevention and cure shall be examined and validated.
- To combat the low level of literacy among PTGs, area and need specific education coupled with skill upgradation shall be given priority.
- Formal schooling shall be strengthened by taking advantage of 'Sarva Shiksha Abhiyan'. Trained tribal youth shall be inducted as teachers.
- Teaching shall be in tribals' mother tongue/dialect
- Considering PTGs' poverty, school-going children shall be provided incentives.
- Emphasis shall be on laid on vocational education and training.
- PTGs shall enjoy the 'right to land'. Any form of land alienation shall be prevented and landless PTGs given priority in land assignment.
- Public distribution system (PDS) shall be introduced to ensure regular food supply. Grain banks shall be established to ensure food availability during crises.
- PTGs' participation in managing forests shall be ensured to meet their economic needs and nourish their emotional attachment to forests.

REFERENCES

Chandra, Kripal : *India's Unequal Citizens : A Study of Other Backward Classes,* Manohar, New Delhi, 1994.

Chandra, Satish : *History of Medieval India*, New Delhi: Orient Longman, 2007.

Koch, Ebba: *Mughal Architecture: An Outline of Its History and Development (1526-1858),* Munich, London, 1991.

Kothari, Rajni: *Politics in India*, Boston, Little, Brown, 1970.

Papadopoulo, A.: *"Islam and Muslim Art"*, New York, Harry N. Abrams, 1979.

Chapter 8

Bhakti Movement

EMERGENCE OF BHAKTI IN BRAHMANISM

Brahmanism had to accept the growing importance of new gods like Siva and Vishnu side by side with Vedic gods like Indra and Varuna. It also assimilated many other popular deities like Vasudeva, Skanda and so on. All these led to the growth of the Bhakti cult. Around the fourth century B.C. the cult of Vasudeva was becoming popular. This is suggested by reference to it by classical authors like Megasthenes who came to the court of Chandgragupta Maurya.

The worshippers of Vasudeva submitted to Bhakti as the proper religious approach and called themselves Bhagavatas. Several epigraphs of the early Christian era bear testimony to the prevalence of the Vasudeva cult in central India and the Deccan. Simultaneously with the cult of Vasudeva arose the sect of Pasupatas, devotees of Pasupati or Siva, a fertility deity. This cult was kept alive in non-brahmanic circles from the days of the Harappan culture.

The popularity of these new gods increased during the Sunga and Kanvaa periods. Patanjali, who lived in the Sunga period, in his Mahabhashya refers to the exhibition and sale of the images of Siva, Skanda and Vishakha. These gods appear on the coins of the Kushana kings, especially Huvishka. An important characteristic of later Brahmanism was its capacity to adopt new trends.

This became necessary to meet the challenge of the 'hentical sects' which were opposed to Brahmanism. Besides adopting new gods,

Brahmanism gradually shifted its emphasis from Vedic ritual to Bhakti, which implied the cultivation and development of a personal relationship between God and the devotee. Thus a monotheistic concept of God,, with either Siva or Vishnu as his manifestation and Bhskti (loyalty and devotion) to him was gaining strength. Soon Bhakti became the dynamic force of later Brahmanism also called Hinduism.

Syncretism of Deities

An important characteristic of the new Brahmanism was its genius to syncretise many local deities and to evolve a monotheistic great God. Syncretism in this context will mean that deities worshipped at different places and by different people were recognised as identical and were worshipped as manifestation of the same supreme deity. Thus Vasudeva was identified with Vishnu, a minor Vedic god and Narayana, a god of obscure origin mentioned in the Brahmana literature.

Then Vishnu was closely connected with the name of Krishna, who represented the fusion between martial hero and a flute-playing pastoral deity. Vishnu could assimilate many other cults-the cult of the 'divine boar' which prevailed among some of the tribes of Malwa, the cult of Parasurama, a Brahamna hero; and Rama, the great hero of the Ramayana. Then Vishnu rose to the status of the Universal God in the Bhagavad Gita.

Similarly, Siva came to be syncretised with the Vedic Rudra and Bhairava, a tribal god and was worshipped in the form of the phallic emblem or linga. With Siva were later associated certain other deities such as Skanda and the elephant-headed Ganesa.

These theistic cults stressed the merit of worship rather than the performance of Vedic sacrifice.

Adaptation of Tribal Rituals

Yet another important feature of later Brahmanism was its adaptation of the tribal rituals keeping the Vedic Yajna rites supreme only in theory. In course of time the merit derived out of these new rituals were equated with the merit of the Vedic Yajna. Further, the sacred spots of the tribals were included as new places of pilgrimage (Tirtha) with suitable myths to make them respectable. The Ithihasas and Puranas are full of such material or stories which inspire bhakti (devotion) to a personal god.

Royal Support to Temples and Theism

The Puranas highlighted the merits acquired by visiting great cult centres like Mathura and Varanasi which were major places of pilgrimage. This gave a stimulus to the institution of the temple. In fact, the Puranas and other texts of the period list numerous places of pilgrimage (tirthas) which drew devotees in large numbers because visiting tirthas would ensure merit.

The temple which housed the deity, became a place of worship and thus drew devotees away from home to an institution which became a public centre. The Gupta age marked the beginning of temple construction. It laid the foundation of the typical styles of Indian temple architecture. Among the few Gupta temples which survive, the Dasavatara temple of Devagarh, the Vishnu temple at Tigawa, and the Siva temple at Bhumara are known for their beauty.

The epic and Puranic stories relating to Rama and Krishna were represented in the temple sculptures. Excellent specimens of them are still found in the Devagarh temple. The Gupta emperors patronised both Shaivism and Vaishnavism. However, the personal religion of most of the Gupta rulers was Vaishnavism which led to the creation of a number of important Vaishnava centres and Vaishnava sculptures in the Gupta period. The idea of the awataras or incarnations of Vishnu in which Vishnu is born on earth as a boar, a fish, or a human being for rescuing earth from a crisis, also seems to have been systematised in the Gupta period.

In the sixth and seventh centuries A.D. Shaivism seems to have replaced Vaishnavism as recipient of royal patronage in northern India. Shaivism counted among its followers supreme plers, foreign as well as indigenous, such as Mihirakula, Yashodharman, Sasanka and Harsha. Pasupata or Shaiva acharyas are frequently mentioned in contemporary records which include inscriptions, and many literary works like those of Varahamihira, Bana and Hiuen Tsang.

SPREAD OF BHAKTI TO THE SOUTH

All the major north Indian religions-Brahmanism, Jainism and Buddhism-travelled southwards. The Brahmanas brought with them the Vedic Yajna cult and the two theistic cults, Vaishnavism and Shaivism. The kings were in favour of the Vedic rituals as they conferred ritual status on them. The theistic cults struck root among the people. However, eventually the devotional theistic cults were to prove stronger than any other religious force in the south, and this was recognized even by royal patrons who extended support to Vaishnavism, Shaivism and their sects.

Among the early chalukya kings of Vatapi some professed Bhagavatism and others, the Pasupata cult. The famous bas-reliefs of Badami testify to the popularity of the theistic cults in the Deccan in the sixth-seventh centuries A.D. Similarly, the Pallavas of Kanchi patronised the two theistic cults as shown by the monolithic rathas (chariots) at Mahabalipuram and many bas-reliefs on them.

Bhakti, centring around the worship of specific deities, began to spread fast in the south through the brahmana settlements and temple centres where the exposition of the epics and the Puranas was institutionalized by means of munificent land grants. Thus Bhakti was popularised among the common people. It is to be noted that the way in which the Brahmanas transformed the earlier religious forms into temple-centred theistic culture in the north was repeated in the south also.

BHAKTI MOVEMENT IN SOUTH INDIA

The final form of theistic Bhakti was largely the result of the influence of the Tamil devotionalism. This devotionalism was a product of the fusion between ecstatic local tribal cults (e.g. Velan Veriyadal) and northern theistic schools. This cross fertilization started at Tiruppati and Kalahasti, which then constituted the northern door of the Tamil country.

Then it developed around Kanchipuram, the Pallava capital and soon reached the region of Madurai, the Pandyan capital. The Tiru Murugu Arruppadai, a famous devotional work on Muruga, the local tribal god who was syncretised with Skanda in this work, is the earliest example of this cross fertilization.

Soon this Tamil devotionalism developed into a great movement when it was adapted to the two theistic cults, Shaivism and Vaishnavism. Then Tamil Bhakti movement was characterized not only by intense ecstatic piety for the deity, but also an aggressive militancy against the heterodox cults which were growing in popularity among the people with royal support.

This movement was spearheaded in the sixth century A.D. by gifted poet-saints who traversed the country many times with great missionary zeal. All their way they sang their hymns, danced and debated with the heterodox cults. Among these hymnal poet-saints the Shaiva saints are called Nayanmar and the Vaishnava saints as Alvars.

This great wave of religious enthusiasm attained its peak in the early seventh century and its triumph was largely achieved in the two centuries that followed. The hymns of the saints of this period are marked by an outspoken hatred against the Buddhists and the Jainas. As a result, public debates, competition in the performance of miracles and tests of the truth of I their doctrines by means of ordeal became the order of the day..I.

There were other reasons for the success and popularity of these hymnal saints. Unlike the Brahmanas who propagated Hinduism through theories and the use of Sanskrit, the hymnal saints sang in easily understood forms using only the popular language, Tamil. Their Bhakti was not a reverence for a transcendent deity, but ecstatic love for an imminent one. Being unable to stand before the force of this Bhakti wave which also attracted royal support, Jainism and Buddhism had to retreat from the South.

PROTEST AND REFORM IN THE BHAKTI MOVEMENT

Whereas the Brahmanas were obsessed with caste regulations, the Bhakti movement not only ignored caste but also included men and women of all castes. Among the Nayanar 'Karaikkal, Amrnai was a woman and Nandanar was a member of the depressed class. Among the Alvars, Andal was a woman and Timppan was a hymnist from a "low caste". Thus the whole movement carried elements of protest and reform. However, it soon became part of the establishment, lost its early character and got engulfed by brahrnanical orthodoxy.

The Bhakti movement grew first under the Pallavas and then under the cholas, Pandyas and the Cheras. Many rock temples were cut and structural temples were built for Siva and Vishnu throughout the Tamil land by almost all the reigning monarchs.

These temples were endowed with vast landed property, often tax-free. Extensive areas of land were donated to the Brahmanas as is evident from the thousands of inscriptions on the walls of the south Indian temples. A prince-priest axis soon emerged.

The monarchs fervently welcomed the rich temple-centered bhakti (or unflinching loyalty) as it suited the monarchical ideology. The

Brahmanas welcomed this as it enabled Brahmanism, with its institutional base in the temple centred agrarian settlements, to emerge as the most dynamic force in south India.

Everywhere the local temple was the nucleus of religious life and a new social formation. In these temples the two arms of the brahmanical religion-the ritualistic Vedic cult and the theistic devotional cult-could meet. The temple-centred Bhakti enabled the all-embracing caste system to attract all the origional tribes of south India within its fold and place them in the hierarchical caste order.

This order fixed the ritual and social status of the mbes with the Brahrnana as the fixed point of reference. The ideology of Bhakti could bring together kings, priests and the common people within a network of understandable social relations. With the increasing patronage of kings and landed magnates, the Bhakti movement soon became part of the establishment. Thus all trances of dissent, protest and reform were obliterated in the tenth century A.D. The Alvars and the Nayanars do not appear any more.

Their place was taken by Vaishnava acharyas, all of whom were Brahmanas or the Saivite acharyas who all came from the rich landed Vellala caste.

THE NIRGUNA-SAGUNA MODEL OF MEDIEVAL BHAKTI MOVEMENT

The *nirguna-saguna* model of the medieval north Indian Bhakti movement emphasizes the primacy of doctrines and theological ideas in the teachings of various Bhakti leaders. This model makes a clear distinction between *nirguni sants*(such as Kabir, Raidas, Dadu etc.) and *saguni* Vaishnava Bhaktas (such as Mirabai, Surdas, Tulsidas, etc.). Modern studies of *nirguni santism* focus on its origins, its uncompromising monotheism and unique perception of God, its rejection of the orthodox Brahmanical and Islamic religions and their scriptures and, finally, its opposition to the Brahmanical caste system. On the other hand, the *saguni* Vaishnavas are seen as accepting the basic premises of the *varna* doctrine and the ritual supremacy of the Brahmans. The *nirguna-saguna* model thus underlines the two-fold theological and social division of the Bhakti movement. The *nirguna-saguna* model was first popularized by Hindi scholars such as Ramchandra Shukla, P.D.Barthwal and Parashuram Chaturvedi. Ramachandra Shukla was the first important Hindi scholar who propounded the notion of *Bhakti Kal* (the Age of Bhakti) and divided the period into two distinct theological categories; Kabir, Raidas, Dadu, etc. were placed in the *nirguna* category (due to their faith in the non-incarnate, formless God) and the Vaishnava devotees of the later period such as Surdas and Tulsidas were placed in the *saguna* category (as they championed the cause of a personal, incarnate god in a human form). Shukla's view of the medieval Bhakti movement as consisting of two distinct theological categories has since been accepted by most of the Hindi scholars irrespective of their differences with him.

P.D. Barthwal in his *The Nirguna School of Hindi Poetry*, produced one of the earliest general works in English on the *sants* and their utterances (*vanis*). His work is particularly important for the information on many obscure *sants*, in particular of the later medieval period. Barthwal's work was later superceded by Parashuram Chaturvedi's encyclopaedic study, *Uttari Bharat Ki Sant Parampara*, which gives an account of most of medieval and modern Indian *Sants*. Both Barthwal and Chaturvedi made a clear distinction, like many scholars before and after them, between *sagun* bhaktas and *nirgun sants*. The last four decades have witnessed a surge of western scholarly interest in medieval *sants*. Most of the Western scholars have depended heavily on the *nirguna-saguna* model popularized by the Hindi scholars. Tracing the doctrinal sources of Guru Nanak's religious thought, W.H. McLeod emphasized that while the religious thought of Guru Nanak was more consistent than that of Kabir, the '*Sant* tradition' or '*Nirguna Sampradaya*'provided the basis for the former's religious teachings. McLeod's expousal of such a position and his reaffirmation of it in his subsequent writings on the Sikh movement has made him the target of criticism by 'the critics of critical scholarship but it must be made clear that McLeod does not equate the *sant* tradition with Vaishnava bhakti and makes a clear distinction between the two theological traditions.

The value of the *nirguna-saguna* oppositional essences for defining the basic contours of the *sant* movement and of the religious culture shaped by it is pressed further by various contributors to the influential volume entitled *The Sants*. The contributors express their debt to the pioneering works of P.D. Barthwal and Parashuram Chaturvedi in no uncertain terms and regard the *nirguna-saguna* categories as foundational undifferentiated and monolithic. Striking the only note of discord, however, John Stratton Hawley points out that though there were differences in the theological learnings of the 'without attributes' group of *sants* and the 'with attributes' group, yet "they all inherited a single, massive bhakti". Elsewhere, much in the manner of medieval antholizers - who included the utterances of both *nirguna sants* and saguna Vaishnavites in the works compiled by them - Hawley subverts the *nirguna-saguna* dichotomy by presenting six 'saints', three of *nirguna* persuasion did the other three belonging to *saguna* leanings, in the scope of a single volume. He cites various instances of mixing up of *nirguna-saguna* categories and of the resultant breach in the theological wall. David Lorenzen, a specialist on Kabir-panth and Kabir legends, strongly supports the view that awareness of *nirguna-saguna* distinction is necessary for studying the values of medieval *sants*. Disagreeing with Hawley, Lorenzen considers the differences between the *nirguna* and *saguna* devotees more fundamental than their similarities. He does not exclude the existence of "considerable overlap" between the two categories but still justifies the distinctionas made by scholars such as Barthwal, Chaturvedi, Vaudeville and McLeod. Lorenzen, however, imparts a new dimension to the *nirguna-saguna* dichotomy by identifying the two categories with two mutually opposite social ideologies of dominance and resistance. His argument is as follows:

"Although the contrast between the *saguni* and *nirguni* traditions is usually defined in theological terms - both by outside observers and by the followers of these two traditions - it is the social ideologies of the two traditions that lie behind and give strength to these differing ideologies. And behind the ideological lie the communities themselves."

Applying the concepts of hegemony and resistance - as formulated by the Italian Marxist, Antonio Gramsci - to the religious ideas of medieval *sants*, Lorenzen concludes that the *saguna* Bhakti was elite, hegemonic and Brahmanical while *nirguna* religion was subaltern, contestory and lowercaste. However, Lorenzen's attempts to fit the *nirguna-saguna* model into his analysis of caste-based dominance and subordination in medieval India have not been entirely successful. Apart from the important qualifications that he himself introduces in his formulation (such as both *nirguna sants* and Vaishnavite devotees sharing common historical roots, popularity of certain Puranic episodes among both of them, presence of lower caste followers is in *saguna* congregations and *nirguna* appropriations of many *saguna* beliefs and practices),18 his approach does not take into account the multiple religious forms- and not just the *nirguna* form – which the *sant*-based religious culture could assume in medieval India. As we shall show in the course of this essay, when we move from the *sants* to their ordinary followers, listeners and later day venerators, the whole picture changes because the ordinary people as creative agents of history give their own meaning to the *sant* teachings. One may additionally question Lorenzen's assumption that all forms of *saguna Bhakti-* particularly its Vaishnavite version- had acquired hegemonic status during the 16th, 17th centuries and had come to serve the ideological needs of the ruling elites. Perhaps a clear distinction needs to be made here between the hegemonic, orthodox Brahmanical system and an ambivalent but increasingly popular Vaishnavite (*saguna*) movement which was pregnant with many possibilities during the 16th-17th centuries. In popular and subversive Vaishnavism, the difference between a *nirguni* sant and a *saguni* Vaishnava became blurred with the result that figures like Kabir and Namdev could be represented as Vaishnavas and nirguni *sants.*

In fact, in this subversive variant of Vaishnavism- which was reflected in the emergence of such religious fraternities as *Bairagis, Mundiyas* and *Satnamis,* not just the difference between *nirguni* and *saguni* but also between Hindu and Muslim became irrelevant.

SANT *VANIS* AND HAGIOGRAPHY

From the issues discussed above, it becomes clear that distinction between the *nirguni* and *saguni* categories of medieval north Indian Bhakti was a historical reality. John Stratton Hawley, who has otherwise focused on the erasure of this distinction in different genres of the Bhakti literature, has also acknowledged that the *nirguna-saguna* distinction "largely works". Sectarian theological boundaries in terms of *nirguni* and *saguni* doctrines did exist in the medieval Bhakti movement. However, Hawley himself has underlined the fact that this distinction was not always honoured in *sant vanis*, hagiographies and anthologies. He cites many poems of "*nirgun* persuasion" in Surdas's *bhramargit.* He also draws our attention to "alignment" between Namdev (a *nirgun sant*) and Surdas (a prominant *saguni* Vaishnava).

It may, however, be argued that the instances cited by Hawley to demonstrate a breach in the *nirguna-saguna* divide do not exhaust the subversive potential of the *sant*-based religious culture and hagiography in giving a short shrift to such theological divisions. Here it is important to shift the focus from the ideas of great *sants* to the aspirations and subversive ways of their ordinary followers who used the symbols of both the categories to oppose and ridicule the contemporary religious and political elites. As the *sant* movement grew in the course of the 16th and 17th centuries, the ordinary people remembered the great *sants* of the 15th and early 16th centuries not so much for their *nirguni* ideas as for their frontal attack on Brahmanical supermacy. The stories about the *sants* emphasize the successful assertion by them of their claims to use those sacred objects, myths and symbols that were regarded as Brahmanical or upper-caste monopoly. The subversive, transgressive and contestory character of these lower caste appropriations is also established by the ceaseless Brahmanical disapproval of them as is evident not only from the representations of Brahmans in the *sant* legends but also from texts such as Tulsidas's *Ramacharitamanasa* which in its portrayal of *Kali Yuga* (Age of Degeneration) denounces the lower castes (*shudras*) for instructing "the twice-born" in spiritual wisdom, putting on the sacred thread, accepting "abominable" alms, indulging in all sorts of prayers, penances and vows, and expounding the Puranas" from an exalted seat". Even as late as the later part of the nineteenth century, the orthodox Brahmans expressed the view that the *panthis* (low-caste, *sant*-based sects) exhibited "a lamentable ignorance of the precise force of philosophical terms - words, the property of opposed systems, being used indiscriminately ... their style is assumed to attract the vulgar, and the teaching is inconsistent and deliberately false". Brahmanical opposition to lower-caste use of various sacred objects, rituals, pilgrimage centres and customs has continued right into the twentieth century.

The limitations of the *nirguna-saguna* oppositional model became even more glaring if we consider the ways in which the images of *nirguni sants* such as Namdev, Kabir and Raidas were constantly fashioned and refashioned by their lower-caste followers. This is evident from the hagiographic narratives about these figures. Anantadas, one of the earliest hagiographers of the great *sants* of the formative period, does not use the *nigruni-saguni* distinction to sing the glory of the great miraculous deeds performed by the *sant*-heroes. It seems that before the followers of the great *sants* of the fifteenth-sixteenth centuries themselves began to record the legendary accounts of their lives, liberal Vaishnavite hagiographers such as Anantadas and Nabhadas took the lead in narrating these tales. First non- Vaishnavite reference to legends about great *sants* are to be found in the utterances of *sants* who were the first generation disciples of Dadu (1544- 1603). But by the end of the sixteenth century, two Vaishnavite hagiographers Anantadas and Nabhadas had already produced the biographical narratives of Kabir, Raidas and some other low-caste *sants* of the early period. Of these two, Anantadas was exclusively concerned with the biographies of Kabir, Namdev, Pipa, Dhanna and Raidas. The authorship of the *Parachais* of all these *sants* has been attributed to him. We have drawn frequently from the *Kabir Parachai* and *Raidas Parachai* of Anantadas. David Lorenzen believes that Anantadas composed these *Parachai* towards the closing years of the sixteenth century while Shukdev Singh is convinced that Raidas Parachai was composed in the year 1588 A.D. (V.S. 1645).40 According to Lorenzen, Anantadas was a Vaishnavite of the Ramanandi stock, though John Stratton Hawley is of the opinion that the 'historical position' of both Anantadas and Ramanand is not clear. It is, however, clear that he was deeply sympathetic to the low-caste *sants* and his *Parachai* perhaps constitute the oldest collection of *sant*-legends.

The Niranjani Panthi recession of Kabir Parachai contains thirteen sections and includes some of the most important episodes in the life of legendary Kabir. These episodes are: Ramanand's acceptance of Kabir as his disciple, God bringing a bullock's load of food to his house, various encounters between him and the Brahmans, his attempts to rid himself of increasing popularity by taking up the company of a prostitute and the resultant encounter with the Brahmans and the local ruler, the continuing Brahmanical hostility and Sultan Sikandar Lodi coming to the rescue of the Brahmans and qazis, persecution of Kabirby Sikandar Lodi in various ways, Kabir's miraculous escapes and acceptance of his greatness by the Sultan, the failure of the *apsara* to seduce Kabir in the face of his unwavering devotion to God, and finally God giving his *darshan* to Kabir. Similarly, the Raidas Parachai narrates various episodes in the life of Raidas: his previous life as a Brahman, his birth in the low-caste *chamar* family, Ramanand making him his disciple, his refusal to accept the philosopher's stone from God (Hari), his encounter with the Brahmans at the royal court becoming a 'political event', his confrontation with the Brahmans over the right to worship the *salagram*, his initiation of Jhali Rani as his disciple leading to another confrontation with the Brahmans, his debate with Kabir, his visit to Chittor and manifesting himself in many identical forms in the feast and finally his taking out the golden sacred thread from within and showing it to the king, Brahmans and others.

It is not difficult to decipher the Vaishnavite flavour in these legendary episodes. During the course of the seventeenth century, this Vaishnavite flavour of the hagiographic accounts of the lives of the *sants* became even more perceptible. However, most of these stories, especially those dealing with confrontation between the defiant *sants* on the one hand and religious authorities (mainly Brahmans) and rulers on the other, had low-caste origins. As the popularity of great *sants* such as Kabir and Raidas increased during the sixteenth and seventeenth centuries, many legends about them developed from below. Liberal-minded and sympathetic Vaishnavite hagiographers like Anantadas (late sixteenth century) and Priyadas (early eighteenth century) only appropriated these stories and reinterpreted them in Vaishnavite terms. Bhaktamal literally means 'The Garland of (Vaishnava) Devotees.' Nabhadas's Bhaktamal44 is the first major narrative of Puranic and historical bhaktas put together. It set the trend for subsequent works of this kind. According to David Lorenzen, Nabhadas, like Anantadas, was a Ramanandi and they were separated from each other by "one spiritual generation".45 Most of the scholars have placed the composition of Nabhadas's Bhaktamal around 1600 A.D., though Lorenzen is inclined to believe that it could have been composed between 1600 A.D. and 1625 A.D. Nabhadas in all likelihood belonged to a low-caste and was clearly sympathetic to devotees, both mythological and historical, who had risen to fame despite their low caste background.

Strictly speaking, Nabhadas's Bhaktamal is not a biographical work. Nor does it tell us many stories about the lives of the devotees. To use Linda Hess's phrase, it rather gives us "thumb nail" sketches of the Puranic and historical bhaktas. He does refer to occasional episodes in the lives of certain individual devotees but such references are brief and assume certain degree of knowledge of events on the part of the listners or readers. Nabhadas glorifies the devotees more in terms of their ideas, values and teachings than in terms of events in their lives. In contrast to the Parachais of Anantadas, there are no references to the happenings, actual or imagined, in the lives of Kabir and Raidas. References to the Puranic devotees are even shorter and more often than not only names are mentioned. The range of *bhaktas* mentioned by him is very wide but his narration is characterized by lack of thick description. His portrayal of Kabir has been termed "very accurate near-contemporary" perception of Kabir. However, for other images of Kabir, especially those that revolve around his supernatural anti-Brahmanical deeds and that reveal how the ordinary people fashioned a Kabir rooted in their daily experiences, we have to depend not on Nabhadas's Bhaktamal but on its subsequent expansion by other hagiographers, on Anantadas's Parachai and on *santic* hagiography.

Nabhadas's Bhaktamal, however, soon became popular among the Vaishnavites and inspired later generations of hagiographers to compose poetical narratives on the lives of the devotees. When another Vaishnavite hagiographer, Priyadas wrote a 'commentary' on Nabhadas's Bhaktamal in the beginning of the eighteenth century, he claimed that in the course of his remembering the name of Chaitanya, Nabhadas himself appeared to him and commanded him to narrate the lives of the *Bhaktas* in greater details. Here one must note that while Nabhadas was a Ramanandi (and hence a Ramaite), Priyadas, as is clear from his above-mentioned claim, was a Krishnaite belonging to the Gaudiya Vaishnava sect of Vrindavan. Nabhadai's bhaktamal overcame various sub-sectarian differences among the Vaishnavites and became a pan-Vaishnavite text *par excellence*. Perhaps only the more sectarian Vaishnavas of the Vallabhite *Pushti Marga* sect seemed to have remained relatively uninfluenced by the popularity of Nabhadas's Bhaktamal. Even the *santic* hariographic narratives, such as Raghodas's Bhaktamal, came to be modelled on Nabhadas's work. Priyadas insists that however great a *bhakta* may be in terms of his all-round devotion, it is necessary for him to keep Nabhadas's Bhaktamal in his heart in order to comprehend the real nature of devotion. Popularity of Nabhadas's Bhaktamal, particularly among Vaishnavites, during the later and late medieval periods is also indicated by the esteem in which the work was held by Mahipati, the author of Marathi hagiographic text, *Bhaktavijaya*. Mahipati, expressing his gratitude to Nabhadas for his information, writes that Nabhaji (i.e. Nabhadas) lived in the "country to the North" and was an incarnation of Brahmadev. He "wrote a great book containing the stories of saints." He again writes that Nabhadas was "a chief jewel among Vaishnavas" and that he wrote "very extraordinary history of the bhaktas"and after reading this book he wrote his own work in Marathi. Referring to the greatness of various Puranic and historical devotees, Charandas, a prominent eighteenth century *sant*, informs us that it is these *Bhaktas* whose devotion was narrated by Nabhadas.

Priyadas composed his *Bhaktirasabodhini* in A.D. 1712. This work has been treated as a commentary on Nabhadas's Bhaktamal but it is more appropriate to look upon it as an expanded version of the original work. It is a full-fledged hagiographic work written by a broad-minded Vaishnava from Vrindavan. While excluding individual devotees who do not find mention in Nabhadas's Bhaktamal or who may have attained fame during the course of the seventeenth century, Priyadas gives detailed narratives of various episodes in the lives of Puranic and historical devotees who have been treated fleetingly by the original author. Some of the great religious figures of the sixteenth century -

such as Guru Nanak, his spiritual successors and Dadu - have been excluded from Priyadas's expanded version perhaps because the original author,Nabhadas deliberately overlooked them. It cannot be argued that Nabhadas was unaware of Guru Nanak who had acquired greater fame by the end of the sixteenth century than many other sixteenth century devotees who have been mentioned in the Bhaktamal. One is tempted to explain this notable exclusion in terms of the growing distinct religious identity of the Sikh movement which may have made it difficult even for such a catholic Vaishnava as Nabhadas to look upon Guru Nanak and other Sikh gurus of the sixteenth century as Vaishnavas. It may also be stressed here that most of the sixteenth century devotees mentioned in Nabhadas's Bhaktamal and Priyadas's Bhaktirasabodhini belonged to, or were associated with, regions which came under increasing Vaishnavite influence during the sixteenth and seventeenth centuries. There is not much evidence to suggest the presence of a strong Vaishnavite movement in the Punjab and north-western part of the country during this period. It may not be far from truth to suggest that for most part of the later and late medieval periods, the region beyond Thaneshwar remained some kind of prohibited zone and terra incognita for the leading Vaishnavite preachers like Vallabhacharya, though some of his followers did establish a branch of *Pushti Marga* in some towns on the bank of river Indus.56 A leading authority on the Krishnaite sects of the Braj regions tells us that the Punjab and north-western India remained largely isolated from the Vaishnavite centres of northern India during the later medieval period. So far as the omission of Dadu in Nabhadas's Bhaktamal is concerned, it was impossible to appropriate the memory of a living, or recently dead, non- Vaishnavite figure while it was relatively easier to do so in the case of temporally distant figures such as Kabir and Raidas. Priyadas could not include Dadu in his *Bhaktirasabodhini* as he was bound by the names provided to him by Nabhadas's Bhaktamal but another Vaishnavite hagiographer of the eighteenth century, Mahipati does mention the name of 'Dadu Pinjari' as a devotee of "perfect delight". It is clear from the above mentioned cases of exclusion that Vaishnavite ideological considerations did play a role in Nabhadas's scheme of things. Most of Priyadas's information on the low-caste *sants* seems to have come from Anantadas's Parachai or from stories that were already in circulation.

The *Bhaktavijaya* of Mahipati (1715-1790) contains large number of verses on the lives of the low caste *sants* of medieval India. There are also the detailed descriptions of the lives of Namdev and other *sants* of medieval Maharashtra. Mahipati was born in family of *Varkari* pilgrims and subjects the lives of Kabir and other *sants* to extreme Vaishnavization. Raidas is mentioned as Rohidas. Mahipati's work clearly indicates that the stories about the lives of major medieval *sants* such as Kabir and Raidas had spread beyond northern India into the Deccan during the course of the seventeenth and eighteenth centuries. Jan Gopal's *Dadu Janma Lila* was written about two decades after the death of Dadu in 1603. The work, which is the first important, full-fledged santic hagiographic account, underwent many interpolations later. The legendary episodes of Dadu's life, particularly his meeting with Akbar, are important for throwing light on the political perceptions of the ordinary followers of the *sants*.

The first important Bhaktamal in the *sant* tradition is that of Raghodas. According to its editor, it was written around 1660 A.D. Most of the scholars are, however, convinced that it could not have been written before the second decade of the 18th century. Raghodas's Bhaktamal is modelled on the Bhaktamal of Nabhadas. It deals with about twelve hundred *sants*. Many of them were the followers of Dadu and other great *sants*. The commentary by Chaturdas was written around 1800 A.D. Another important Bhaktamal in the Dadupanthi tradition is that of Brahmadas. Most of the Kabirpanthi sectarian literature consists of various 'sagars' and 'bodhs'. Most of them were composed in the early 19th century, though *Anuragsagar* is believed to have been written in the late eighteenth century. *Anuragsagar* is the earliest work written by the Kabirpanthis of Chhatisgarh. The work soon came to acquire different forms and many interpolations have crept into it. The most important aspect of this work is that it offers considerable information on early Kabirpanthi notions of cosmos and time. It also mentions various incarnations of Kabir in previous *Yugas*.

It is important to point out that althoiugh the Vaishnavite hagiographic accounts of the *sants* do contain ideological bias and add Vaishnavite flavour to various episodes in the lives of the *sants*, they are still important from the viewpoint of identifying non-Brahmanical elements in the legends. What is required is to remove the superficial Vaishnavite coating and penetrate beneath it. Moreover, we should remember that there were spheres where Vaishnavite and santic interests converged - both were against orthodox Brahmans and their dominance. The Shaivite and Smarta Brahmans are scoffed at as much in the Vaishnavite hagiography as in the *santic* versons. Most of the hagiographic accounts, whether composed by Vaishnavas such as Priyadas or by *Santic* ideologues such as Raghodas, clearly overlook the *nirguni-saguni* distinction while narrating the episodes in the lives of the great *sants*. What they highlight is the confrontation between the *sants* and politicalreligious elites in busy market-places, temples and pilgrimage centres. Vaishnava symbols and artifacts are shown as being more helpful to the *sants* than to the Brahmans.

BRAHMANICAL REACTION AND VAISHNAVITE CONSERVATISM

In the absence of any direct evidence, it is difficult to surmise the extent to which the all-pervasive prevalence of the vibrant *sant*-inspired religious culture of the seventeenth century eroded the ideological and cultural basis of Brahamanism. We begin to come across large body of archival evidence which shows that the Rajput and Maratha states of the eighteenth century sought to enforce caste rules and religous norms rigourously. It may be pointed out that the increasing attempts of the eighteenth century states to regulate the society in accordance with the principles of Brahmanical ideology could not have been undertaken without the prior violation, transgression and subversion of caste and religious norms.

Historians have highlighted various measures introduced by the eighteenth century Rajput and Maratha states to punish such violations. Brahamanical influence increased under the Peshwa rule. A.R. Kulkarni has cited many cases where the Peshwa state enforced rigid caste regulations with the help of various bodies of Brahmans such as Brahma Sabha, Dharma Sabha etc. Peshwa Narayan Rao deprived the Prabhus, who had been uplifted from the shudra status to that of Kshatriyas, were deprived of their newly acquired caste identity and were prohibited the use of Vedic *mantras* and ceremonies. The Peshwa state tightened the functioning of the caste system, suppressed the lower castes and enforced religious discipline. The worships of God Vitthala at Pandharpur, which was popular among all sections of the society, was brought under the control of Peshwa state and the 'untouchable' social groups were prohibited to enter the main temple there and threatened with punishment if they violated the state regulation.

Evidence for similar acts of state suppression of religious assertion by the lower castes has come from eighteenth century Rajasthan as well. Sawai Raja Jai Singh, who was one of the most powerful rulers in northern India during the first half of the eighteenth century, attempted to revive and strengthen the Vedic system of worship in accordance with orthodox Brahmanical system. He imposed restrictions on various non-conformist religious communities such as Vairagis, Sanyasis and Ramanandis. The Vairagis were told not to carry arms and both the Vairagis and Nagas were made to pledge that they would not fight against each other. Various Vaishnavite groups were required to come to terms with the Vedic mode of orthodox Brahmanical worship. Various Vaishnavite sects of the sixteenth and seventeenth centuries had emerged in opposition to the orthodox Brahmanical mode of worship. The Vaishnavites were clearly hostile towards the Shaktas and Smartas, as is evident from the Nabhadas's Bhaktamal and the Vallabhite *Vartas*. The additude of the 17th century Vaishnavites towards the Vedas and Vedic forms of worship was one of indifference, if not defiance. Vaishnavite preachers such as Tulasidas did acknowledge the authority of the Vedas and even invoked it in their narratives. Such a practice, however, should be viewed in terms of their attempts to impart legitimacy to various innovations in religious beliefs and practices. Another important feature of the seventeenth century Vaishnavite religious culture was its liberal attitude towards the lower castes.

The eighteenth century states increasingly prevented the liberal-minded Vaishnavite sects from carrying out their religious innovations. From the *sammatipatras* (bonds) signed between the leaders of various sects and the Jaipur state authorities, it becomes evident that the Vaishnavites and non- Brahmanical sects came under increasing pressure from the state to give up their religious and social radicalism. The practice of allowing the *shudras* to worship *salagram* was prevalent among many Vaishnavite groups. The eighteenth century Jaipur state clearly considered such a practice contrary to the Vedic principles and asked the Vaishnavite leaders to bring it to an end. The Vaishnavite were also required not to associate with the *shudras.* The activities of various non-Brahmanical sects such as Laldasis (or Lalpanthis) and Dadupanthis were also restricted by the Jaipur state of the eighteenth century. Laldasis or Lalpanthis were the low-caste followers of Laldas, a seventeenth century Meo *sant* whose teachings were similar to those of Kabir. The Jaipur state of the eighteenth century required the Lalpanthis to give an undertaking that they would observe the principles of Vaishnava *dharma.* Most stringent Brahmanical restrictions were imposed on the Dadupanthis. They were made to agree that they "would follow the principles of *shastras* as desired by the Maharaja and would have no contacts with the Muslims." This is very significant because throughout the seventeenth century Dadupanth was a non-Brahmanical community of *sants* and their followers. It is quite clear that the eighteenth century Jaipur state tried to curb the subversive practices of the Dadupanthis and imposed Brahmanical system of values on them. There is an interesting evidence from the late eighteenth century Jodhpur Kingdom which clearly shows state's concern for caste and religious discipline in the society. The state required the local officials to prevent the persons belonging to the lowest castes from carrying the pitchers filled with the holy water from the Ganges while persons belonging to 'Hindu' castes such as Rajputs, Jats and Malis were allowed to do so.

Strengthening of the state control over the transgressive religious practices of the lower castes and resurgence of a Brahmanical ideology which gained sustenance from the Rajput and Maratha States of the eighteenth century were not the only factors that constrained the growth of non- Brahmanical sects. Vaishnavism, which had largely ignored the ties of caste and recruited its adherents from all castes including the lowest, was increasingly acquiring a conservative character during the eighteenth century. Although the Vaishnavite movement never questioned caste as the basic principle of ordering society, many Vaishnavite sects of the seventeenth century developed an egalitarian orientation. David Lorenzen has suggested that religious and social conservatism began to grow in the Ramanandi order in its early phase. Such a view, however, is not borne out by facts. During most of the 16th century, the Ramanandi order retained its liberal religious character and recruited persons of both sexes and castes including 'untouchables'. Ramanandi hagiographers such as Anantadas and Nabhadas glorified the values and deeds of many low-caste devotees. The great Vaishnavite preacher, Ramanand came to be represented in popular memory as the Brahman teacher of various low caste *sants*. The Vaishnavite congregations of the seventeenth century had a participatory character and were open to all castes and social groups. As is evident from the testimonies of texts such as the *Vallabhite Vartas* Bhaktamal of Nabhadas, Anantadas's Parachais and Tulasidas's *Ramcharitmanas*, the seventeenth century Vaishnavite sects accomodated rather yjsm excluded lower castes. The names of many lower caste followers of the *Pushti Margi* preachers have been mentioned in the *Do Sau Bavan Vaishnavan Ki Varta*.

Vaishnavism was gradually becoming a state ideology during the eighteenth century. In lieu of state patronage, the Vaishnavites had to abserve the caste rules and give up its liberal and sympathetic attitutde towards the lower castes. Citing the case of transformation of Vaishnavism into a state ideology in later medieval Maharashtra, D.D. Koshambi points out that while originally Bhakti began as a form of protest against oppression prepetuated through Brahmanical superstitions, the feudal order ultimately imposed its own limitations and "the reforms and its struggle was never conciously directed against ferdalism so that its very success meant feudal patronage and ultimately feudal decay by diversion of democratic movement into the dismal channels of conquest." While Nabhadas's Bhaktamal and the early eighteenth century commentary by Priyadas reflect the great capacity of seventeenth century Vaishnavites to accomodate the lower castes and glorify the lower caste Bhaktas, most of the eighteenth century is marked by growing Vaishnavite conservatism. Even the Vairagi sect which incorporated people from different castes and religions in its fold during the seventeenth century, became socially restrictive in the eighteenth century. The Ramanandis began to seek royal patronage to defend their newly acquired prestige and religious power. The eighteenth century states, in turn, increasingly patronised conservative Vaishnavite sects and ascetic orders.

Paradoxically, while various Vaishnavite sects such as Ramanandis and Vairagis increasingly became status quoist and developed full-fledged Brahmanical tendencies, popular Vaishnavism reached new heights in the course of the eighteenth century. Vaishnavite preachers and story-tellers took the Rama and Krishna cults to regions which had hitherto been beyond the influence of Vaishnavism. The *Ramcharitmanas* of Tulasidas was slowly but steadily acquiring the status of a "social epic" in various regions of northern India. It was read, sung and enacted on various occasions and became popular among the common people and elites alike. Different sections of society interpreted its contents in different ways. While the ruling elites used it to maintain status quo, the oppressed people, particularly peasants, interpreted its contents in subversive ways, especially during times of crisis and hardship. The *Ramcharitmanas* made available a language that enabled the oppressed social groups to vent their feelings against the agents of the state. In an important study, Philip Lutgendorf has emphasized the increasing popularity of the *Ramcharitmanas* from eighteenth century onwards. The *Manas-Katha* tradition and the *Ramleelas* (dramatized enactment of the episodes described in the *Ramcharitmanas*) played important role in making the epic popular among the peasants and other oppressed groups. The facts that the epic contained many passages which denigrate the lower castes and women and which advocate an ideal social order based on the hierarchical concept of *varna-ashrama-dharma* became irrelevant as the epic could be read and understood differently by different sectionsof society. While the elites could interpret the concept of *Ramraj* in terms of a hierarchical socio-political order in which the lower castes would know their limits, the common people belonging to the lower casts and peasantry could understand the same concept in terms of an ideal society in which all would be free and equal irrespective of their caste and class. By the end of the eighteenth and beginning of the nineteenth century, Krishnaite and Ramaite forms of Vaishnavism had become popular among many sections of the subordinate social groups in various parts of northern India. The popularity of Vaishnavism seriously restricted the scope of non-Brahmanical sects. However, in regions where Vaishnavism was not very popular (such as western Rajasthan and the Punjab), non- Brahmanical religions continued to spread among the common people. This, to some extent, explains the growing popularity of the Sikh movement in the Punjab and Bishnoi religion in western Rajasthan.

REFERENCES

Creswell, K. A. C.: *A Short Account of Early Muslim Architecture*, Aldershot, Adlohoc, 1989.

Crowe, S.: "*The Gardens of Mughal India*", Oxford, London, 1972.

Kumar, Pradip : *Social Mobility and Caste Violence: A Study of the Gujarat Riots*, Delhi, Adjanta Publications, 1985.

Lai, K.S., *History of the Khaljis*, Asia Publishing House, Bombay, 1967.

Peter Jackson - *Delhi Sultanate: A Political and Military History*, Cambridge University Press,1999.

Chapter 9

Art and Culture of Mughal

MUGHAL PAINTING

Mughal painting reflects an exclusive combination of Indian, Persian and Islamic styles. As the name suggests, these paintings evolved as well as developed during the rule of Mughal Emperors in India, between 16th to 19th century. The Mughal paintings of India revolved around themes, like battles, court scenes, receptions, legendary stories, hunting scenes, wildlife, portraits, etc. The Victoria and Albert Museums of London house a large and impressive collection of Mughal paintings.

ABU AL-HASAN (MUGHAL PAINTER)

Abu al-Hasan (b. 1589, d. c. 1630), from Delhi, India, was a Mughal painter under the reign of Jahangir.

Abu al-Hasan was the son of Aqa Reza of Herat in western Afghanistan, a city with an artistic tradition. Aqa Reza had taken up employment with Jahangir before the latter's accession to the throne of the Mughal empire.

Abu al-Hasan was initially trained by the emperor himself in his large studios and workshops but soon surpassed his father and his employer. Jahangir siad of him that he had no equal and bestowed the title *Nadir-uz-Saman* ("Wonder of the Age") on him.

Abu al-Hasan's main task was the documentation of events at the imperial court, which resulted in many superb portraits. Not many of

Abu al-Hasan's paintings survived, but those that identify him as the artist show that he also worked on a range of subjects including some everyday scenes.

The most famous painting associated with his name, "Squirrels in a Plane Tree" held in the British Library is a masterful depiction of animal posture and movement that could only have been derived from direct observation. Since the painting depicts European squirrels unknown in India his work suggests that Jahangir's zoo may have held a few of these animals. Alternatively Abu al-Hasan may have accompanied Jahangir on one of his travels. The signature on the painting is confusing;*Nadir al-Asr* ("Miracle of the Age") is the title of Ustad Mansur, not of Abu al-Hasan, but the painting is definitely not Ustad Mansur's style. It is possible that both painters collaborated on this painting.

This illustration by the Mughal court artists Miskin and Shankar depicts Adham Khan, foster brother of the Mughal emperor Akbar (r.1556–1605), being thrown from the palace walls at Agra, north-west India. This was his punishment for having burst into the private apartments of the palace with his companions, one of whom had stabbed the emperor's prime minister to death. The different episodes of the incident are shown concurrently. Akbar emerges from his sleeping quarters, sword in hand, having been awoken by the commotion. He orders the immediate death of Adham Khan, who is thrown from the terrace.

The painting is from the Akbarnama (Book of Akbar), commissioned by Akbar as the official chronicle of his reign. The Akbarnama was written in Persian by his court historian and biographer, Abul Fazal, between 1590 and 1596, and the V&A's partial copy of the manuscript is thought to have been illustrated between about 1592 and 1595. This is thought to be the earliest illustrated version of the text, and drew upon the expertise of some of the best royal artists of the time. Many of these are listed by Abul Fazal in the third volume of the text, the A'in-i Akbari, and some of these names appear in the V&A illustrations, written in red ink beneath the pictures, showing that this was a royal copy made for Akbar himself. After his death, the manuscript remained in the library of his son Jahangir, from whom it was inherited by Shah Jahan. The V&A purchased the manuscript in 1896 from Frances Clarke, the widow of Major General John Clarke, who bought it in India while serving as Commissioner of Oudh between 1858 and 1862.

MUGHAL MINIATURES REVEAL THE BIG PICTURE

In the world of the visual arts of India, Robert Skelton needs no introduction. As one of the foremost postwar authorities on Indian painting and fine objects, he started as a young and enthusiastic scholar in the 1950s at the Victoria and Albert Museum under William G. Archer, who had been in the Indian Civil Service before the war. Until this time, Western scholarship on India was expected to be in the hands of those who had served there, but times were changing and a new breed of scholar with a fresh viewpoint was emerging.

Archer soon recognised Skelton's sharp and critical powers of observation, which led to a thorough re-evaluation of the museum's Mughal miniatures. Skelton was later in charge of the Indian collections and nurtured many young scholars, not just in the museum, but worldwide. It is not surprising that he is admired by all those involved with Indian art.

Arts of Mughal India is a finely produced volume presenting a number of essays, mainly, but not exclusively, on Indian painting, written by Skelton's eminent friends and colleagues. The book opens with reminiscences by three old friends, Pramod Chandra, Simon Digby and Stuart Cary Welch, and is followed by a select bibliography of Skelton's publications that may not appear extensive but shows his wide knowledge of all aspects of Indian art and includes a paper on Shah Jahan's wine cup, one of the V&A's finest Mughal jade objects, obtained through his efforts. The essays follow. Daniel Ehnbom discusses a single painting from the *Hamzanama,* a magical and heroic tale of the legendary Persian hero Amir Hamza. The work, apparently painted in the early days of Akbar's court, is almost entirely Persian in style and detail, and Ehnbom recalls the formative influence of Persian artists, in this case the celebrated Mir Sayyid 'Ali, on Mughal court painting.

In the next essay, Welch demonstrates a similar influence through the illustrations of the *Shahnama,* the great Persian epic that was at the time also regarded as history, illustrated by Mir Sayyid 'Ali. Welch compares the *Shahnama* illustration with another painting attributed to Mir Sayyid 'Ali and comments on the extent of the influence on Indian art of the older Persian masters at the height of their powers. This paper should have perhaps been the opening essay.

Linda York Leach's essay is on the illustrations of a royal copy of the *Akbarnama,* an official history of the Emperor Akbar, many illustrated copies of which were produced in the Mughal court in the late 16th century and given to princes and courtiers. Persian influence is still present in this example, but elements such as costumes and architectural features are Indian.

In spite of the early Mughals' leanings towards Persia, book illustration had long antecedents in pre-Mughal India, for both Hindu and Muslim works.

The influence of such illustrations on Mughal works is explored in essays by B. N. Goswamy on a series of paintings of the time of Akbar depicting the Hindu goddess Devi Mahatmya, and by Asok Kumar Das on paintings related to a number of copies of the *Razmnama,* a Persian translation of the *Mahabharata* epic. Non-Muslim regional book illustration is presented in essays by Shridhar Andhare and Catherine Glynn, while Joachim K. Bautze studies the Rajput wall-paintings at Karwar, Rajasthan. This is a pioneering work on the subject because Rajasthan is a region where there are many Rajput palaces with fine wall paintings awaiting investigation, among them the private rooms of the palace at the fort of Nagaur.

For Mughal painting in its maturity, we should turn to studies presented by Terence McInerney, John Seyller and Milo Cleveland Beach. Friedericke Weis introduces yet another influence on later Mughal art, European imports to India through Portuguese trade; and Barbara Brend writes on the possible influence of European botanical illustration.

Europeans and Mughal India are also represented in a number of essays. Nuno Vassallo e Silva goes back a step and discusses the treasures presented by the Portuguese to the Sultan of Gujarat even before the appearance of the Mughals. None of these well-documented treasures has survived, but the records are of considerable interest for understanding the initial attitude of the Portuguese towards the local powers. Gauvin Alexander Bailey, on the other hand, discusses the Catholic churches founded by Portuguese Jesuit missions in Mughal India. Ebba Koch, in turn, looks at the influence of Mughal painting in Europe, not just through Rembrandt's well-known version of a Mughal miniature, but through a detailed study of the Mughal-style wall paintings at the Schonbrunn Palace at Vienna. These paintings, although Europeanised, are clearly based on specific Mughal miniatures.

Other aspects of the arts are not neglected. Manuel Keene studies Mughal jewellery, and Rai Anand Krishna a group of Rajasthani painted panels from Jaisalmer. Navina N. Haidar Haykel writes on painted and lacquered papier-mache objects, mainly pen boxes, of the late 17th and early 18th century that are closely linked with Iranian traditions of the same period.

There is much to study here, particularly on the Iranian side. If Mughal painting originally owes much to the earlier Persian masters, at the end of the Mughal period and after their fall there seems to have been a migration of Indian artists to Iran, but little attention has been paid to their influence, evident in pen box decoration and miniature painting. The book ends with essays by Debra Diamond and J. P. Losty on late-Mughal cartography, a subject that provides a wealth of material for those interested in the architecture and urban planning of the period.

Credit for the production of this attractive volume should go to the editors, colleagues of Skelton who have also each contributed a paper.

Rosemary Crill writes on a piece of 17th or early 18th-century chintz *(qalamkari)* painted and dyed with floral borders and animal and birds surrounding a medallion in the middle. Through comparative material, she demonstrates how far textile design in India benefited from the international textile trade, which spread patterns and design worldwide.

What could have perhaps been added is the close similarity of the treatment of the birds and even the background colours of this textile with those of the wall paintings of Ali Qapu at Isfahan. Susan Stronge's contribution is on Robert Hughes, a merchant and amateur artist in India during the reign of the Emperor Jahangir. With the help of an Armenian, who apparently knew English and Persian, Hughes produced a little-known Persian dictionary with Persian words transliterated in Roman letters. For philologists, this book could be a mine of information on how Persian was pronounced in Mughal India.

Finally, Andrew Topsfield discusses the representation of court musicians in the paintings of the Udaipur Rajputs in the late 17th and early 18th century. Through a number of paintings, he surveys court traditions concerning music and musicians. His work is a rare attempt to reinvestigate cultural history not just through written material but through physical evidence-a useful model for young scholars to begin looking at Indian miniatures not only as art objects but in a wider perspective, as documents of social and cultural history.

Admirers of Indian visual arts will find this book an up-to-date and informative work with finely produced illustrations. It will serve as a reference tool for scholars for years to come.

MUSIC IN MUGHAL INDIA

Tansen the famous singer at Akbar's court is credited with having enriched the Hindustani school by composing many new melodies or ragas. One of the most popular of these was the raga Darbari. Jahangir and ShahJahan continued patronizing music in the royal court. New styles of singing such as the khayal and thumri became popular. However music in all forms continued to be patronized by Aurangzeb's queens and by the nobles. That is the reason for largest number of books on classical Indian music in Persian were written during Aurangzeb's reign. But some of the most important developments in the field of music took place only in the 18 century during the reign of Muhammad Shah.

Tansen

Considered as the greatest musician in India, Tansen (1506-1589) is instrumental in the creation of the classical music that dominates the north of India. He was considered as one of the Navaratnas (Nine Gems) in the court of Emperor Akbar. Tansen was born in a Hindu family in a place called Gwalior located in Madhya Pradesh. His father was a famous poet by the name of Mukund Mishra. Tansen was named Tannu Mishra when he was born. To know more about the fascinating life history of this great musician, go through this biography of Mian Tansen.

He received the prefix "Mian" from Emperor Akbar. As a young boy, Tansen learnt music from his Guru, Shri Haridas Swamy. He was considered to be a legendary teacher of that time. It is said that Tansen has no equal apart from his teacher. Such was his passion for music that he is said to have performed astonishing miracles merely by singing. He could bring rain by singing in a particular Raag known as Megh Malhar. Similarly he could start a fire by singing in Raag Deepak. He has also composed several Ragas that have been the foundation of classical music like Bhairav, Darbari Todi, Darbari Kanada, Malhar, Sarang and Rageshwari.

There is no particular evidence of the origin of each and every school of music. Since he is the greatest musician, every school of music tries to trace its origin from him. The Dhrupad style of music is likely to have been started by him and his Guru. Some of his important works on music are the Rajmala and Sangeet Sara. Such was the power of his music that when he used to sing in the court of Akbar, candles used to light up automatically. Even today, Tansen is considered to be the greatest of all and there is no comparison when it comes to his style of singing. His contribution to the world of music is priceless and is still worshipped by leading singers and composers of the world.

PERSIAN INFLUENCE ON MUGHAL MUSIC

The advent of Islamic rule under the Delhi Sultanate and later the Mughal Empire over northern India caused considerable cultural interchange. Increasingly, musicians received patronage in the courts of the new rulers, who in their turn, started taking increasing interest in local music forms. While the initial generations may have been rooted in cultural traditions outside India, they gradually adopted many aspects from their kingdoms which retained the traditional Hindu culture. This helped spur the fusion of Hindu and Muslim ideas to bring forth new forms of musical synthesis like qawwali and khayal.

The most influential musician from the Delhi Sultanate period was Amir Khusrau (1253-1325), sometimes called the father of modern Hindustani classical music. A prolific composer in Persian, Turkish, Arabic, as well as Braj Bhasha, he is credited with systematizing many aspects of Hindustani music, and also introducing several ragas such as Yaman Kalyan, Zeelaf and Sarpada. He created the qawwali genre, which fuses Persian melody and beat on a dhrupad like structure. A number of instruments (such as the sitar and tabla) were also introduced in his time.

Amir Khusrau is sometimes credited with the origins of the khayal form, but the record of his compositions do not appear to support this. The compositions by the court musician Niyamat Khan (*Sadarang*) in the court of Muhammad Shah 'Rangiley' bear a closer affinity to the modern khyal, and suggests that while khyal already existed in some form, 'Sadarang' may have been the father of modern day khyal.

Much of the musical forms innovated by these pioneers merged with the Hindu tradition, composed in the popular language of the people (as opposed to Sanskrit) in the work of composers like Kabir or Nanak. This can be seen as part of a larger Bhakti tradition, (strongly related to the Vaishnavite movement) which remained influential across several centuries; notable figures include Jayadeva (11th century), Vidyapati

(1375 AD), Chandidas (14th-15th century), and Meerabai (1555-1603 AD).

As the Mughal Empire came into closer contact with Hindus, especially under Jalal ud-Din Akbar, music and dance also flourished. Particularly, the legendary musician Tansen is recognized as having introduced a number of innovations, ragas as well as particular compositions. Legend has it that upon his rendition of a night-time raga in the morning, the entire city fell under a hush and clouds gathered in the sky, or that he could light fires by singing raga Deepak, which is supposed to be composed of notes in high octaves.

At the royal house of Gwalior, Raja Mansingh Tomar (1486-1516 AD) also participated in the shift from Sanskrit to the local idiom (Hindi) as the language for classical songs. He himself penned several volumes of compositions on religious and secular themes, and was also responsible for the major compilation, the *Mankutuhal* (book of curiosity), which outlined the major forms of music prevalent at the time. In particular, the musical form known as dhrupad saw considerable development in his court and remained a strong point of the Gwalior gharana for many centuries.

After the dissolution of the Mughal empire, the patronage of music continued in smaller princely kingdoms like Lucknow, Patiala, and Banaras, giving rise to the diversity of styles that is today known as gharanas. Many musician families obtained large grants of land which made them self sufficient, at least for a few generations (e.g. the Sham Chaurasia gharana). Meanwhile the Bhakti and Sufi traditions continued to develop, and interact with the different gharanas and groups.

MUGHAL CONTRIBUTION TO INDIAN LITERATURE

The Mughals established a mighty empire that dominated India for more than two centuries. Their passion for literature and knowledge commissioned excellent literary works. They add luster and wealth to the literatures of India.

Printing in India

Most of the Indian literatures were in palm leaves till the arrival of the printing technology in the sixteenth century. Printing was a turning point in the Indian history. It came with the missionary movement of the Portuguese and others. Fifty-nine years after the landing of Vasco da Gama in India, the printing press opened its account at Goa, a few decades after the beginning of the 16th century. Within a hundred years of the printing of Gutenberg's Bible in Germany, India initiated its groping towards fashioning of types for the many Indian languages.

Mughal Empire which was established in the north in the sixteenth century and the Vijayanagara Empire in the south witnessed the changes that were brought by the printing technology in India.

Mughal Contribution To Literature

There was tremendous literary activity during the Mughal period, because with the return of a stable and prosperous empire. There was once again patronage for the literary works. Languages like Persian, Sanskrit, Hindi and Urdu saw tremendous creative activity as did many vernacular languages. The Mughal Emperors, themselves interested in literature, encouraged literary contributions. Vast number of works were written during the period of the Mughals.

The Three Categories of Contributions

We can easily divide the contributions of the Mughals into three categories: historical works, translations, poetry and novels. Our understanding of the Mughal period was greatly enhanced by these books, and most of the historical works of this period provide us with a fairly reliable source of information. The important historical works written in this time were Ain-I-Akbari, and Akbarnama by Abul Fazal, the Tarikh-I-Alfi by Mulla Daud. Akbar, though was not educated in any formal educational institution, could contribute much to literature.

Jehangir possessed a keen interest in literature, and his autobiography is one of the finest amongst the Mughal emperors. During his reign important historical works like Maasir-I-Jahangir, the Igbalnamah-I-Jahangiri and the Zubud-ut-Tawaikh were written.

Great Translations

Many important works in translation were also written during this period, with the translation of the epics, the Mahabharata and the Ramayana taking place. Many of the Vedas were also translated and several previous historical books were also translated. All this translation added to the wealth of Indian literature and spread ancient knowledge to a greater audience. This renewed interest in Indian literature would be an important tool used by the social reformers of the eighteenth century to educate the people about what the ancient texts really said as opposed to the distorted interpretations that were being followed.

New Contributions

The Mughal empire encouraged a large number of poets and writers and hence there were a lot of new contributions published in this era.

During the reign of Akbar, Jehangir and Shah Jahan the literary people had tremendous patronage and many remarkable works were composed. Since the Mughal emperors had integrated themselves into Indian society, they patronized many Indian languages leading to some good quality literature being developed for these languages. The main themes of the period were essentially religious, covering most of the major religions of the period.

One of the fine Hindu works composed during this time was Ramcharitmanasa (the life of Rama) by Tulsidasa, which was a simplified version of the Ramayana. In Bengal there was a lot of work being created in Vaishnava literature. Writers like Krishnada and Kaviraj were popular authors of the time. Many biographies were also written during this period.

Valuable Contributions

The Mughals established a mighty empire that dominated India for more than two centuries. Their passion for nature and literature contributed much for the Indian literature. Books were very precious to the Mughal kings. Expensive and laborious contributions were as marked the symbols of royal wealth, power and intelligence.

At the height of the Mughal power, the imperial studios hummed with the activity of hundreds papermakers, printers and business people of books. Today we can see and enjoy the books and manuscripts illustrated with exquisite miniature paintings of the Mughal Emperors treasured by museums around the world. The Mughal contribution to the Indian literatures is really great.

BEGINNINGS OF MUGHAL ARCHITECTURE

By 1544, Humayun reached Iran and found refuge in the Safavid court of Shah Tahmasp. The affiliation between the deposed Mughal and this Safavid king was not a comfortable one, since Shah Tahmasp insisted that Humayun embrace Shiism just as Babur had been forced to do some years earlier. However, Shah Tahmasp's support eventually enabled Humayun to regain the Mughal throne in 1555. These years in Iran introduced Humayun not only to Safavid painters and painting but also to the architecture of Herat and Samarqand and to the Timurid-Safavid Iranian customs that Babur had so admired.

Humayun's Patronage

With the exclusion of a single engraved mosque in Agra, no other surviving structure beyond a doubt ensues from Humayun's disdain. Some hold that the Delhi Purana Qalca, its mosque and octagonal pavilion also are his. Despite the dearth of remaining buildings from Humayun's time, contemporary sources refer to his architectural output. They describe, for instance, his unique conceptions, even though they are based on Timurid design concepts. One of them was a floating palace formed from four barges each bearing an inward facing arch and attached in such a fashion that an octagonal pool formed the central portion. Moreover, he designed three-storied collapsible palaces, gilded and domed.

More conventional palaces were built at Gwalior, Agra and Delhi. Neither the Gwalior palace, built of chiselled stones, nor the multistoried Agra palace, with its octagonal tank, associated via subterranean passages to other parts of the palaces, survives. Much controversy centres around Humayun's role in erecting the fortified enclosure at present called Delhi's Purana Qalca. Humayun began a walled city and royal palace on this site in 1533. The city, named Din-Panah or Refuge of Religion, was auspiciously located upon the age-old site called Indraprastha, long linked with the conventional Hindu epic Mahabharata. The city was also situated in very close propinquity to the shrine of Delhi's to the highest degree revered saint, Nizam al-Din Auliya. The choice of the site must have been made with its history in mind, for Humayun, superstitious yet religious, sought advice from learned men in addition to astrologers. Even after Humayun's victorious return to India in 1555, this site remained symbolic for the Mughals, for, as we shall see, Humayun's tomb was built in this same area.

Khwand Amir, a noble in Humayun's court, reports that by 1534 the "walls, bastions, ramparts and gates" of Humayun's Din-Panah were nearly came to end, adding that it was hoped that the "great and lofty buildings" of the city soon would be finished. It is difficult to tell from Khwand Amir's bombastic prose exactly how much of the city in reality was ready by 1534; moreover, it is impossible to judge how much was came to end before Sher Shah's accession to the Delhi throne in 1540, for Humayun was constantly engaged in defending the Mughal domain and struggling to maintain his crown.

Sher Shah believably came to end the fort and built its inner Qalca-i Kuhna mosque. Humayun nearly certainly constructed the fort's small octagonal pavilion, called the Sher Mandal and customarily linked with the library upon whose steps Humayun fatally fell in 1556, less than a year after his successful return to India. Abu al-Fazl, the official chronicler of Humayun's son and successor, Akbar, writes that the building in which Humayun had his fatal accident had only recently been came to end, presumably by Humayun. The pavilion's design, close to Timurid garden pavilions and unlike Sultanate architectural forms, suggests Mughal disdain. So does the visual aspect of the net pendentives in the structure's vaulting.

The sole engraved monument belonging to Humayun's disdain is a mosque in Agra known after the name of its locality, Kachpura. Two inscriptions show that the mosque was came to end in 1530, the year of Humayun's accession to the throne. Its location, across the Jumna from the land on which the Taj Mahal was later constructed, may have been the site of the Hasht Behisht garden, or Garden of Eight Paradises, used for Babur's court.

This garden also to the highest degree likely sustained to serve as Humayun's court until he built his Delhi citadel. Like Babur's mosques, this one in Kachpura is mentioned in no text. It resembles Babur's Panipat mosque in general plan and visual aspect, even though the central pishtaq is much higher and the central vaulted chamber achieves a larger sense of open space than did the only slightly former Mughal mosques. The open character of the central bay with low flanking bays recollects former Timurid mosques, for instance the Jamic mosque at Nishapur. As at Babur's Panipat mosque, stucco covers a brick core. On Humayun's mosque, eight-pointed stars and lozenge forms are imprinted into the rectangular frontage; possibly these were once painted to emphasize the design, evoking the brightly coloured glazed tile decoration of Herat and Samarqand. The mosque at present is ruined, so it is unclear how various bays initially composed the double-aisled side wings. The inner central bay is surmounted by a dome supported on kite-shaped pedentives and net squinches. The smaller domes of the resulting side wings are similarly supported. While no traces of enclosure walls and entrance gates remain, they were nearly certainly part of the original plan. The overall visual aspect and plan of this structure suggests that it, like Babur's Panipat mosque, was intended to emulate older Timurid forms.

NON-IMPERIAL ARCHITECTURE UNDER BABUR AND HUMAYUN

Architecture erected in the Delhi region by those close to Babur and Humayun comes out little shaped by Timurid concepts; rather, what remains reflects the older Lodi style. To the highest degree important examples are at the shrine (dargah) around the tomb of Nizam al-Din Auliya. Belonging to the Chishti order, Nizam al-Din is Delhi's to the highest degree esteemed Muslim saint. This shrine gained renewed importance in the Mughal period. In it is the tomb of Amir Khusrau (d. 1325), regardedthet famous Persian poet of Hindustan.

This tomb was restored by Babur's brother-in-law, who provided an engraved marble slab next to an open-air grave. In Humayun's reign, in 1531-32, a red sandstone screened enclosure was constructed around the grave. This screen, carved with geometric and floral forms, recollects Lodi-period tombs, for instance that of Yusuf Qattal, also in Delhi. Other monuments of this time comprise the mosque of Ghazanfar, built in 1528-29 during Babur's reign near the Delhi airport in Palam. In another part of Delhi, Malvianagar, a residential centre for spiritual study (khanqah) was constructed in 1534-35 to honor Shaikh Farid al-Din Ganj-i Shakar, a long deceased saint. That makes it contemporary with Humayun's Din-Panah, even though it reveals no awareness of new royal forms. Both the mosque and khanqah are squat single-aisled three-bayed structures notable for neither their proportions nor decoration. Inscriptions show that mosques, tombs and other structures sustained to be erected by men of all ranks and classes outside of Delhi during the early Mughal period. Nevertheless, few of these remain in their original state. Like subimperial monuments in the Delhi area, they reveal little or no Timurid impact. For instance, the tomb of Tardi Kochak in Hisar, dated 1537-38 by a stucco inscription incised on its frontage, is a square-plan structure whose frontage is articulated by a series of slightly recessed niches intimately resembling the Lodi-period tombs of Delhi.

One more structure suggests the persistence of the older Lodi style. It is a small three-bayed single-aisled mosque in Fatehabad (Hisar District, Haryana), called the Humayuni mosque. An inscription now detached from the structure bears the date 1539 and describes the construction of a mosque during Humayun's reign. This is believably the very mosque keyed out in the inscription. Even though another inscription on the mosque shows that it was renovated in the nineteenth century, characteristics from the time of Humayun are quite apparent. Small glazed tiles on the east frontage, for instance, are reminiscent of those on two sixteenth-century buildings in Hansi, about 30 km away: the Barsi gate restored in 1522 and the tomb of Ali Mir Tijara. Ibn Khaldun, the fourteenth-century Islamic political thinker and historian, observed that the founders of dynasties usually channel substantial effort into consolidating their political strength, leaving little time for panoptic architectural construction. Nonetheless, the architecture of both Babur and Humayun sowed the seeds for future construction under the Mughals. This is particularly true for the forms of works constructed, even though the purpose and meaning will change somewhat as the state matures and evolves its unique notions of legitimacy. Babur introduced the char bagh garden, which for him was a visual metaphor for his ability to control and order the arid Indian plains and eventually its population. Later on such gardens gain even larger popularity, particularly when used as a paradisical setting for funereal monuments. Before his conquest of India, Babur had constructed no mosques. In Hindustan, nevertheless, he constructed mosques, believably for the reason that of his newly acquired role as a warrior in the cause of Islam. Humayun, too, constructed at least one mosque; nevertheless, his construction of palaces and pleasure pavilions speculated his obvious selfindulgence. The palace and its role as the centre of regal ceremony, progressively important in each king's interpretation of the nature of Mughal kingship, continues as a chief architectural form through the eighteenth century. Babur and Humayun, each keenly aware of their Timurid inheritance, attempted to introduce Timurid-motivated architectural forms and spatial conceptions into India. Even though the outcome was not necessarily successful, the ideology behind such forms is maintained by their Mughal successors.

HISTORY OF MUGHAL PAINTING

Indian Mughal paintings originated during the rule of Mughal Emperor, Humayun (1530-1540). When he came back to India from the exile, he also brought along two excellent Persian artists, Mir-Sayyid Ali and Abd-us-samad. With time, their art got influenced by the local styles and gradually; it gave rise to the Mughal painting of

India. The earliest example of the Mughal style is the Tutinama ('Tales of a Parrot') Painting, now in the Cleveland Museum of Art. Then, there is the 'Princess of the House of Timur', a painting redone numerous times.

Growth of Mughal Painting

Mughal paintings of India developed as well as prospered under the rule of Mughal Emperors, Akbar, Jahangir and Shah Jahan.

Under Akbar

Mughal painting experienced large-scale growth under the reign of Emperor Akbar. During that time, hundreds of artists used to paint under the direction of the two Persian artists. Since the Emperor was fond of tales, one can see the paintings mainly being based on the Mahabharata, Ramayana and Persian epics. Mughal paintings also started illustrating an enhanced naturalism, with animal tales, landscape, portraits, etc.

Under Jahangir

Emperor Jahangir reigned from 1605 to 1627 and extended great support to various art forms, especially paintings. This period saw more and more refinement in brushwork, along with the use of much lighter and subdued colours. The main themes of the Mughal paintings revolved around the events from Jahangir's own life, along with portraits, birds, flowers, animals, etc. One of the most popular examples of Mughal paintings of this time include the pictorial illustrations of the Jehangir-nama, the biography of Emperor Jahangir.

Under Shah Jahan

The grace and refinement of the Jahangir period was seen at the time of Emperor Shah Jahan (1628-1658). However, the sensitivity of the paintings was replaced by coldness and rigidity. The themes of that time revolved around musical parties, lovers on terraces and gardens, ascetics gathered around a fire, etc.

Decline of Mughal Painting

The trend that was seen during the time of Shah Jahan was also found under the rule of Aurangzeb (1658-1707). However, the emperor did not pay too much attention on the growth of the Mughal paintings. Still, the art form continued to survive with the support received from its other patrons. However, gradually, because of diminishing support, a declining trend set in. The time of Muhammad Shah, (1719-1748), did experience a brief revival of the Mughal paintings. Nonetheless, with the arrival of Shah Alam II (1759-1806), the art almost became extinct and another school of painting, known as Rajput paintings, started evolving.

JAHANGIR'S LOVE OF PAINTING

Mughal Emperor Jahangir was a great patron of painting from the days of his Viceroyalty. He patronised many great painters of the time including Mansoor, Abul Hasan, Daswant and Basawan. He acknowledged that his liking for painting was so strong that he was able to judge which painter had executed which work. He also stated that if there was a picture containing many portraits drawn by different artists he was able to identify the artists from the stroke of the brushes.

Once, British Ambassador Thomas Roe arrived in the court of Jahangir and the Emperor asked him to identify the original European Painting placed alongside five copies of it, made by the Indians. This completely foxed the Ambassador much to the delight of the Emperor highlighting the artistic merit of the Indian painters.

KHWAJA ABDUS SAMAD

Khwaja Abdus Samad (16th century) was an Iranian painter and one of the founders of the Mughal school of painting in India. He was born in Shiraz.

Early in life, Samad became known for his painting and calligraphy. Samad met the Mughal emperor Humayun in Tabriz, where he was invited to come with the emperor, though he was unable to accompany the emperor at that time. In 1548, he came to the temporary Mughal capital, Kabul where he was hired by Humayun to teach himself and his son Akbar, how to draw. Samad was thus one of the first to become a member of the imperial atelier (imperial art studio) of India.

A few of his works executed during this period is located in the Royal Library of the Golestan palace in Tehran. One such miniature painting created by Samad depicts Akbar giving a miniature painting to his father Humayun. This painting looks very typical of Persian paintings of that time, but it also contains aspects that would go on to influence future Indian painting.

While at the atelier, Samad supervised (along with Mir Sayyid Ali) the illustrations that were done for the Hamzanama-about 1,400 large paintings (although it is uncertain whether Samad himself painted any of them). Also in the course of teaching at the atelier, Samad taught Dasvant and Basavan, two Hindu men who went on to become famous Mughal painters.

In 1576, Akbar put Samad in charge of the Fatehpur Sikri mint. In 1584, Akbar made him dewan of Multan. He was given a *mansab* of 400 and honoured with the title of *Shirin Qalam* (sweet pen). More of Samad's work can be seen in the illustrations found in the 1595 manuscript of the Khamseh of Nezami, today located in the British Museum.

THE MUGHAL LITERATURE

There was tremendous literary activity during the Mughal period, because with the return of a stable and prosperous empire, there was once again patronage for their work. Languages like Persian, Sanskrit, Hindi and Urdu saw tremendous creative activity as did many vernacular languages.

Persian literature received a lot of attention as it was the court language. A vast number of works were written during the period of the Mughals. Broadly one can divide them into three categories, historical works, translations, poetry and novels. Our understanding of the Mughal period was greatly enhanced by these books, and most of the historical works of this period provide us with a fairly reliable source of information.

The important historical works written in this time were *Ain-I-Akbari,* and *Akbarnamath* by Abul Fazal, the *Tarikh-I-Alfi* by Mulla Daud. Jehangir possessed a keen interest in literature, and his autobiography is one of the finest amongst the Mughal emperors. During his reign important historical works like *Maasir-I-Jahangir*, the *Igbalnamah-I-Jahangiri* and the *Zubud-ut-Tawaikh* were written.

Many important works in translation were also written during this period, with the translation of the epics, the Mahabharata and the Ramayana taking place. Many of the Vedas were also translated and several previous historical books were also translated. All this translation added to the wealth of Indian literature and spread ancient knowledge to a greater audience. This renewed interest in Indian literature would be an important tool used by the social reformers of the eighteenth century to educate the people about what the ancient texts really said as opposed to the distorted interpretations that were being followed. The

Mughal empire had a large number of poets and writers and hence there was a lot of work published in this era. Especially during the reign of Akbar, Jehangir and Shah Jahan they had tremendous patronage and many remarkable works were composed. Since the Mughal emperors had integrated themselves into Indian society, they patronized many Indian languages leading to some good quality literature being developed for these languages.

The main themes of the period were essentially religious, covering most of the major religions of the period. One of the fine Hindu works composed during this time was *Ramcharitmanasa* (the pool of Rama's life) by Tulsidasa, which was a simplified version of the Ramayana. In Bengal there was a lot of work being created in Vaishnava literature. Writers like *Krishnada* and *Kaviraj* were popular authors of the time. Many biographies were written, especially of the great saint Chaitanya Deya. The keen interest in literature that the Mughal emperors had led to the establishment of many great libraries which became repositories of tremendous knowledge. The works were properly filed and locating information was very easy. The art of calligraphy also reached a level of excellence. Literary activity did not decline with the Mughal empire and flourished even in the twilight years of the Mughal empire, in fact some of the later Mughals were better poets and writers than they were capable emperors.

LITERATURE IN MUGHAL EMPIRE

The Mughal period saw great developments in the field of literature. Many Mughal emperors and members of the royal family were great men of letters. Babar the first Mughal emperor was one of the pioneers of Turkish poetry and also the author of a very valuable autobiography in Turkish Babar Nama which was later translated into Persian. Gulbadan Begum sister of Humayun wrote the Humayun Nama. Jahangir the great connoisseur of painting wrote his autobiography the Tuzuk-i-Jahangiri. Aurangzeb also was a prolific writer and the last Mughal emperor Bahadur Shah Zafar was a notable Urdu poet.

Hindi literature made significant progress during Akbar's reign. Tulsidas and the Surdas wrote in this period. Keshavdas a great poet wrote on themes of love. Rahim's dohas or couplets are extremely popular. It was also in Akbar's time that the great Sanskrit work on styles of writing, the Alankarashekhara by Keshava Misra appeared. This was the period of many notable writings in the Persian language. Abul Fazal wrote the Ain-i-Akbari and Akbar Nama. Abul Fazal's brother Faizi was a great poet of Persian and was responsible for the translation of many Sanskrit works into Persian. Akbar had started a whole dept for translation of works like Mahabharata, the Ramayana, the Atharva –Veda, the Bhagvad Gita and the Panchatantra.

Many important historical works were produced under the emperors after Akbar. Some of the important historians were Abdul Hamid Lahori, Khafi Khan, Muhammad Kazim and Sujan Rai Bhandari. Literature in modern Indian languages also continued to grow. The famous book of Bihari called the Satsai in Hindi belongs to this period. One of the most significant developments during the medieval period was the birth of the Urdu language. This new language soon developed one of the richest literatures as a modern Indian language. It produced great poets like Wali, Mir Dard, Mir Taqi Mir. Nazir Akbarabadi, Asadullah Khan Ghalib. Many original prose works in Urdu were written like Muhammad Hussain Azad's Darbar-i-Akbari. The Urdu novel was one of the earliest development in the Indian languages. Urdu became the language of the urban people of northern India and the Deccan.

REFERENCES

Currie, P.M.: *The Shrine and Cult of Muin-ul-din Chishti of Ajmer*, Oxford, Delhi, 1989.

Curtin, P. : *Cross-cultural Trade in World History,* Cambridge, 1994.

MacIver R.M. : *Society, An Introductory Analysis*, Rinehart and Company, New York 1949.

Mandal, B.B.: *Industrialisation and Social Disorganisation:* Concept Publications: New Delhi, 1985.

Chapter 10

Self Respect and Social Condition in Medieval Society

The Hindus hated the Muslims and called them Mlechchhas. They were not prepared to interdine with them or to have marriage relations. There was a feeling among the Hindus that by doing so they would fall in life. Most of the Hindus cared for their self-respect. Their superiority was undoubted. They were known for their love for justice and were not prepared to give it up in actual life. In their professions, they were known for honesty and worthy of confidence.

In all spheres of life, Hindus were respected for their qualities of head and heart. It is true that the religious and intellectual leaders of the Hindus were not influenced by Muslim conquest of India and they maintained their standard of nobility and superiority, but the ordinary Hindu was affected by Muslim conquest. On account of lack of independence, there was a fall in Hindu society.

The Sultans of Delhi and other Muslim rulers regarded the Hindus as their enemies. With a few exceptions, no Hindu was given any position of responsibility in the state by the Muslim rulers. Even the right to life was given to them if they agreed to pay Jizya. For political reasons, Ala-ud-Din Khalji treated the Hindus of the Doab with great severity. He humiliated the Khuts, Chaudharies and Muqaddams. No Hindu could raise his head. There was no sign of any gold or silver coin or even Jital in their houses. They could not ride on horse. They had no arms or good clothes, Birani tells us that their lot bad become so bad that their wives were forced to work as maid servants in the houses of the Muslims. The Muslims state offered many concessions to convert the Hindus to Islam. Ibn-Batuta tells us that when a Hindu desired to become a Muslim, he was taken in the presence of the Sultan who gave him valuable clothes and articles of gold. The orthodox Muslims hated the Hindus. When the condition of Hindus improved a little during the reign of Khusrau, Birani wrote in sadness that the Hindus had again begun to live in comfort and had become happy. Brahamanas were not taxed to Jizya but Firuz Tughlaq imposed Jizya even on the Brahamanas. Sikandar Lodi also started persecuting the Hindus and their condition became miserable.

In Hindu society, there were four principal castes (Brahamanas, Kshatriyas, Vaisyas and Sudras) in order of rank and status, and indefinite number of so-called mixed castes of varying status and the despised castes who were placed at the bottom of society. The old position of the Brahamanas and Kshatriyas was materially affected by the Muslim conquest of India. The Brahamanas lost their royal patronage. They got no job in administration. They were no longer prosperous. They lost the opportunity of earning a lot of money by officiating as priests in sacrifices. The result was that the new Smritis laid down that they could pursue agriculture through hired labour. In times of special distress, they could themselves cultivate the fields. Both agriculture and trade were the occupations of the people of all castes. In view of the change, the rank and file among the Brahamanas could not devote the same time and attention to Vedic studies and spiritual and intellectual pursuits as they used to do in the past. The new commentaries on the Smritis allowed them to give less time to their original occupation and content themselves with the study of just a part of the Vedas in which they were interested and in some cases with that of the Puranas alone. This was an admission of the decline of the Vedic studies during the Sultanate period and the importance of the Brahamanas. There was also a change in the attitude of the Brahamanas towards the Sudras. The latter were allowed to listen to recitations of the Puranas. It was made permissible to eat the food of certain Sudra castes under some special circumstances. The Sudras were allowed to engage themselves in some of the prohibited articles of sale, including meat.

The Kshatriyas lost not only political power but also the opportunity of earning their livelihood as soldiers. Except in Rajasthan, Central India and the Himalayan region in the North, West, many of the Kshatriyas sank into the status of local landlords serving as intermediaries in the revenue system organised by the Muslim rulers. Guru Nanak has referred to the demoralisation of the Kshatriyas in these words: "The Kshatriyas have forsaken their religion and adopted the language of the Malechchas." This refers to the acceptance of service by the Kshatriyas under the Muslim rulers and their imitation of Muslim manners and customs. The changed position of the Kshatriyas had a direct impact on Hindu society as a whole. On account of the elimination of the normal rivalry of the Kshatriyas, the authority and personal influence of the Brahamanas increased among the Hindu masses. However, that is not wholly true because the Brahamanas themselves were weakened as they could not look upto political power for support and patronage. The Brahamans continued to be the unofficial guides of Hindu society.

The picture of the condition of the Vaisyas and Sudras and the untouchable given by Al-Biruni seems to be exaggerated. The Sudras were divided into two categories. Those of the lower category were looked down upon as interior, as the untouchables. The number of mixed castes had gone up to 64 and those were divided into two groups, Those belonging to the Anuloma group (born of higher caste males and lower caste females) were considered twice-born and were entitled to the sacred thread and other sacraments. Those belonging to the Pratiloma group (born of lower caste fathers and higher caste mothers) were considered as belonging to low castes. The lower orders of society were discriminated against and even despised, Detailed rules were prescribed to avoid contact with the despised castes. Purification by bathing with clothes on was prescribed for touching a Chandala. Different penances were to be undertaken by a Brahman for conversing, or sleeping on the same bed, or going in company with a Chandala, for looking at or touching a Chandala, for drawing water from a tank owned by Chandala, for drinking water from a well from which water had been drawn in a Chandala vessel, for eating the food of a Chandala or living for some time in the same house with a Chandala, for the entrance of a Chandala in the house of a Brahmana etc.

The caste rules and the rules governing the relations between the various castes as laid down in the Shastras were not strictly followed. Some Brahmans followed the occupation of the Kshatriyas and some Sudras, "in the teeth of the canonical rule forbidding the lower Varnas to take up the functions of the higher ones, assumed the Kshatriya's occupation of ruling and fighting." In the seventh century A.D Sind was ruled by a Sudra dynasty. There were some Sudra rulers in other parts of the country.

The common practice was to marry in one's own caste but inter-caste marriages were not unknown. It was laid down in the Shastras that the marriage of girls of inferior castes with the twice-born or higher caste males was forbidden in the Kaliyuga, but such marriages did take place, though they were considered inferior and undesirable. Although Al-Biruni does not mention the Kayastha caste, yet it had come into existence as an important caste in the later half of the 9th century A.D. The individuals of the caste had risen "to the highest public offices in different tracts" in the eleventh and following centuries.

It is true that the caste system was in many respects a cruel and immoral system but was so deeply rooted in Hindu society that it could not be shaken even by Medieval religious reformers. Guru Nanak condemned the caste system as "folly" but inspite of that it continued. Even the Sikh Gurus who were Khatris did not marry non-Khatri girls. Chaitanya stood for removing all distinctions based on caste and religion but be himself observed practices and after his death Bengal Vaishnavism developed on traditional Hindu lines.

The caste system was in a sense a disruptive force but it was also a cohesive force in so far as it assured every Hindu of a recognised professional or occupational status. It promoted social integration in a limited sense as it assigned rights and duties to every individual and ensured a working harmony between the socio-religious and economic structures.

The view of Dr. K.M. Ashraf is that the caste system was "a contributory factor in the establishment of the foreign Muslim rule." (Life and Conditions of the People of Hindustan, p. 108). The view of Habib and Nizami is that the social system of the Hindus and the invidious caste distinctions "rendered the whole military organisation rickety and weak" (Comprehensive History of India, Vol. V, pp. 185-86). This view is not accepted by Prof. A.C. Banerjee. He points out that the first Arab raid in Sind took place in or about 643 A.D. and the Kingdom of Dahir fell in 712. The Caliphs failed to extend their dominions beyond Sind. The invasions of Sabuktagin and Sultan Mahmud resulted only in the annexation of a part of the Punjab and that too in the eleventh century A.D. The Indian campaigns of Mohammad Ghori covered a period of over thirty years (1175-1206). It took the Khaljis and the Tughlaqs more than thirty years to accomplish the partial subjugation of South India. The Rajput princes successfully resisted the Muslims till the days of Akbar. The primary cause of the loss of independence by India was not the caste system but the lack of unity among the Hindu princes, it was due to their lack of political vision and the absence of the ideal of imperialism. They did not keep themselves breast of the developments in the art of warfare in Central

Asia. The Hindus also suffered from their superiority complex which kept them isolated from other countries.

The position of women in the Sultanate period was not as high as it used to be in ancient India. No women was allowed to enjoy an independent status. Before marriage, she was under the strict supervision of her father. After marriage, she was under the supervision of her husband and after his death, she was under the supervision of her grown-up sons. However, it was laid down that a husband must honour his wife and provide her with gifts of ornaments and good food. If the husband went abroad, he was required to provide for the maintenance of his wife, during his absence. Even if a husband left his wife for some valid reason, he was required to make provision for her maintenance. Even if a wife was guilty of adultery, she had to be provided for. If a husband in-treated his wife, he was punished by the state. Inspite of this, the position of women worsened during the Sultanate period. On account of fear from Muslims and other kinds of high-handedness, new rules were made to enforce early marriage. It was laid down that girls should be married at the age of 7, 10 and at the most 12 years. A marriage at or after the age of puberty was considered a bad marriage and a matter of sin for her parents. The revocation of marriage was permitted in certain special circumstances.

The seclusion of Hindu women came in the wake of the Muslim conquest of Northern India. Child marriage and Purdah brought about the segregation of girls and a degradation in the condition of Hindu women during Medieval India.

Sati was common, but not compulsory. Al-Biruni tells us that a widow had to choose between two alternatives viz remaining a widow all her life or burning herself on the funeral pyre of her dead husband and she usually chose the latter alternative. Ibn Batuta who has given an eye witness account of Sati in Malwa, tell us that the custom was highly esteemed but not obligatory. According to him, under a law made by the Sultans of Delhi, permission had to be-obtained before burning a widow.

The institution of Devadasis in principal temples was in existence. A large number of beautiful maidens were maintained for music and song in important temples in most parts of the country. Al-Biruni writes that while the priests were opposed to the institution of Devadasis, the kings maintained them for the sake of revenue. Women were allowed to possess certain kinds of property, besides their Stridhana. Contrary to the Smriti rule of the perpetual dependence of women, princesses and queens wielded great political authority. There were instances of

Hindu women who ruled over, certain parts of the country at that time, particularly in Kashmir and South India. Queen Rudramba successfully ruled the Kakatiya kingdom for forty years. Polygamy was permitted. Rulers and princes were allowed to have many wives but the common people were monogamous.

The birth of a daughter was not considered to be auspicious. It is stated that when a daughter was born to Amir Khusrau, the great poet, it was considered to be an unfortunate occasion.

The Hindus celebrated many festivals such as Holi, Dussehra, Raksha-Bandhan, Vasant etc. The Muslim rulers put many restrictions on their celebration. Slavery was fairly common. Slaves were bought and sold. They were also distributed as ordinary gifts or presents among friends.

The customs of religious suicide by the Hindus prevailed during the Sultanate period. It was considered a great religious merit to commit suicide at certain sacred places such as Prayag and Kashi. Hindu devotees cut off their limbs or their necks with sharp swords in the fulfilment of their vows before their deities. Ibn-Batuta tells us that the Hindus committed suicide by drowning themselves voluntarily into the Ganges as an act of spiritual merit. The Hindus also went on religious pilgrimages to Prayag, Puri, Konarak, Gaya, Kashi, Dwarka and other holy places. Cow was worshipped by the Hindus all over India.

The Hindus had a high standard of honesty. The foreign travellers bear testimony to the high character of the Hindus. The people paid their debts without going to a court of law. If a debtor could not pay his debt during his life-time, he made it obligatory on his sons and grandsons to pay that amount. The people in general were superstitious. They had great faith in omens, lucky stars, auspicious and inauspicious moments and days. On the whole, the Hindus were honest and just. They were true to their word and their engagements. This is confirmed by Idrisi, Al-Biruni and Marco Polo.

The people were fond of music, dance and drama. The common musical instruments were flute, Vina and drums. Stringed instruments and trumpets were common. Boys and girls played with balls and enjoyed the swing. Indoor games like chess, were common.

The people in general were vegetarian. That was due to the influence of Buddhism, Jainism and Vaishnavism. The killing of an animal was considered sinful. Slowly and slowly, the custom of meat-eating became popular with the Kshatriyas. The Sudras took meat openly. The Tantrikas and the Shaktas also encouraged the use of meat and fish.

There were some people among the Hindus who ate the meat of the dead animals. They were considered to be very low in society and were forced to live outside the villages and cities. Slowly, the use of wine and opium became popular among the higher castes. People put great emphasis on the preparation of food. Special dishes were prepared on the occasion of festivals and other auspicious occasions. The common food was rice, wheat, barley, gram etc. Great emphasis was put on the use of milk, butter, ghee and sugar in eating. Both the Hindus and Muslims were known for their treatment of guests.

People took great interest in decoration. People of all types and classes put on ornaments which were of different metals and qualities. Jewels were inland in ornaments. Sometimes holes were made in the ears and nose to put on ornaments. People used various kinds of clothes. Those were made of cotton, wool and silk. The rich put on costly clothes while the poor used ordinary clothes.

The Muslim population of Northern India consisted of many elements. Mohammad Ghori came with Turkish adventurers and they were followed by other foreigners who came for employment. The army of Qutub-ud-Din Aibak was composed of Turks, Ghurids, Khorasanis and Khaljis. The Afghans served in the armies of Sultan Mahmud and Mohammad Ghori. Balban employed Afghans in suppressing the people of Mewat. A large number of foreigners came to India on account of Mongol invasions. The Mongol converts were called "New Muslims". The Abyssinians also came to India. Jamaluddin Yaqut who was liked by Queen Raziya, was an Abyssinian. The Abyssinians also seized the throne of Bengal in the late 15th century A.D. Mohammad Tughlaq gave facilities to those who came from outside India. Barani tells us that people from different parts of the world came to India such as Khorasan, Iraq, Khwarizm, Seistan, Herat and Damascus. Barbosa tells us that foreigners from many lands such as Arabs, Mameluks, Persians and Khorasanis lived in the coastal towns, particularly in Gujarat. Many Arab traders settled in Chittagong. Men of learning from Arabia, Persia and Bukhara took up their residence at Agra during the reign of Sikandar Lodi. These various elements were united by the single faith of Islam. There were also inter-marriages among them. Social intercourse and the identity of political interests also united them and they permanently settled in India.

The Turks, the Persians, the Arabs, the Abyssinians and the Egyptians constituted an exclusive ruling oligarchy. The Turk was the most jealous guardians of the foreign aristocrats. He monopolised power in Hindustan and played the role of the leader of the Muslims in Asia.

He believed in the policy of racialism and rigidly excluded the Indian Muslim community from a share in power and employment in the state. Balban openly despised "low-born non-Turks". As a very large number of persons migrated into India from Central Asia, there was a mixing up of the Muslims of different races and nationalities. During the reign of Alauddin Khalji, the policy of associating Indian converts with the administration was adopted. Alauddin Khalji appointed Malik Kafur as his Deputy. Firuz Tughlaq's Prime Minister was Khan-i-Jahan Maqbul who was a convert from Hinduism to Islam.

To begin with, the number of converts to Islam must have been small but with the passage of time their number increased. Most of the Hindus who were converted to Islam came from low castes and they were not admitted to the aristocracy of the Muslim conquerors. They were also not given any social and economic privileges.

There was a great deal of antipathy among the Muslims on account of their religious differences, particularly among the Sunnis and Shias. This rivalry and enmity continued throughout the medieval period. The Afghans were known as the sworn enemies of the Mughals and they looked upon them as usurpers. Foreign settlers in India preferred urban areas where military and civil employment was available to them. Some of them settled in rural areas to look after the lands assigned to them. However, the vast majority of the Muslims in rural areas were converts from Hinduism. Most of them belonged to lower castes and they continued to pursue their old occupations. They were not admitted to the social and political privileges of foreigners who were affiliated to the ruling class and had more money.

As regards social divisions among the Muslims, Barani refers to persons of low birth and high birth and contempt for the low-born. He refers to artists, merchants, clerks, soldiers, cultivators, Bazaris and Darveshes. In Fatawa-i-Jahandari, there are references to religious scholars, mystics, physicians, astrologers, artisans, shopkeepers, merchants, caravan workers, courtesans, musicians, dancers, buffoons, tavern-keepers, jugglers, story tellers, jokers and wrestlers. Tarikh-i-Mubarak Shahi refers to Amirs, Maliks. Ulama, Sadat, Mashaikh, beggars, artisans, money-lenders and cultivators. Khavand Mir's Humayun Nama refers to Ahi-i-Daulat comprising the royal family, nobility and the army, Ahl-i-Saadat comprising the Ulama, Qazis, the Sayyids, men of learning and men of letters and Ahl-i-Murad consisting of those-who catered for pleasures comprising musicians, minstrels and dancers.

There was a privileged class in Muslim society consisting of the

Umara or the nobility and the Ulama or the theologians together with other religious groups. The nobles (Ahl-i-Suyuf or "men of the sword") were mostly of foreign origin. They derived their nobility not from birth but from the favour of the Sultan. In the 13th century, many of them were initially slaves. The sons and relatives of the Sultan formed a special section of the nobility. They stood at the top of the hierarchy and enjoyed exceptional prestige and privileges. The men of the sword constituted a military aristocracy. The title of Khan was the privilege of those who belonged to the highest grade. Some of them were given the title of Ulugh Khan-i-Azam. The nobles of the second grade were given the title of Malik and those of the third grade were designated as Amir. The term Amir was also used in a generic sense to indicate all the holders of important military and civil posts. Military officers of lower ranks were called Sarkhails and Sipahsalars but they were not recognised as nobles. On paper, there was a descending hierarchy from Khan downwards but in actual practice, it began to disrupt quite early. In the 14th and 15th centuries, it lost all its significance.

The highest posts and large revenue assignments were monopolised by the nobles and that enabled them to live in luxury. Those at the top copied their royal masters. They lived in palatial houses, richly decorated and furnished. They used costly tapestries and carpets imported from foreign countries, gold and silver dishes, exquisite glass and china etc. They maintained in their stables fine horses. Many of them maintained elephants. A Fil-Khan-was a familiar adjunct to the palaces of the big nobles. A large number of slaves and domestic servants, both males and femaales, were maintained by them. They were known for their lavish hospitality and charity. In theory, neither the office nor the revenue assignment to any noble was permanent or hereditary. There was no scope for the development of a hereditary nobility.

The Ahl-i-Qalam or "men of the pen" formed the second privileged class. The term Ulama covered various groups such as theologians, ascetics, Sayids, Pirs and their descendants. They did belong to the nobility but they enjoyed wealth and influence in varying degrees. Theologians were collectively known as Dastar-Bandan. They were shown a lot of respect although many of them did not deserve it. Barani puts the Ulama into two categories. Ulama-i-Akhirat (those who kept themselves aloof from wordly temptations and Ulama-i-Dunya (those who coveted worldly prizes). The people did not enquire whether a particular theologian belonged to the first category or the second category. They respected every Ulama. The Ulama were regarded as the heirs of the Prophet. The laws of the Shariat were enforced by them and things illegal and not sanctioned by the Shariat were suppressed by them. The religion of God stood firm due to them. The best kings and the best nobles were those who visited the doors of the Ulama and the worst Ulama were those who visited the doors of the kings and the nobles. The Ulama were much superior in dignity and status to others. The Sayyids claimed descent from the Prophet through his daughter Fatima. They commanded special respect in Muslim society. Even Timur protected the lives of Sayyids during his invasion of India although his policy was one of general slaughter. A Sayyid accused of misappropriating state revenue was discharged by Sikandar Lodi and was allowed to keep to himself his dishonest gains. The Sayyids put on a pointed cap (Kulah) and they were known as Kulah-Daran.

There was a widely prevalent belief in Pirs and Shaikhs as spiritual guides in Muslim society. Partly as a result of the decay of the spiritual and moral influence of the Ulama on account of their degeneration as a class, the Pirzadas (descendants of Pirs) and Mukhdumzadas (descendants of Shaikhs) took over to a large extent the spiritual guidance of Muslims. They were practically worshipped. Some nobles of King Bahlol Lodi offered their heads to the son of their Pir if he chose to sit on them.

Next to the two privileged classes, there was a middle class whose income was from small holdings of land and services in lower posts under the state of the nobles. Energetic and ambitious men of the middle class found opportunities for ascending to the highest class, the nobility. If fortune turned against them, they were reduced to the level of cultivators of land.

The lowest strata of Muslim society were composed mainly of artisans, shop-keepers, clerks and petty traders. At the bottom there were Qalandars and other beggars. Most of them were of Hindu origin. In most cases, the change of religion did not involve any change either in their occupation or in the place of their work. They continued their old religious and social ideas and prejudices. Converts from Hinduism were looked down upon and non-Indian extraction was a special claim to distinction in society. The result was that many Hindus who were converted to Islam and became rich or well-placed in life, claimed foreign origin in order to gain a higher social status.

The Muslims were essentially a city people. They dreaded village life Their main profession was in the army and in the offices of the state. Some of them were engaged in trade and commerce. A large number of them were engaged as shop keepers and teachers in primary schools. The Muslims of Indian origin followed handicrafts and petty trades in cities. A small number of them took to agriculture. There were also

Muslim butchers, water carriers, corpse-washers engravers, painters, illuminators and physicians, some of them were calligraphists and copyists of the Quran, A large number of them were weavers, washermen, barbers, carpenters, blacksmiths, tailors and woodcutters.

Domestic servants and slaves were employed in the royal household and in every rich and respectable Muslim family. Barani writes that the royal slaves were supposed to confer power and dignity on the Sultan. They were employed rot only in domestic and menial work but also in war. Barani was aware of the danger of the use of slaves for military and political purposes. He wrote, "Most of the slaves are wreckless and shameless. There can be no permanent security against their revolt." Afif tells us that after the death of Firuz Tughlaq, his slaves "became so bold that they unhesitatingly severed the heads of the princes of his family and hung them at the Darbar Gate." In private households, there was practically no distinction between domestic servants and slaves. War was probably the most important source of the supply of slaves.

Prisoners of war who were mostly Hindus, were reduced to slavery. Hasan Nizami tells us that after the victory of Kutbuddin Aibak at Kalinjar, 50,000 men were made slaves. Slaves were also imported from Africa and West and Central Asian countries. They were also procured from certain parts of India, Ibn-Batuta tells us that slaves from Assam were worth several times more than others. There were markets for the sale of slaves. Barani refers to such a market in Delhi. The regulations of Ala-ud-Din Khalji fixed the prices of slaves. The prices of male and female and handsome men and women slaves varied. Ibn Bututa found many slave girls in Bengal. A slave in the service of the Sultan was usually manumitted after some time and was provided with an honourable position. But that was not always so. Mohammad Ghori did not manumit either Qutb-uddin Aibak or any of his senior slaves. It is doubtful even if Balban was manumitted. Firuz Tughlaq had 180,000 slaves but it cannot be said how many were raised to high tank. The promotion of a slave so high office was usually a political device and not a generous recognition of the principle of social equality. Being dependent on his royal master, a talented slave could be used as a trustworthy agent and was, therefore, preferable to nobles. A slave could be set free only when he and his master came to an agreement that the former would pay the latter an appropriate part of his earnings and the Qazi confirmed the agreement.

The mere acceptance of Islam did not bring freedom to a non-Muslim slave although in theory a Muslim could not be enslaved. There was a custom among the Muslims that if a slave girl gave birth to a child from her master she ceased to be a slave and became the wife of the master and she also got a share in the property of her master. Slavery was not considered to be bad in Muslim society. Some slaves took pride in being the slaves of some big person. They got every opportunity to rise in life.

Slavery made very little contribution of the economic development of the country. The Indian slaves were engaged in domestic and menial work and contributed merely to the luxurious style of living of their masters.

Muslim women in India did not possess the privileged position which was occupied by Arab women. They occupied a subordinate position and were at the mercy of their husbands who could marry at least four wives at a time according to the Shariat. No women in a Muslim household could claim to be the mistress of her house. However, Muslim women were treated well as the honour of the family was supposed to depend upon the chastity of womenfolk. They observed strict Purdah. Muslim women of the upper class did not go out without a Burkah. Muslims were very jealous about their wives and they did not allow even their near relations to look at them. Women of the higher classes were taught the Quran and other religious books, There were a number of highly educated and talented women in medieval India.

Women of the lower classes assisted their husbands in the cultivation of land. They looked after cows and bullocks, poultry-keeping etc. They did not observe Purdah.

In one way, there was a fall in the morals of the Muslims in India. Drinking and gambling became very common among them, Balban imposed many restrictions on the use of intoxicants. The same was done by Ala-ud-Din Khalji. But inspite of that, the Muslims indulged in those evil habits in excess. There was some improvement during the reign of Mohammad Tughlaq but corruption became rampant during the reign of Firuz Tughlaq.

There were many causes for the decline of morals among the Muslims. One reason was that they acquired a lot of wealth without much effort. When the Muslims defeated the Hindu rulers, a lot of money fell into their hands. They got gold, silver, diamonds etc. in large quantities. The result was that the Muslims wasted their riches on beautiful women and drinking and that led to a decline in their morals.

Another reason was that the Sultans of Delhi did not possess high moral character. Many of them were really bad. They thought of nothing except beautiful women and drinking. Sultan Kaiqubad lived a licentious life. He required more beautiful women. The same was the case with Mubarak Shah (1316-20). He was also a man of no character. If such was the condition of the Sultans, their nobles tried to copy them and thereby lost their character.

As a result of their permanent residence of India, the social life of the Muslims who came from foreign countries became Indianised in very many ways. There developed among the Muslim aristocrats something like the caste system, particularly in the matter of marriage. The Muslims borrowed from the Hindus the use of umbrellas and elephants as emblems of authority. They also borrowed from them the use of rings, necklaces and earring. They started using rich spices for cooking food. They also borrowed from the Hindus the practice of chewing the betel-leaf. They borrowed headgears known as Chira and Pag from the Rajputs, The Muslims were accustomed to the use of coarse cloth in their original homelands but when they came to India they started using fine cotton and silk fabrics. The Muslim rulers and nobles started employing professional gesters after the fushion of the Hindus, The Muslims came to have belief in astrology as the Hindus did. Some of the marriage ceremonies and customs of the Hindus were adopted by the Muslims. Music is forbidden in Islam. It was banned by Iltutmish but it was patronised by Balban and Firuz Shah Tughlaq. It is said that when Firuz Shah Tughlaq ascended the throne, he entertained the public for three weeks with music. The Qawwali music became popular among the Muslims.

REFERENCES

Duboi, Abbe: *Hindu Manners, Customs and Ceremonies*, Fifth Indian Impression, CUP, 1985.

Dutt, Sukumar : *Buddhist Monks and Monasteries of India*, George Allen and Unwin, London, 1962.

Mervin Lapidus, *Muslim Cities in the Later Middle Ages,* Cambridge, Mass, 1967.

Michell, George, and Mark Zebrowski: *Architecture and Art of the Deccan Sultanates,* Cambridge, London, 1999.

Prussin, L. Hatumere: *Islamic Design in West Africa,* Berkeley, 1986.

Bibliography

Armand Maass: *Social Problems as Social Movements.* Philadelphia: Lippincott, 1975.

Augustine, P.A.: *Social Equality in Indian Society*, New Delhi, Concept 1991

Baird, Robert: *Religion in Medieval India*, New Delhi, Manohar, 1981.

Basham, A.L.: *A Cultural History of India*, Oxford, Clarendon Press, 1975.

Bérinstain, Valérie : *India and the Mughal Dynasty*, New York: Abrams, 1998.

Bernard, Jessie: *Social Problems at Midcentury: Role, Status and Stress in a Context of Abundance,* New York: Holt, Rinehart and Winston, 1957.

Bosworth, C.E., *The Ghaznavids*, Edinburgh University Press, Edinburgh, 1963.

Brend, Barbara : *The Emperor Akbar's Khamsa of Nizami*, London: British Library, 1995.

Chandra, Kripal : *India's Unequal Citizens : A Study of Other Backward Classes,* Manohar, New Delhi, 1994.

Chandra, Satish : *History of Medieval India*, New Delhi: Orient Longman, 2007.

Creswell, K. A. C.: *A Short Account of Early Muslim Architecture*, Aldershot, Adlohoc, 1989.

Crowe, S.: *"The Gardens of Mughal India"*, Oxford, London, 1972.

Currie, P.M.: *The Shrine and Cult of Muin-ul-din Chishti of Ajmer*, Oxford, Delhi, 1989.

Duboi, Abbe: *Hindu Manners, Customs and Ceremonies*, Fifth Indian Impression, CUP, 1985.

Dutt, Sukumar : *Buddhist Monks and Monasteries of India*, George Allen and Unwin, London, 1962.

Edwin, M.: *Social Pathology A Systematic Approach to the Theory of Sociopathic Behaviour,* New York: McGraw-Hill, 1951.

Elizabeth B.: *Paradise as a Garden In Persia and Mughal India*. New York, George Braziller, 1979.

Evans, T.F. : *On Three Copper Cakes found at Bryndu*, Oxford, Anglesey, 1873.

Habibullah, A. B. M.: *The Foundations of Muslim Rule in India.* Lahore, 1945.

Heimann, Betty: *Facets of Indian Thought*, Geroge Allen & Unwin, London, 1964.

Ikram, S.M. : *Muslim Civilization in India*, New York:Columbia University Press, 1964.

Koch, Ebba: *Mughal Architecture: An Outline of Its History and Development (1526-1858),* Munich, London, 1991.

Kumar, Pradip : *Social Mobility and Caste Violence: A Study of the Gujarat Riots*, Delhi, Adjanta Publications, 1985.

Mandal, B.B.: *Industrialisation and Social Disorganisation:* Concept Publications: New Delhi, 1985.

Mervin Lapidus, *Muslim Cities in the Later Middle Ages,* Cambridge, Mass, 1967.

Michell, George, and Mark Zebrowski: *Architecture and Art of the Deccan Sultanates,* Cambridge, London, 1999.

Oommen, T.K.: *Protest and Change: Studies in Social Movements*, New Delhi, Sage, 1990.

Peter Jackson - *Delhi Sultanate: A Political and Military History*, Cambridge University Press,1999.

Prussin, L. Hatumere: *Islamic Design in West Africa,* Berkeley, 1986.

Qureshi, I. H.: *The Administration of the Sultanate of Delhi.* Lahore, 1944.

Richards, J. F. : *The Mughal Empire*, New York: Cambridge University Press, 1993.

Roy, S. : *The Story of Indian Archaeology*, 1784–1947, Archaeological Survey of India, New Delhi, 1961.

Sharma, K. L.: *Caste, Class and Social Movements*, Rawat Publications, Jaipur, 1986.

Singh, Gopal: *A History of the Sikh People, 1469-1978*, New Delhi, World Sikh University Press, 1979.

Stephen Carr.: *Archaeology and Monumental Remains of Delhi*, Calcutta, 1876.

Thapar, R. *: Asoka and the Decline of the Mauryas,* Oxford, 1961.

Tillotson, G. H. R.: *Mughal India*, New York, Penguin Books, 1990

Vohra, Ranbir: *The Making of India: A Historical Survey,* Armonk, M. E. Sharp, 1997.

Warmington, E.H. *: The Commerce between the Roman Empire and India,* Cambridge, 1928.

Index

148/SR

H-5